Architecture as a Way of Seeing and Learning

DESIGN RESEARCH IN ARCHITECTURE

Since the Renaissance a number of architect-scholars have created methods of intellectual scrutiny of architectural design that rely upon the interplay of drawings, models, textual analysis, intellectual ideas and cultural insights. Yet there is still no cohesive framework or outlet for design research in architecture. This innovative book series – still the only one of its kind – showcases the very best proponents of architectural design research from around the globe, drawing on a range of exemplar positions between practice and academia.

Featuring work from Early Career Researchers and leading architect-scholars in practice and academia, books in the series vary in tone and structure, covering aspects such as design method, visual representation, reasoned critique, social processes and strategies for action. The series is deliberately inclusive to encourage a vibrant, novel approach, and is openly international. Each book combines serious historical or theoretical research with creative propositions expressed through drawings, models or texts; indeed, it is the symbiotic interplay between these components that forms the basis for design research in architecture. Now is a fertile time for design research and this book series acts as the heart of these investigations.

Architecture as a Way of Seeing and Learning

The built environment as an added educator in East African refugee camps

Nerea Amorós Elorduy

UCLPRESS

First published in 2021 by
UCL Press
University College London
Gower Street
London WC1E 6BT

Available to download free: www.uclpress.co..uk

A CIP catalogue record for this book is available from The British Library.

ISBN: 978-1-80008-012-6 (Pbk.)
ISBN: 978-1-80008-011-9 (PDF)
DOI: https://doi.org/10.14324/111.9781800080119

Contents

List of figures

Foreword

My architectural work in the refugee camps of Rwanda incited me to start a PhD at the beginning of 2015 on the role the built environment had on encamped children's development. I began work in the country as an intern with the United Nations Children's Fund (UNICEF) as part of Rwanda's national Early Childhood Development Task Force[1] in February 2011. I contributed to develop an incremental, modular design for early childhood development (ECD) centres. This initial prototype was subsequently tested in different communities across the country in 2011 and 2012[2] and went on to become the basis for the first work of Active Social Architecture (ASA) Studio,[3] the architectural practice I co-founded in Kigali in 2012, which built more than 20 of these centres across rural Rwanda from 2012 to 2014. ASA Studio worked for UNICEF and the United Nations High Commissioner for Refugees (UNHCR) to develop two ECD centres in the two newest refugee camps at the time: one in Kigeme and one in Mugombwa.[4]

These ECD centres were the first built interventions I had developed in a refugee camp setting. Each experience examined the potential role of architecture, participatory processes and ECD interventions in refugee camp settings. I also attempted – but failed – to develop a speculative collaboration between the UNHCR and the School of Architecture in Rwanda, where I lectured from 2011 to 2014. Such cooperation intended to investigate the potential of having local creative minds continuously involved in the well-being of camp inhabitants and their local hosts rather than resorting to one-time foreign consultants, as was common practice. In 2014, we sold ASA Studio, and I went on to undertake this research.

The PhD research project that inspired this book explored the role of architecture, refugees and built environment professionals in the making and maintenance of refugee camps in East Africa. It was initially aimed at measuring the impact that the design of ECD centres had on young children's development. However, as I began to search for case studies, I became aware of the lack of information on educational facilities, child development and the built environment within refugee camps in East Africa.[5] I also realised it is necessary to emphasise the socio-political role of the built environment within refugee camps. Prompted by both realisations, I decided to focus my research on investigating the kaleidoscopic and multi-authored built environments of the camps as a whole and their effects on young children's learning, rather than focus on a technical appraisal of formal educational facilities alone.

This book is a study of the whole built environment of seven refugee camps in Southwest Uganda, Northwest Kenya and Rwanda as a learning source for young children. It shows that there is a need for a more focused, inclusive and participatory approach towards refugee assistance. This book tries to shed light on the relevance that the built environment, its creation and development have on humanitarian policy and practice, on geopolitics, on the study of refugee camps and, most importantly, on the lives of encamped refugees and their direct local hosts, especially young children. Principally, with this book, I tried to test if and how architecture and the built environment could help to improve the lives of those inhabiting and surrounding the long-term refugee camps of Eastern Africa.

With this book, I do not expect or hope to suddenly transform refugee camp planning and refugee education policies and practices. I desire to inject a sense of urgency into the topics concerning the built environment, the refugees' voice, the development of young children and the need to decolonise the study and practice of refugee assistance in these East African camps.

Notes

1. Ministry of Education Government of Rwanda, 'Integrated early childhood development strategic plan 2011–2016', 5.
2. UNICEF developed an ECD centre in Kayonza in June 2012; ASA developed a second iteration of the model in Nyabiondo, Bugesera, in October 2012.
3. I co-founded ASA with Tomà Berlanda. We were both lecturers at the Department of Architecture at the College of Science and Technology at the University of Rwanda (Former KIST) at the time.
4. This improvement of the refugee educational facilities coincided with the Rwanda Ministry of Education taking over the coordination of education within the camps. In addition, since 2015, UNICEF is using ASA's design of ECD centres to develop ECD centres at Mahama refugee camp, established in April 2015 in the east of the country.
5. At the time of writing this book, there was no database that agglomerated the world's refugee camps, their position and size and the number and quality of their educational facilities. Yet, there are increasingly websites, large data sets and reports that accumulate information on specific ongoing emergencies.

Acknowledgements

This book is the result of a collective effort made possible thanks to the generosity of many individuals and institutions. I first want to thank UCL Press for promoting high-quality open-source publications and for accepting this work for publication under a relevant series.

I was able to undertake my research full-time thanks to a scholarship award from the La Caixa Foundation, which generously sponsored two years of my PhD work. In addition, the fieldwork trips, which constituted the bulk of my research, were made possible thanks to the Architecture Research Fund and the Bartlett Student Conference Fund from the Bartlett Faculty of the Built environment at UCL, the travel bursary of the British Association for International and Comparative Education, and the Beacon Bursary from UCL Culture.

I was also lucky to be accompanied on this research journey by some incredibly talented people. Joan Amorós was a source of energy, happiness, logistical mastery and gifted filming and photographing skills during most of the fieldwork trips. Lloyd Price, Mary Dain and Mercé Torrelles brought their expertise and vitality to the field and to the writing table. Thanks also to Marta Elorduy for being an unparalleled hard worker and for her reviews, patience and advice, and to Matt Smith, who made the three and a half years of PhD research a fun adventure and a possibility with his hard work, serenity and support and who endured all my trips.

Many other family, PhD colleagues, friends, friends of friends and selfless strangers also helped this research with ideas and discussions, hosting my team and me and providing advice and support at all stages of the process.

I would like to express my gratitude to Professors Murray Fraser and Jonathan Hill for their tireless work at developing excellence in research by architectural design. I would also like to thank Professor Camillo Boano and Dr Tejendra Pherali for contributing with incredibly valuable insights and guidance. I also express my gratitude to the staff at the Bartlett School of Architecture.

My research assistants have been critical to this research. They volunteered their time and accompanied me on long trips over bumpy dirt roads, walking tirelessly to visit refugee homes and remote ECD centres and accompanying young children on transect walks. Their vitality and willingness and their aim of improving their own countries have and continue to be a source of inspiration. Sincere thanks to Flavia Gwiza, Frank Bagenzi, Yves Twizeyimana, Murwanashyaka Shaffy,

Aziz Farid, Emmanuel Nyirikindi, Thierry Iraguha, Mugabo Medard, Theophile Uwayezu, Jackson Opolot, Moses Magala, Justicia Tegyeka, Tiffanie Kateizi, Etta Madette, Dolphine Kerubo, Asya Esajee, Victor Iyakaremye, Lydia Kanakulya and Moses Mawa.

This research was also made possible by the UNHCR Rwanda and Uganda, UNICEF Rwanda and Kenya, the Lutheran World Federation in Kenya, and the Windle Trust in Uganda to whom I would like to offer my thanks. Very special thanks go to Luca Ginoulhiach and Tomà Berlanda who believed in me in 2011 and have always given me advice and opened doors in order to make this research and other work a possibility. I am deeply grateful to the team of *imigongo* artisans who spent two full weeks in Kiziba working hand in hand with refugees and my team of research assistants. Thanks too to the former Ministry of Disaster Management and Refugee Affairs (Rwanda), the Office of the Prime Minister (Uganda) and the Department for Refugee Affairs for granting me access to all the camps visited. My deep appreciation also goes to the College of Science and Technology in Rwanda, to the Ugandan Martyrs University and to the head of department, Dr Mark Olweny, and the University of Nairobi, especially Professor Musau Kimeu.

My biggest recognition and appreciation goes to all the refugee parents, caregivers, mother leaders, youth and community mobilisers, elected camp leaders and the children at Nakivale, Kyangwali, Kyaka II, Kakuma, Kiziba, Kigeme and Mugombwa refugee camps. They generously opened their homes, nursery schools and playgrounds to my research team, shared their opinions, ideas and desires with us and enjoyed their participation in the diverse activities we developed. I wish them the best as they continue to work to improve their lives and those of the youngest camp inhabitants.

Introduction | the spatial and educational paradox of the long-term refugee camp

At the beginning of 2020, 66 long-term refugee camps[1] existed along the East African Rift.[2] Some, such as Nakivale in Southwest Uganda, were established as early as 1958. Around two million refugees lived in these camps in 2020, with roughly half a million of them being younger than six years old.[3] Over the years, millions of children have been born and have grown up in these camps. Yet, it is unknown how their surrounding built environments affect their learning and development.

I started to work designing and evaluating early childhood development (ECD) facilities – inside and outside the refugee camps – in Rwanda in 2011 when I also began teaching at the country's first school of architecture. Like many professionals involved in humanitarian assistance, I want to understand the impact of my work and ensure that I provide what the users of my

I.1 Nyabiheke refugee camp, Gatsibo, Western Province, Rwanda. September 2015.
© Amorós Elorduy.

I.1

designs want and need. In 2015, I decided to investigate how the architecture of the formal ECD facilities in the long-term camps in the region affected young children's learning. As I was studying with former architecture undergraduates at the ECD centres of the Congolese camps in Rwanda – which my architectural firm Active Social Architecture (ASA) had built – I realised that their weight on young children's learning was relatively small. The homes, streets, common areas and public sanitation facilities carried the brunt of the influence on the lives of the young refugees.

Indeed, is it not the case that we all remember the feeling of the floor where we played with our siblings when we were young? And how tall the counters were at our grandma's kitchen when we tried to help her cook? That recognition made me recall this quote from Peter Zumthor that highlights how unforgettable our first experiences with architecture are:

'There was a time when I experienced architecture without thinking about it. Sometimes I can almost feel a particular door handle in my hand, a piece of metal shaped like the back of a spoon. I used to take hold of it when I went into my aunt's garden. That door handle still seems to me like a special sign of entry into a world of different moods and smells. I remember the sound of the gravel under my feet, the soft gleam of the waxed oak staircase, I can hear the heavy front door closing behind me as I walk along the dark corridor and enter the kitchen, the only really brightly lit room in the house'.[4]

I realised that I needed to shift focus and explore the whole built environment of the camps – both inside and outside the formal schooling facilities – if I was to understand how architecture was affecting the young refugees. Unfortunately, the camps' spaces seemed to be forming mostly negative skills, attitudes and behaviours. That insight made me want to explore further how architecture could transform what were meagre learning environments into stimulating added educators.

Foregrounding built and learning environments—Over the years, I have noticed an extreme lack of information about East African camps, especially in their built environments. I have indeed suffered from it when trying to develop my work. Apart from a few academic works such as Manuel Herz's about Western Sahara and Chad,[5] Bran Jansen[6] and Anooradha Iyer Siddiqi[7] about Kenya, there is a shortage of scholarship – which also comes mostly from European scholars – about the camps' built environments. These works become almost non-existent when concerning learning settings and when looking at the built realm through a socio-political lens.[8] Moreover, the refugee's voice is missing in most studies, humanitarian policies and interventions, which suffer from an excess of standardised guidelines and toolkits. I thought it was time to create contextualised knowledge – nuanced, situated and participatory – to describe, study and transform the East African long-term camps, to help decolonise the refugee studies field and to uncover biases and hidden agencies in refugee assistance.

I tackled the task by using architecture as a means to create new knowledge collectively, include more local voices and speculate – through highly participatory approaches – on how to improve the current educational landscape for the millions of young children living in these camps. Besides, while practising – especially building ECD facilities – in the refugee camps, I was faced with the moral dilemma of contributing to their creation and maintenance. Participatory approaches help me reflect on the highly political role of practising in the camps.[9]

In this book, the reader will find an architect's take on the questions that many academics and humanitarian workers are already asking.[10] Is it relevant to look at camps through an urban lens and focus on their built environment? Which analytical benefits can architectural and design tools provide to refugee assistance? And which advantages can assemblage thinking and situated knowledges bring about in analysing, understanding and transforming long-term refugee camps?

With this work, I want to build upon what Bran Jansen calls a 'modest urban turn'[11] in refugee camp studies, the emerging attention on the built environment in the last decade. This body of literature aims to bring nuance and contextualisation to the field, focusing on the camps' urbanity.

Especially, the Middle Eastern cases are gaining from the new centrality of the built environment, which is bringing valuable insight about push-pull factors for forced migration, concepts of belonging and the relationships between encamped refugees and direct local hosts and is contributing to exploring the role of the refugees in their own assistance in these settings. Alas, this attention has not yet reached the least visible cases in Eastern Africa. Studies, policies and strategies in the region have for decades largely ignored the built environment's relevance, assuming it as a contextual side topic. This disregard might be due in part to the insufficient humanitarian funding, a focus[12] mostly on what is perceived to be life-saving and resulting from the humanitarian and the space of exception narratives, which have led the scholarship on camps for decades.[13]

You might be wondering why am I – moreover why should you be – interested in the built environment as a learning resource for young children? Humanitarian institutions did not anticipate that camps would become long-term living and learning environments for millions of young children. In fact, my personal experience shows that many camp planners in the region still hardly foresee the physical infrastructures they design as permanent devices. Instead, they mainly plan camps as efficient tools for movement control, epidemic prevention, food distribution and temporary shelter.

Moreover, as camp spaces have been considered non-places, limbo and transitional for decades, not only the built environment but also matters such as child development and everyday life have been left aside. In addition, as humanitarian educational programmes lack enough funding and suffer from an overarching Anglo-European bias – mainly due to a lack of situated knowledges – they promote a narrow approach to education, emphasising formal schooling with standards devised in Geneva and overlooking the learning that happens outside the school environment. Moreover, as ECD has only recently gathered momentum in refugee assistance,[14] the information available on learning environments for young children is mostly technical, with an excess of standards and construction guidelines focused on formal educational facilities alone.

What really should trigger your interest are the impacts of this neglect. It is now internationally acknowledged that children's initial years are critical for their socio-emotional, cognitive and physical development.[15] It has also been proven that children absorb from experiencing the social and built environments that surround them. The built environment holds a potential that we must understand.[16] Knowing which spatial qualities are relevant to young children's learning can inform policies and interventions as ECD gains momentum and new alternatives to camps are being built. It is a matter that affects millions of young humans globally, and the long-term camps show that it will continue to do so.

To understand to what degree camps are acting as learning environments, I draw from post-structuralist literature that has, over the years, widened the conception of learning, describing it as diverse, composed of direct content-based education and learning by experience.[17] Since the 1950s, work in the learning environments field has increasingly studied the built and natural environments outside the school setting as a useful learning source.[18] This literature is, by nature, interdisciplinary[19] and has included architects and designers[20] since the 1970s.

The body of learning environment works I reflect upon, and I want to collaborate with, consider education and learning environments as complex, nuanced and contextualised – as tools that can be both freeing and oppressive. Especially when there are unbalanced power relations, conflict and extreme deprivation – such as the case of refugee camps – education and learning environments can harm and be used as a tool of the powerful to repress, indoctrinate and eradicate pre-existing and traditional knowledge.[21]

The refugee's role—Not surprisingly, given the decades-long humanitarian consideration of refugees as dependent victims, there is an extreme lack of involvement of refugees and surrounding populations in planning the refugee camp spaces in East Africa.[22] This lack of engagement is exacerbated by a shortage of aid for long-term crises, poor humanitarian institutional memory due to the continuous movement of personnel and short-term funding, restrictive host government policies and economic and geopolitical stakes. In my experience, it is also because most humanitarian relief workers – which count few built environment professionals in their ranks – are unfamiliar with thinking and talking about the built environment as a relevant factor in their work.

Despite refugees not being included in the official management and construction of the camps, they are their primary makers, especially as camps become long term. Yet, there is scarce research about refugee-led actions. Due to my long-term engagement in the topic, I have been fortunate to observe the refugee-led spatial appropriations in Rwanda's long-term refugee camps since 2011.[23] In particular, I have experienced it in real time in the Mugombwa refugee camp, as I have been involved there from its establishment in 2013.

For the same reasons as those stated above, the refugees' perspective is lacking in knowledge production cycles. Academia and practice rely heavily on foreign-led accounts – mostly Anglo-European researchers and institutions – based too often on short-term engagements in 'the field'. The perceptions, views and actions of the encamped and their direct local hosts, especially children and their support networks – mainly women – are still largely overlooked.

In this book, I want to shed some light on the effects that the inclusion of the refugees' voice – both adults and children – can have for the discussion about refugee assistance, particularly focusing on the built and learning environments. As part of my research and practice journey, together with my teams, we have collected respondents' proposals to make the camps stimulating child-friendly learning environments.[24] The analysis of the information I gathered and created exposes the refugees' crucial role in the production of the camps' built environments and the relevance of their voice to transform the long-term camps and develop real alternatives to camps.

Integrating theory and practice—I strive to stand aware of my baggage and inherent biases throughout my work, creating a constant dialogue with my peers, assistants, informants and contexts. My identity as a young female architect born and raised in Barcelona affects access to certain areas and people, the types of responses I obtain, the information I collect and its analysis. It also limits my position as I seek to decolonise refugee camp research[25] and camp management, as well as architectural design and research in the region. I try to challenge assumptions – the readers', mine and those of the humanitarian system/host government assemblages.

Specifically, writing this book, I was motivated by Bruno Latour's concepts of the 'new deal' and the 'collective experiment'[26] and Dona Haraway's 'Situated Knowledges: The Science Question in Feminism of Partial and the Privilege'.[27] Both authors state that optimal policies cannot be universal or extracted from partial information and views – a common trait amongst humanitarian policies; they should be context specific and draw from various factors. They require local actors' participation to contextualise data and existing knowledge and tailor solutions best suited to their environment. It was relevant to involve refugees, direct local hosts, local artists, architects, academics, institutions, and foreign participants' in order to achieve my goals.

The collective experiment I have tried to undertake is rooted in a post-structural conception of the built environment and the world. I have used assemblage thinking[28] to grasp the interconnectedness of actors and the long-term camps' ever-changing nature. This theory has helped me understand seven long-term refugee camps in East Africa as proto-urban settlements and learning assemblages in continuous evolution. It has allowed detail and contextualisation, opening the door to create situated bits of knowledge to contend narratives of camps as solely humanitarian spaces, as spaces of exception, limbo and non-places.

Architecture as a way of seeing and learning—My experience is that architecture can be – and should more often be – used as an exploratory and analytic tool of social phenomenon. I will try to persuade the reader about it with the different spatial experimentations that I describe in this book.

In the first chapter, 'The urban turn: informality, co-modification and assemblage,' I explain how the long-term camp prevalence triggered an urban turn in refugee camp studies at the end of the twentieth century. The urban turn comprises a body of works that use post-structuralist urban theory to explore the camps' power dynamics. I outline the possibilities this movement provides for the study of the phenomenon in East Africa. I make a case for studying the long-term camps as a typology in its own right as proto-urban spaces and as learning environments. I draw from works that analyse the embodiment of Lefebvre's 'right to the city' in urban settings in former colonies – particularly in Sub-Saharan Africa – through local perspectives. I reference Asef Bayat's concept of the 'quiet encroachment of the ordinary',[29] James Scott's notions of 'everyday life' and 'survival practices',[30] Teresa Caldeira's 'peripheral urbanisation'[31] and Edgar Pieterse's 'radical incrementalism'.[32]

In the following two chapters, I try to convey to the reader the considerable challenges that children face living in the long-term refugee camps that I describe, and how they extract both positive and negative learning from their surroundings. I lead the reader through a multi-scalar spatial mapping and analysis of Nakivale, Kyangwali, Kyaka II, Kakuma, Kiziba, Kigeme and Mugombwa refugee camps. These seven camps represent three of the principal conflict areas in the region (the Horn of Africa, the Great Lakes and South Sudan),[33] encompass three nation states, 12 refugee origins, six decades of encampment practice and a wide variety of physical characteristics. These long-term refugee camps include various ages,[34] sizes, population densities, regional climates, geographies and host country refugee policies. Moreover, these camps host large proportions of young children.

Particularly, in the chapter 'Ever-evolving assemblages: the built environment of seven East African long-term camps', I map, dissect and finally reassemble the seven camps' spatial characteristics on regional, country and landscape scales. It becomes apparent how their evolution influences, and is influenced by, a complex array of factors, including the education of young children living in these camps and the refugees' agency. I present to the reader six spatial characteristics of the camps as relevant to their evolution: growing heterogeneity and complexity, co-functioning/interconnectedness, ever becoming, porosity, land scarcity and weak

I.2 Diagram of all the actors included in this research.
© Amorós Elorduy.

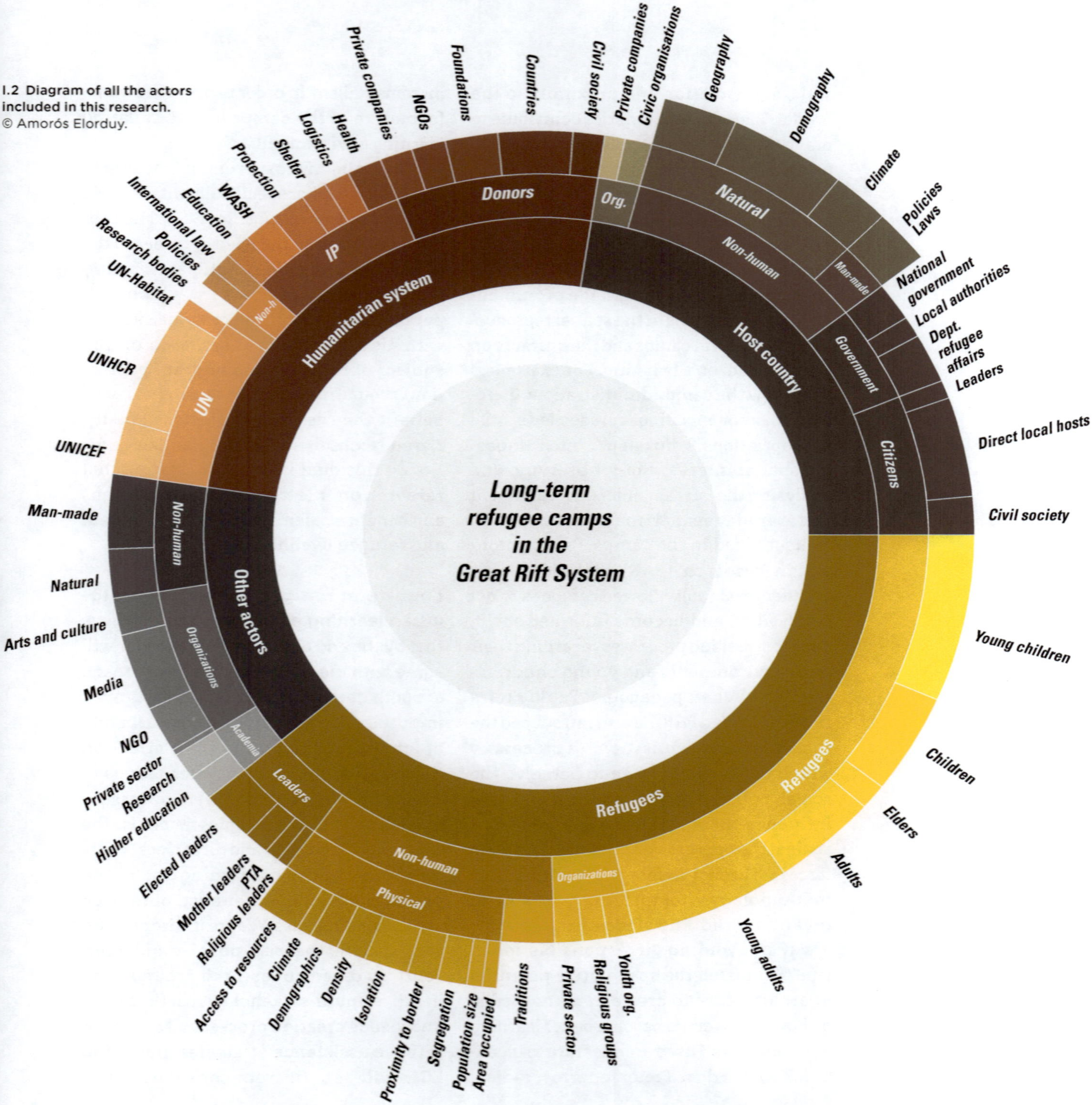

soils, and isolation and proximity to the border. These characteristics contribute to make the long-term camps ever-changing, proto-urban and learning assemblages for young children.

Exploring an architecture of opportunity, in the third chapter, 'Refugee-led spatial interventions: observed, imagined and speculated', I bring to light the prominent position of refugees in the spatial reproduction of long-term camps and their effects on young children's learning. For example, I show how the camp administrations disregard, allow or encourage refugee-led spatial appropriations. I dig deeper into refugee-led spatial interventions, observing and analysing the current quiet encroachment and everyday spatial transformations that refugees lead in the camps. Participatory action research (PAR) methods using architectural tools allowed refugees to get involved in, and become informed about, decision-making processes regarding their built environments and young children's learning. When pedagogist Paulo Freire first introduced PAR, he also introduced the theory of 'conscientisation' – a process by which participants learn to perceive the social, political and economic forces that influence them and learn to take action against the oppressive components of such forces.[35] Through Lefebvre's 'transduction' methodology, '[to] introduce "rigour in invention and knowledge in utopia" as a way of avoiding "irresponsible idealism"',[36] I tested the speculative potential of architecture to create new knowledge on how camps could become better learning environments. I used architecture to incentivise what Edgar Pieterse terms 'radical incrementalism' in order to begin the transformation of the camps into stimulating learning environments.[37]

The collective experiment I recount in this book complies specifically with refugee camp research ethics. In 1986, Harrell-Bond emphasised the need to research the humanitarian system's anti-participatory ideologies and practices,[38] which still persist. David Turton took this idea further with his assertion that research on the subject of refugees and migrant populations should, in addition to causing no harm, benefit the research subjects.[39] Finally, Karen Jacobsen and Loren Landau questioned this dual imperative, stating that research on this topic should be rigorous and benefit academia, policy development and refugee livelihoods.[40]

Long-term refugee camps are proto-urban learning environments—I believe that by the end of the book, the reader will agree with me that its topic and approach are both timely and vital. It is of the utmost importance to explore the proto-urbanity of long-term camps and their effect on lifelong learning as new 'alternatives to camps'[41] are created. It is also necessary that humanitarian strategies recognise the centrality of refugees and direct local hosts on young children's learning and in the production and maintenance of refugee assistance strategies. We are in dire need for case-specific theories, policies and interventions based on research grounded on iterative, multi-stakeholder, participatory knowledge creation processes. Moreover, refugee assistance strategies, including ECD, will benefit from considering the whole built environment as one of its various relevant tools, and from including local creative minds, arts and crafts, both as a universal language and as tools to involve more actors and create positive change. My work might be of use to policy and practice on several fronts, including new refugee assistance strategies, refugee ECD, long-term camp maintenance in East Africa and research by architectural design.

I expect to persuade the reader that a more contextualised, inclusive and participatory approach towards creating and coordinating spatial strategies of refugee assistance is attainable. An architecture of opportunity could improve the lives of those inhabiting the long-term refugee camps and the newly created 'alternatives to camps'. It could transform the long-term camps in East Africa into vibrant schools without walls.

Notes

1. By 'long-term refugee camps', I mean those that have lasted more than three years and host more than 5,000 refugees from the so-called protracted refugee situations. These include refugee settlements (as they are called in Uganda). I encompass refugee settlements and camps because of their primary role in physically containing refugees, even though in the political humanitarian arena they distinguish between the two terms, stating that settlements leave more freedom to refugees.
2. Macgregor, 'History of the development of the East African Rift System', 2015.
3. UNHCR, 'Population statistics', 2020, population figures updated for the end of 2018.
4. Zumthor, 'A way of looking at things', 9.
5. Herz, *From Camp to City*; Herz, 'Refugee camps in Chad'.
6. Hilhorst and Jansen, 'Humanitarian space as arena', 2010.
7. Siddiqi, 'L'historire architecturale d'un territoire non identifie'.
8. Fresia and Von Kanel, 'Beyond space of exception?', 2015.
9. 'Space becomes a medium for politics. Refugee camps are probably the most direct translation of politics into space. Any political strategy or decision has immediate consequence on a spatial dimension in the camp. And any spatial modification, on whatever scale, immediately resonates on a political and demographic level. The camp is politics having become space'. Herz, 'Refugee camps or ideal-cities in dust and dirt', 2005, 318.
10. Jansen, 'The protracted refugee camp', 2015; Minca, 2015; Herz, 'Refugee camps or ideal cities in dust and dirt', 2005; Sanyal, 'Urbanizing refuge', 2014; Grbac, 'Civitas, polis, and urbs'; Ramadan, 'Spatialising the refugee camp', 2013; Agier, 'Afterword: What contemporary camps tell us', 2016.
11. Jansen, 'The protracted refugee camp', 2015, 1.
12. The humanitarian and development modes of aid have different approaches and goals. While the former tends to rely on quick fixes for emergency situations usually in 'fragile' contexts, the latter focuses on sustainable approaches for long-term solutions and works in more stable situations. These two modes of aid are narrowing their positions, affording the recognition of education as a necessary tool in humanitarian relief.
13. On the one hand, humanitarian publications lead the 'humanitarian space and space of protection' reading. These works apply a structuralist and technocratic approach to the creation, maintenance and representation of refugee camps and frame the camps' physical spaces as of almost purely apolitical protection. On the other hand, European political scientists, anthropologists and sociologists initiated the 'space of exception and non-place' reading during the 1990s. Many Euro-American academics and mainstream media publications still use it.
14. Dryden-Peterson, 'Refugee education: A global review'; Dryden-Peterson, 'Refugee education: The crossroads of globalization'.
15. UNICEF, 'Building better brains'; Cappa, 'The formative years'.
16. Montessori, *The Absorbent Mind*; Dewey, 'Experience and education', 1986.
17. Dewey; Coombs, *World Educational Crisis*.
18. Ward and Fyson, *Streetwork: The Exploding School*.
19. Bronfenbrenner, *The Ecology of Human Development*.

20. Ward, 'The child in the city', 1978; David and Weinstein, 'The built environment and children's development'.
21. Bush and Saltarelli, *The Two Faces of Education in Ethnic Conflict*; UNESCO, 'The hidden crisis'; Paulson, *Education, Conflict and Development*.
22. Cooper, 'What do we know about out-of-school youths?' 2005.
23. I first visited Nyabiheke, Kiziba and Gihembe refugee camps in August 2011 for a project to improve primary education facilities in these camps with UNICEF and UNHCR Rwanda.
24. With my research team, we asked respondents about their opinions to improve young children's learning in three different areas: (1) the whole settlement – the streets, common spaces and WASH facilities; (2) the homes; and (3) the educational facilities – ECD, pre-primary and maternelle.
25. Smith, *Decolonizing Methodologies*.
26. Latour, 'From the world of science to the world of research?', 1998.
27. Haraway, 'Situated knowledges', 2009, 583–4.
28. Deleuze and Guattari presented the assemblage theory in 1987 with the publication of *Mille Plateaux: Capitalisme et Schizophrénie*. Assemblage theory presumes that a fixed, linear, hierarchical and stable ontology for the social world does not exist. It rejects the interpretation of the social and natural worlds as made up of finite and definable organisms and considers conceptualisation as a reductionist generalisation and a synthesis to facilitate analysis. Assemblage theory proposes instead that natural and social formations are assemblages of complex configurations that are interrelated, composed of other complex configurations, and that in turn create more extended configurations.
29. Bayat, 'From "dangerous classes" to "quiet rebels"', 2000; Bayat, 'The quiet encroachment of the ordinary', 2007.
30. Scott, 'Preface'.
31. Caldeira, 'Peripheral urbanization', 2016.
32. Pieterse, *City Futures*.
33. The conflicts in the Great Lakes loosely includes Rwanda, Burundi, Eastern Democratic Republic of Congo (DRC) and Uganda, particularly Rwanda's internal wars (1950s–1990s), Burundi's internal wars (1950s–ongoing), Eastern DRC's decades-long internal and external conflicts (1960s–ongoing) and Uganda's internal conflicts (1960s–1990s). The South Sudan conflicts include South Sudan, Sudan and Uganda, specifically: Uganda–Sudan (1960s–1980s), the South of Sudan conflict against Sudan (1980s–2000s) and the South Sudan internal conflict (2010s–ongoing). The Horn of Africa conflict includes mainly Somalia, Ethiopia and Eritrea and Djibouti: Somalia–Ethiopia (1990s), Somalia's internal conflicts (1990s-ongoing), Eritrea–Ethiopia war (1990s–ongoing) and Eritrea's and Ethiopia's authoritarian regimes (1990s–ongoing).
34. The seven case studies in this book are: Nakivale (est. 1958), Kyangwali (est. 1964) and Kyaka II (est. 1983) in Southwest Uganda; Kakuma (est. 1992) in Northwest Kenya; and Kiziba (est. 1997), Kigeme (est. 2005) and Mugombwa (est. 2013) in Rwanda.
35. Freire, *Education for Critical Consciousness*.
36. Lefebvre in Petcou and Petrescu, 'R-URBAN or how to co-produce a resilient city', 2015, 256.
37. Pieterse, *City Future*, 6.
38. Harrell-Bond, *Imposing Aid*, 3.
39. Turton, 'Refugees, forced resettlers and other forced migrants'.
40. Jacobsen and Landau, 'The dual imperative in refugee research', 2003.
41. UNHCR, 'Policy on alternatives to camps'; UNHCR, 'Comprehensive refugee response framework'; UNHCR, 'UNHCR policy on refugee protection and solutions in urban areas'.

The urban turn | informality, co-modification and assemblage

The study of refugee camps started in earnest in the 1980s and currently holds a sizeable and varied body of works. However, not all the contexts, camps and topics receive the same attention. The built environment is still a surprisingly elusive topic, and most East African long-term camps are shockingly understudied in a field packed with European philosophers, social scientists and humanitarians.

It is not clear why the built environment has not gained traction in the field until recently and why its professionals seem to have failed to collaborate in its study. Some causes might stem from the compartmentalisation of both academic studies and humanitarian practice. For example, architecture and urban planning studies are usually historical, theoretical and archival investigations, with architectural design research incorporated only recently. Moreover, humanitarian practice and refugee camp studies tend to think of the built environment and its professionals as just technical support to other programmes rather than relevant in their own right.

Despite a lack of focus on the built environment, it is inevitable for most refugee camp studies to touch upon it in one way or another, as encampment is a spatial answer to humanitarian assistance. Amongst existing works, there are mainly three conceptualisations of the physical space of refugee camps: as a humanitarian space and a space of protection, as a space of exception and non-place and a relatively new conceptualisation as a proto-urban space. On the one hand, humanitarian publications lead the 'humanitarian space and space of protection' reading. These works apply a structuralist and technocratic approach to creating, maintaining and representing refugee camps. They frame the camps' spaces as almost purely apolitical protection. On the other hand, European political scientists, anthropologists and sociologists initiated the 'space of exception and non-place' reading during the 1990s. Many Euro-American academics and mainstream media publications still use it.[1]

Both conceptualisations are partial representations of the camps and are insufficient to characterise, study and manage long-term refugee camps nowadays. These incomplete views simplify the spatial complexity and variability of refugee camps to depict an abstract and universalised 'camp' whose analysis can produce broadly transferable knowledge and generate global policy recommendations. These structuralist conceptualisations are useful to a degree in international refugee assistance and advocacy strategies. Yet, they tend to miss

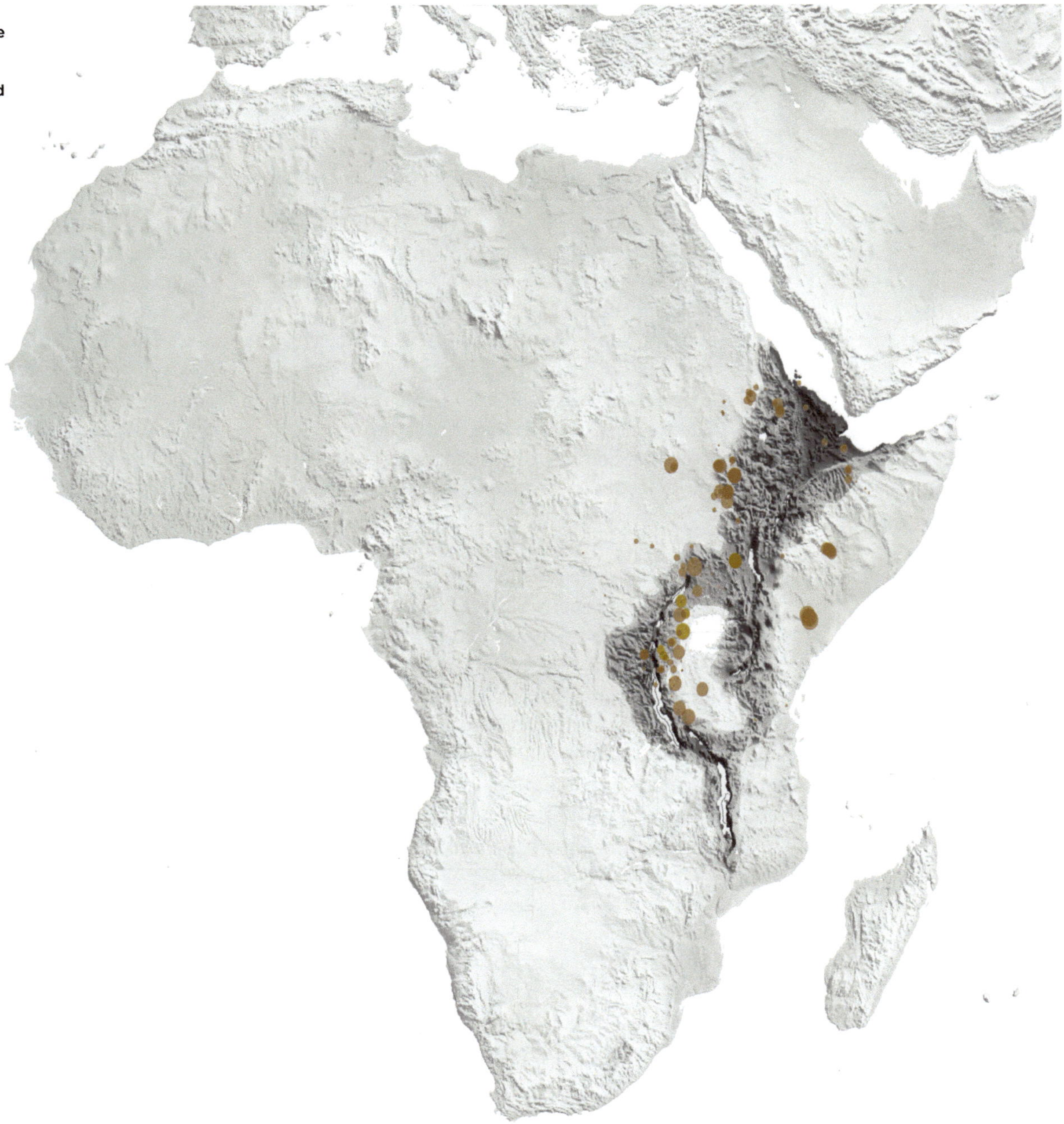

1.1 Map of the African continent showing the East African Rift with the current locations of internally displaced people and refugees registered with the United Nations High Commissioner for Refugees (UNHCR) and the International Organization for Migration. © Amorós Elorduy.

1.1

out on the diversity of actors that create, maintain and reproduce the long-term camp spaces and overlook their influence on inhabitants and direct local hosts, especially the effects on young children's learning.

Since the early 2000s, an 'urban turn' in the literature has presented camps as what I call 'proto-urban spaces'. Post-structuralist authors from varied disciplines lead this branch of works, which include – in addition to humanities and social sciences academics – geographers, architects and urban planners, with a relevant representation of authors that aim at decolonising the field.[2] Urban turn works are especially prevalent in highly visible cases, such as the Palestinian camps in Lebanon, and bring to the forefront the complexity, variability and overlapping authorships of the long-term camp spaces. The urban turn approach renders visible human and non-human actors largely bereft of agency and overlooked under discourses of humanitarian spaces and spaces of exception.

In the following pages, I lead the reader through the evolution of the camp space conceptions in academic discourse and in humanitarian practice, which derived in the current urban turn. I highlight three cross-cutting themes on spatial modifications and place-making in vulnerable urban settlements, which also apply to the refugee camp: informality, co-modification and assemblage thinking. To conclude, I discuss how an urban turn could benefit East African refugee camps, specifically its long-term ones.

The long-term camp and the nascence of the urban turn—Refugee camps have for decades been studied from either a structuralist or a humanitarian standpoint. Both narratives have generalised and simplified the 'camp',[3] the 'refugee' and 'education' into easily managed concepts. These works explain camp life as a relationship between two main actors: the poor and powerless refugees and the either harsh or saviour camp management. The limits of these frameworks for the analysis of refugee camps surfaced in the late 1990s as long-term camps became prevalent, and development and humanitarian efforts started to intermingle.[4]

The 66 existing East African long-term refugee camps are a testament to the refugee camp model failing in its goal of becoming a transitional space of protection. With the turn of the century, it became clear that refugee camps tended to become oxymora: lasting spaces of control and confinement. Long-term camps defy standardised, hierarchical and totalising definitions.

The vast majority of camps become long term due to geopolitics, long-lasting conflicts and a lack of plausible durable solutions for refugees.[5] As camps prolong in time, they pose threats to refugees and their surrounding communities. Despite this, the humanitarian system/host government assemblage continues to replicate this model, partly due to global politics and socio-economic factors, and partly due to assumptions rooted in incomplete and biased information.

The long-term camps pose a paradox that ripples through socio-political, spatial and educational fields. These camps are sites of humanitarian assistance, conflict, political action and everyday life. These camps are a transitional solution turned long-term

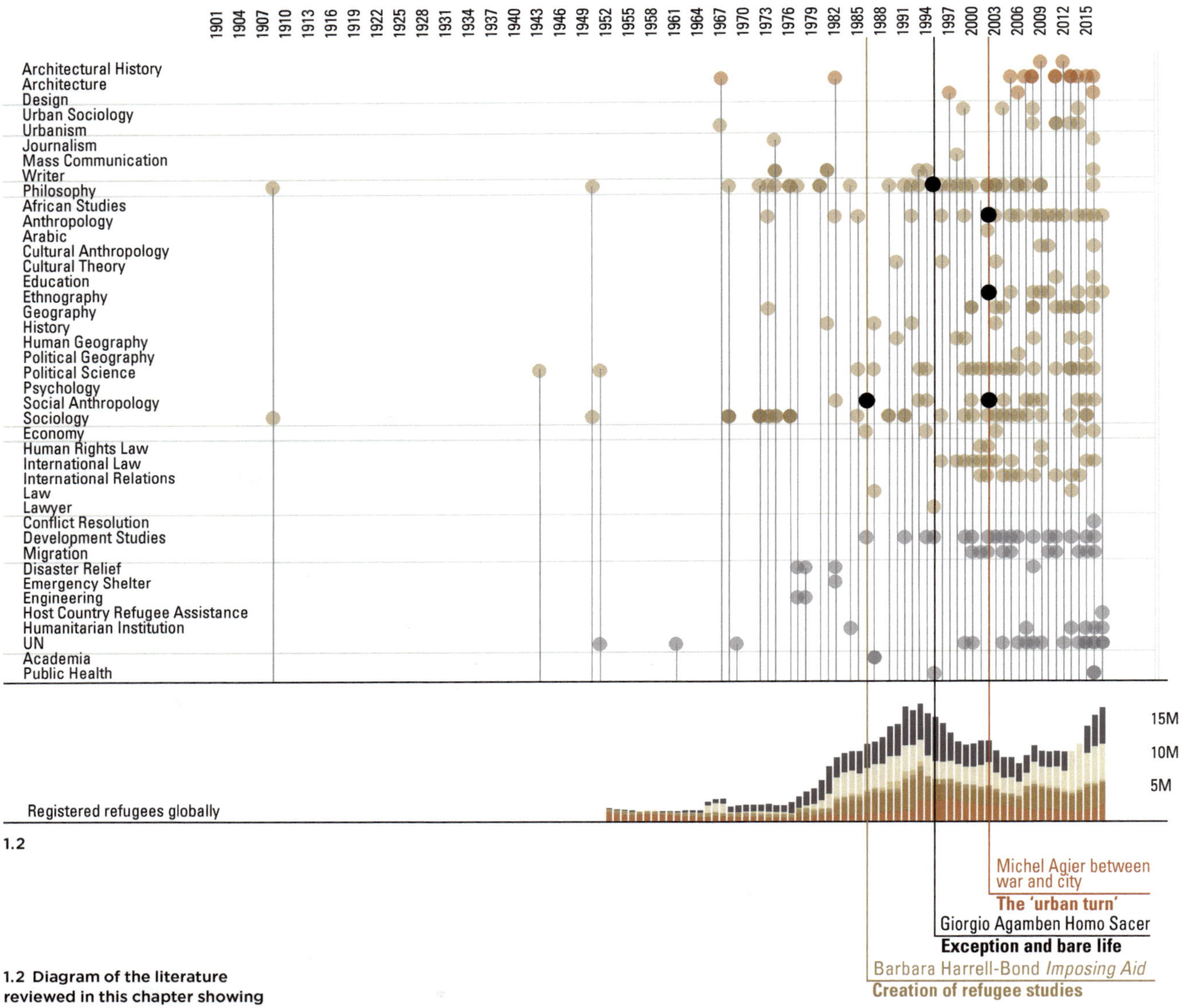

1.2

1.2 Diagram of the literature reviewed in this chapter showing the growth of refugee camp studies' texts from the 1970s onwards (coinciding with the growth of registered refugees globally) and the incorporation of built environment experts into the discussion. The diagram highlights three main points of inflexion relevant to this study: Barbara Harrell-Bond's push for a refugee studies centre at Oxford University, Giorgio Agamben's *Homo Sacer* book and Michel Agier's discussion on camps as cities. © Amorós Elorduy.

problem. They result from a continuous co-modification camp-inhabitant-neighbour, not just the outcome of humanitarian planners and host government policies. In this book, East African long-term camps are cosmopolitan; they are proto-urban environments.[6] They cultivate socio-political and economic interactions, and within them, refugees and their direct local hosts consistently exercise their Lefebvrian 'right to the city'.[7] They are also learning environments. Yet, the learning that young children gain from them is rather negative, and the formal education provided is then crippled, as camps prevent refugees from furthering that education or its use for gainful work.[8] The long-term camps are not – some have never been – standardised and transitional settlements.

Why call them proto-urban rather than thoroughly urban? Despite the move by some academics and humanitarians to recognise these as not just 'humanitarian' spaces or 'limbo', many researchers and practitioners, including most host governments, are reluctant to admit them as urban. Such recognition could legitimise these spaces as permanent – as 'cities' – and their inhabitants as citizens. The current governing structure in these settlements largely prevents refugees' political participation within the nation states that host them and the accountability of the humanitarian organisations that de facto govern them. Besides, my experience, the information I have collected on them and the literature on the topic demonstrate that these settings' political community is not fully formed. There is no real refugee representation in the camps' management. These camps are not a polis, not yet.[9]

These camps suffer from limited, biased – both geographically and disciplinary – and inconsistent information, insufficient to build sturdy and contextualised frameworks to develop appropriate policies. Being understudied affects the lesser-known camps, such as those in Southwest Uganda and Rwanda particularly. A lack of interest and political motivation, accessibility hurdles, limited pre-existing information, a dominance of European-based scholarship that focuses heavily on the Middle East and a scarcity of resources cause this weak pool of knowledge.[10] Besides, the current explosion of big data and remote sensing technologies[11] facilitate the generation of information on understudied camps. Yet, they promote an outsider standpoint. The lack of situated knowledges, the top-down perspective of the Euro-American lenses and the heightened visibility of the Middle East cases tend to guide mainstream thought, inform humanitarian practise and policy, and influence further studies globally. The humanitarian system's lack of resources and organisational loopholes exacerbate this.[12] In East Africa, even the limited and recent literature that offers more nuanced and complex views falls through the cracks of a weak network of existing research and an insufficient humanitarian institutional memory.[13]

In response to the long-term camp phenomenon, in the early 2000s, ethnographers, anthropologists, geographers, architects and urbanists began a body of 'multidisciplinary, multi-scalar, multi-sited'[14] studies. These works promoted an increasingly post-structuralist understanding of the long-term camps, associating their particular socio-spatial organisation with different urban life forms. This move afforded the consideration of these settlements as complex proto-urban assemblages where all components are agents of change.[15] Paraphrasing cultural anthropologist Bram Jansen, these works created an urban turn in refugee camp studies:

'[This shift not] only highlight[ed] the emergence of vibrant and diverse markets, cosmopolitanism and self-management, in places deemed bleak and dependent. It also showed how the academic gaze has moved beyond emergency epistemes and humanitarian and normative discourses, to recognise "normalisation of the geography of the camp", in which people settle down, engage in economic lives and re-form a political body'.[16]

By the mid-2000s, refugee camp studies' scholars started to explore the built environment as a transformative force. Increasingly since the early 2010s, this line of enquiry enabled the inclusion of the concept 'urban', highlighting the agency of both the refugee camps' built environments and their inhabitants. These works dwell in the camps' complexity, bringing out the insufficiency of the structuralist and the humanitarian discourses to define and study them. Moreover, these studies denounce the humanitarian/host government assemblage's inertia to maintain power relationships and assumptions. This awareness is a necessary step towards analysing and changing inactions by the powerful.

As sociologists Giovanni Picker and Silvia Pasquetti point out,[17] Michel Agier's work *Between War and City: Towards an Urban Anthropology of Refugee Camps*[18] kick-started the discussion about the analytical benefits of drawing from comparative literature on cities to study the camps. Agier states that the long-term camps become functional cities due to the complexity and length of the economic and social agreements they trigger:

'... the camps gradually become the sites of an enduring organisation of space, social life and system of power that exist nowhere else. These are paradoxical devices, hybrids that, for lack of an appropriate term, I shall call city-camps (camps-villes). ... It constitutes a "relatively large, dense, and permanent settlement of socially heterogeneous individuals", creates opportunities for encounters, exchanges and reworkings of identity among all who live there. In this sense, the humanitarian device of the camps produces cities, "de la ville", if one considers the city from the point of view of its essential complexity. ... Can the refugee camp become a city in the sense of a space of urban sociability, an urbs, and indeed in the sense of a political space, a polis?'[19]

The hypothesis of a camp as a city allowed researchers to study long-term refugee camps as 'city-like, with complex social arrangements and economic activities'.[20] Philosopher Zygmunt Bauman suggests that with this consideration, 'Agier returns to the refugees their human subjectivity, of which they have been expropriated by the dominant discourses'.[21]

Most scholars agree on some generic city traits that relate to the long-term refugee camps' urbanity such as size, density, heterogeneity and social hierarchies. However, the contested definition of 'city' complicates its use as an analytic tool.[22] Particularly, in regions of the third urban wave, as is the African continent, growing numbers of urban scholars challenge the use of the terms 'city', 'metropolis' and 'megacities' as Euro-American constructs.[23] Amongst refugee studies scholars, Liisa Malkki opposes the use of the term 'city' to analyse camps and instead explores the idea of camps as urban-like, political and identity-creating places.[24] I align with Manuel Herz and call them proto-urban.[25]

Once the 'city' dispute was acknowledged and urban turn works focused on urban traits, they allowed a growing body of authors such as Claudio Minca,[26] Iris Katz,[27] Romola Sanyal,[28] Peter Grbac[29] and many others[30] to bridge the gap between humanitarian spaces and urban environments. These texts borrow from urban theory, urban planning and architecture. These increasingly post-structural studies unveil the myriad of human and non-human actors that participate in camps' evolution. They create space for discussions about camp inhabitants' agency and their role in the camps' spatial re-production. For example, in his work *Civitas, Polis, and Urbs*, Grbac defends that conceiving refugee camps as urban spaces can allow the inhabitants' agency to be fully acknowledged.[31] The geographer Sanyal elaborates on that by suggesting that refugees' actions 'transgress the boundaries of place and non-place'.[32] Both authors focus on Palestinian refugee camps and try to respond to the camps' preconceptions as anomalies, violations, non-places and ghettoes expressed by structuralist studies.

This urban turn in academia began to influence humanitarian refugee assistance practice from the 2010s[33] when the international community started to acknowledge the relevance of the physical space on refugee assistance and the protracted nature of refugee camps.[34] In 2014, the humanitarian assemblage drafted and accepted an *Alternative to Camps* policy[35] seeking new 'durable solutions' connected to new spatial forms of assistance.[36] In 2016, the international community recognised the complexity, length of existence and variability of conditions amongst refugees and refugee camps with the signing of the *New York Declaration for Refugees and Migrants* which included the proposal of a Global Compact on Refugees and facilitated the development of the Comprehensive Refugee Response Framework (CRRF).[37] The CRRF aims to welcome refugees in national policies, providing a more contextualised response to their assistance.

Looking at the refugee camps through the lenses of post-structural urban theory affords an understanding of the camps' built environments as a key player in political, social, economic and educational actions within the camps and their broader networks.[38] Specifically, three cross-cutting issues from urban theory appear useful in the analysis of long-term refugee camps: informality, co-modification and assemblage thinking. I understand informality as a fluid, elastic and adaptative means of creating, not as opposed to formality but as inherent in the urban. I assume co-modification as natural in the urban realm, particularly as the multiple human and non-human actors are agents of change and influence each other. Finally, I conceive assemblage thinking as a post-structural framework for analysing social complexity, emphasising non-linear approaches to social systems based on mutability, exchangeability and interconnectedness.[39]

Informality—Geographer Romola Sanyal has been instrumental in the inclusion of informality as a line of enquiry in the study of refugee camps and refugee settlements in urban areas.[40] Borrowing from urban planners and theorists such as Nazer Alsayyad[41] and AbdouMaliq Simone,[42] Sanyal applies notions of urban informality and decolonisation to describe and study the socio-political, economic and physical connotations of long-term spaces of refuge. She outlines parallels between informal settlements and long-term refugee settlements, sustaining that the boundaries between the global and the urban marginal are blurring. Her work aims to demystify the universal and generic ideas that present refugee spaces solely as Agambean bare life spaces and Foucauldian biopolitics.[43]

Another geographer, Diana Martin, compares urban informality and long-term encampment spaces following anthropologist Arjun Appadurai's steps. Martin uses the suffix '-scape' to coin the term 'campscapes',[44] which 'gives the idea of fluidity, of something elastic. It indicates dispersal and non-static boundaries. The notion of "campscape" seems to better render the image of what is the refugee camp today in its relation with its surroundings as the exception has transcended the camp's shape'.[45] In addition, anthropologist Ilana Feldman, while not mentioning informality per se, describes the informal development processes of long-term refugee camps in the Middle East.[46]

In the East African context, economic studies are the only ones looking at informality, and they have little regard for the production of space.[47] Jansen's[48] and Anooradha Iyer Siddiqi's works[49] about the Kenyan camps – the most visible of the East African camps – look at their development and mention informal processes of construction while not dwelling on them.

Co-modification—The inclusion of post-structuralist logics in refugee camp studies has allowed diverse types of power and a variety of actors into the discussion. It has afforded refugees, direct local hosts and the built environment to show their agency as they exercise what philosopher and sociologist Henri Lefebvre called the 'right to the city'. This notion discussed how city space and inhabitants are co-constitutive and use their agency to modify each other.[50] In the camps, human actors transform the physical spaces while simultaneously those alter the identity of refugees, surrounding communities, host governments and the perception others have of them. Urban turn literature presents co-modification in three discrete fields: political, economic and sociocultural.

In the political arena, the discussion in African soil explores the contested role of space as an actor that enhances or tames refugees' political aspirations and negotiations. One example of this is Elisabeth Holzer's work. She explains how Liberian refugees – particularly women – appropriated Buduburam refugee camp's open spaces[51] to demonstrate against its administrators.[52] As a consequence of this occupation, the humanitarian institutions' perception of these refugees changed from victims to political dissidents with implications for their asylum status. Another example is Manuel Herz's work about Western Sahara's camps in Tindouf. He sustains how these camps' mere existence – not created or run by the

United Nations High Commissioner for Refugees – allowed Saharawi refugees to 'build' a Saharawi state with ministries. These health and education services would have been unthinkable before the exile.[53] In Tanzania, both Liisa Malkki's[54] and Simon Turner's works[55] focus on the misconceptions held by the humanitarian system, host governments and the media about refugees. Particularly, Malkki reflects on the refugees' heterogeneity and how the physical setting influenced their cultural and political identity. In her case study in northern Tanzania, encamped refugees developed a more robust conception of their Burundian identity than their urban counterparts.

In the economic arena, Peter Mwangi Kagwanja and Marc-Antoine Pérouse de Montclos study the socio-economic opportunities that Dadaab's built environments, their geographic location and their media visibility afforded.[56] Rahul Oka presents these same camps' informal economy as a result and necessity of the humanitarian aid operation and the physical spaces it created in Kenya.[57] Alexander Betts and his team developed a similar work for the camps in Southwest Uganda in 2015.[58]

In the sociocultural arena, a remarkable topic is the interaction between refugee camps and neighbouring communities. For example, Holzer points out how, in Buduburam, 'the influx of people and resources transformed the camp environs and surrounding villages into an urban space. In the ensuing years, Buduburam became host to a diverse array of nationalities'.[59]

In the Rwandan, Southwest Ugandan and Northwest Kenyan camps that I describe here, there is a continuous co-modification between studies, policies, physical spaces, laws, media, aid, refugees, camps, authorities, regulations, culture, geography, traditions and education. I focus primarily on how the co-modifications between camp inhabitant, direct local hosts, built environment and natural environment affect young children's learning. In these camps, learning environments come to the fore as main characters in young children's learning, especially their learning by experience. Precisely, the informal learning environments – homes, streets and common areas – gain responsibility in the education and holistic development of children born and raised in these long-term camps.

Assemblage thinking—It is unsurprising that the notion of 'assemblage', put forward by Deleuze and Guattari in the late 1980s,[60] emerged strongly amongst urban turn studies. The first works that applied assemblage thinking to refugee camps focused on the Palestinian camps in Lebanon and began in the mid-2000s.[61] For example, Adam Ramadan described the Palestinian refugee camps as assemblages of human and non-human actors, analysing time–space particularities with a critical take on Agamben's 'space of exception'.[62] Also, political scientist Nasser Abourahme developed 'a reading of the camp as a material assemblage that brings subjects and objects, people and things into mutually constitutive relations'.[63]

Several other urban turn authors have used the concept of space as an assemblage. For example, Siddiqi and Anoma

Pieris use it to analyse long-term refugee camps in Kenya and Sri Lanka, respectively.[64] Anthropologist Julie Marie Peteet highlights the interconnectedness and assemblic nature of camps, which draws from culture and traditions in countries of origin and the routes refugees have taken and merges that with the camps' contextual situations. She describes the Palestinian refugee camps in Lebanon as 'profoundly shaped by and referenced to places of origin and residence, multiple boundaries, and routes of travel between them'.[65]

Critics of assemblage thinking state that it can easily fall in relativism and fail to acknowledge enough power differences. However, Ramadan, Peteet and Abourahme show that the theory enables them to account for differences of power within and between assemblages. As Ramadan puts it, 'in absence of a single sovereign, different actors and organisations in the camps compete for power and influence among the population through force of arms, provision of services and resources, or the power of political ideas'.[66] This theoretical approach brings to the fore different types of power and agency hidden under humanitarian and structural accounts. Assemblage thinking affords authors to move away from binomial conventions such as powerful–vulnerable, state–individual and humanitarian system–refugee victim.

By questioning the conventionally powerful – the humanitarian system and the host country – and using situated bits of knowledge, studies can help unveil hidden power dynamics. For example, in the seven camps I describe in depth in the next two chapters, different power struggles stand out: refugee leadership, gangs, religious leaders and commercial lobbies. Particularly in the education field, assemblage thinking unveils the hegemony of non-formal and informal educational systems and facilities that operate in addition to, or instead of, the humanitarian system's formal ones.

East African urban turn – a way forward?—Since the urban turn appeared, there is a growing interest in the human and social dimensions of refugee camps' built environments. Studies worldwide are starting to draw from comparative literature on urban theory, urban planning and architecture. However, works on hyper-visible cases prevail, and humanitarian aid is slow to incorporate the learning gathered from the urban turn into practice. One of the issues with the urban turn in refugee studies is the evasive definition of 'urban'. The urban dilemma leads to the question of whether defining refugee camps as urban might ease their study and benefit refugees and the assistance given to them. Besides, there is resistance – mainly by the humanitarian system/host government assemblage – to accept these spaces as urban, since the term 'urban' conveys normalcy and permanence.[67]

Most long-term camps in Eastern Africa were established before the humanitarian camp planning guidelines were in place. Their material evolution assimilates in many ways that of informal settlements in the region. Therefore, it is fitting to study them through an urban lens. They have developed organic settlement patterns, responding to material means, geography, pre-existing community alliances,[68] length of exile, humanitarian system's resources and refugees' daily activities that have modified and continue to change these spaces. In the particular examples portrayed in this book,[69] Uganda follows a settlement rather than a camp model,[70] and humanitarian planning was not introduced in the camps in Rwanda and Kenya until 2005 with the establishment of Kigeme and Kakuma phase III.

This particular urban turn study incorporates human and non-human actors previously bereft of voice into the conversation. It might help understand biases and assumptions, power imbalances and colonial baggage embedded in East Africa's refugee assistance policies – policies that use spatial strategies as their go-to tool to control, assist and manage displaced people.

Giving centrality to the urban may allow a better understanding of the built environment as a powerful and socially charged tool and its use to tackle oppression and improve assistance, young children's learning and refugee livelihoods. The three cross-cutting issues extracted from post-structural urban theory – informality, co-modification and assemblage thinking – highlight the built environment as a critical factor influencing life in the camps. These post-structural lenses underline the relevance of the camps' built environments as added educators, bringing to the fore refugees' actions on young children's learning.

The ensemble of urban turn works and the current humanitarian system's discussions about diversifying spatial strategies of assistance[71] are opening up to nuance and various voices, providing an added path to take, which is more empathic and contextualised.

Notes

1. Diken and Laustsen, *The Culture of Exception*; Diken, 'From refugee camps to gated communities', 2004.
2. Paraphrasing cultural anthropologist Bram Jansen, I call the 'urban turn' the epistemic and ontological shift that occurred in refugee camp studies that associated long-term refugee camps with urbanisation. The inclusion of geographers, architects, urban planners and urban theorists into the study of refugee camps brought with it this new perspective. Jansen, 'The protracted refugee camp', 2015.
3. Diken, 'From refugee camps to gated communities', 2004; Diken and Laustsen, 'The camp', 2006.
4. The development–aid divide owed to the different approaches and goals of the humanitarian and development modes of aid. While the former relies on quick fixes for emergency situations, usually in fragile contexts, the later focuses on sustainable approaches for long-term solutions and works in more stable countries. With the acknowledgement of the long-term camp oxymoron, the protractedness of the refugee crises and with the adoption of the sustainable development goals by the international community, these two modes of aid started to narrow their positions. By the mid-2000s, the approximation of both aid approaches afforded the recognition of education as a necessary tool in humanitarian relief and enabled policies such as the 'alternative to camps'.
5. Feldman, 'What is a camp?', 2014; Jansen, 'The protracted refugee camp', 2015; Napier-Moore, 'Entrenched relations'.
6. I use the term 'urban' to mean 'within or of distinctly demarcated human settlements'. I specifically use the term 'proto-urban' borrowing from Manuel Herz who uses it to refer to the long-term refugee camps in the Western Sahara. Herz, 'Refugee camps of the Western Sahara', 2013, 383.
7. Lefebvre, *Le Droit à La Ville*.
8. The countries that tend to encamp refugees also tend to prevent them from taking gainful work, and it was not until the late 2010s when some camps started to provide some form of secondary education and vocational training

opportunities. Dryden-Peterson, 'Refugee education: A global review'.
9. Jansen, 'The accidental city', 2009; Agier and Lecadet, *Un Monde de Camps*; Feldman, 'What is a camp?', 2014; Jansen, 'The protracted refugee camp', 2015.
10. Refugee camps that receive a lot of media attention, such as the Dadaab camps in Kenya, often attract more focus and funding than the least visible to the international community and mainstream media.
11. OpenStreetMap, 'Humanitarian Openstreetmap Team'.
12. Loescher, 'The UNHCR at 50', 26–7.
13. Loescher, 6.
14. Agier, 'Afterword: What contemporary camps tell us', 2016, 461.
15. Grbac, 'Civitas, polis, and urbs'; Sanyal, 'Refugees and the city', 2012.
16. Jansen, 'The protracted refugee camp', 2015, 1.
17. Picker and Pasquetti, 'Durable camps', 2015.
18. Agier, 'Between war and city', 2002.
19. Agier, 322.
20. Sanyal, 'Refugees and the city', 2012, 634.
21. Bauman, 'In the lowly nowherevilles of liquid modernity', 2002, 343.
22. Vincent-Geslin et al., *Translating the City*.
23. Pieterse, 'Grasping the unknowable', 2011; Pieterse, 'Introduction: Rogue urbanisms', 2011; Simone, 'Movement: The Zawiyyah as the city'.
24. Malkki, *Purity and Exile*.
25. Herz, 'Refugee camps of the Western Sahara', 2013, 383.
26. Minca, 'Geographies of the camp', 2015.
27. Katz, 'Between bare life and everyday life', 2017.
28. Sanyal, 'Refugees and the city', 2012.
29. Grbac, 'Reimagining the refugee camp as the city'.
30. Abourahme, 'Assembling and spilling-over', 2015; Abourahme and Hilal, 'The production of space'; Peteet, *Landscape of Hope and Despair*; Petti and Hilal, 'Architecture of exile'; Isin and Rygiel, 'Of other global cities'; Martin, 'From spaces of exception to "campscapes"', 2015.
31. Grbac, 'Civitas, polis, and urbs', 4.
32. Sanyal, 'Squatting in camps', 2011, 880.
33. The United Nations High Commissioner for Refugees (UNHCR)'s 2014 policy on alternatives to camps has prompted collaboration between the UNHCR and UN-Habitat for the establishment of Kalobeyei refugee camp in northern Kenya. UN-Habitat is applying practices it develops in informal urban contexts to the implementation of Kalobeyei.
34. UNHCR, 'Protracted refugee situations'; UNHCR, 'Protracted refugee situations: The search for practical solutions'; UNHCR, 'Protracted refugee situations: Revisiting the problem'.
35. UNHCR, Policy on alternatives to camps.
36. UNHCR, 'Kalobeyei settlement'; UNHCR Rwanda, 'Mahama refugee camp, one year on'; Ennead et al., 'Rethinking refugee communities'.
37. United Nations, *New York Declaration for Refugees and Migrants*; UNHCR, 'Comprehensive refugee response framework'.
38. Iveson and Fincher, '"Just diversity" in the city of difference', 408.
39. 'Both assemblage thinking and ANT have much to say about the spatial dimensions of power and politics. That is because both approaches are concerned with why orders emerge in particular ways, how they hold together, somewhat precariously, how they reach across or mold space and how they fall apart'. Müller, 'Assemblages and actor-network', 2015, 27.
40. Sanyal, 'Urbanizing refuge', 2014.
41. Roy and AlSayyad, *Urban Informality*.
42. Simone, 'Cities and change'.
43. Sanyal, 'Urbanizing refuge', 2014; Sanyal, 'Refugees and the city', 2012.
44. Appadurai, 'Grassroots globalization and research imagination', 2000.
45. Martin, 'From spaces of exception to "campscapes"', 2015, 14.
46. Feldman, 'What is a camp?', 2014.
47. Oka, 'Unlikely cities in the desert', 2011; Oka, 'Coping with the refugee wait', 2014; Betts and Omata, *Refugee Economies*.
48. Jansen, 'The accidental city', 2009; Jansen, 'The protracted refugee camp', 2015.
49. Siddiqi, 'L'historire architecturale d'un territoire non identifie'.
50. Lefebvre, *Le Droit à La Ville*.
51. Buduburam is a long-term refugee camp established in 1989 in Ghana to host refugees fleeing the Liberian civil war.
52. Holzer, *The Concerned Women of Buduburam*.
53. Herz, *From Camp to City*.
54. Malkki, *Purity and Exile*.
55. Turner, 'The barriers of innocence'.
56. Kagwanja and Pérouse de Montclos, 'Refugee camps or cities?', 2000.
57. Oka, 'Unlikely cities in the desert', 2011.
58. Betts and Omata, *Refugee Economies*.
59. Holzer, 'What happens to law in a refugee camp?', 2013, 852.

60. Deleuze and Guattari, *A Thousand Plateaus*.
61. Peteet, 'Producing place, spatializing identity, 1948–68'.
62. Ramadan, 'Spatialising the refugee camp', 2013.
63. Abourahme, 'Assembling and spilling-over', 2015, 200.
64. Siddiqi, 'L'historire architecturale d'un territoire non identifie'; Pieris, 'Encampments', 2014.
65. Peteet, *Landscape of Hope and Despair*, 25.
66. Ramadan, 'Spatialising the refugee camp', 2013, 72.
67. Bauman, 'In the lowly nowherevilles of liquid modernity', 2002; Jansen, 'The protracted refugee camp', 2015; Grbac, 'Reimagining the refugee camp as the city'.
68. Chkam, 'Aid and the perpetuation of refugee camps', 2016, 83.
69. The seven camps presented in this book are: Nakivale (est. 1958), Kyangwali (est. 1964) and Kyaka II (est. 1983) in Southwest Uganda; Kakuma (est. 1992) in Northwest Kenya; and Kiziba (est. 1997), Kigeme (est. 2005) and Mugombwa (est. 2013) in Rwanda.
70. The Ugandan government and UNHCR call the strategies of refugee containment in the country 'settlements'. 'A "settlement" differs from a "camp" in that it is of a more permanent nature (characterised by infrastructure such as schools, hospitals, brick buildings, boreholes etc.) in which refugees are expected to become self-sufficient over time. "Camps" are often spontaneous and temporary creations (structures of mud and wattle) in which refugees almost exclusively depend on relief handouts'. Bagenda, Naggaga and Smith, 'Land problems in Nakivale settlement', 5. However, even if more loosely contained than in other countries, refugees' freedoms are still curtailed in these so-called settlements.
71. UNHCR, 'The implementation of UNHCR's policy on refugee protection and solutions in urban areas'; UNHCR, Policy on alternatives to camps; United Nations, *New York Declaration for Refugees and Migrants*; UNHCR, 'Comprehensive refugee response framework'.

Ever-evolving assemblages | the built environment of seven East African long-term camps

The beginning of refugee encampment policies in Eastern Africa—Simultaneously inhabited by different nomad and sedentary cultures, Eastern Africa has experienced regional and global migrations for millennia.[1] Mobility patterns across the continent were usual and somewhat fluid until the colonial partition of Sub-Saharan Africa in the late nineteenth century. The liberation from European colonial rule created new nation states with permanent and impermeable political borders. Due to the 1951 refugee convention,[2] many of those crossing the new borders were classified as refugees.

Influenced by their European colonisers, some of the soon-to-be-independent nation states began to house these refugees in specially devised isolated rural settlements in the late 1950s. This move supposed a change in former settlement

2.1 Kiziba refugee camp, Karongi district, Western region, Rwanda. September 2017. © Amorós Elorduy.

2.1

patterns that usually saw migrants settled in places of their choosing through negotiations and struggles.[3] In the early 1960s, due mostly to new conflicts in the young countries, East African refugee numbers grew exponentially,[4] and the United Nations High Commissioner for Refugees (UNHCR) became involved in the region's refugee assistance.[5] The UNHCR consolidated and standardised the refugee settlements established in some countries by colonising powers and created new ones.

Initially, 'villagisation' theories[6] promoted by the International Bank for Reconstruction and Development – the forerunner to the World Bank – underpinned the UNHCR's rationale behind encamping refugee populations on the continent. Villagisation implied that uprooting and condensing populations in 'villages'[7] would ensure the agricultural and technological development desired by both the Bank and the new states' governments.[8] As is evident in numerous studies, these social engineering strategies and theories failed. Despite that, the UNHCR borrowed from these and other spatial forms of extortion happening at the time – concentration camps, prisoners of war camps and forced labour camps – to develop 'agricultural' refugee settlements. With these large, isolated settlements, the UNHCR aimed to instil a sense of belonging to refugees and to ease their assistance, economic independence and control.[9] These agricultural camps evolved into the planned isolated camps that we are used to seeing in the mainstream media.

The continuation of encampment and its effects on young children—Ever since its creation,[10] the UNHCR has presented the spatial containment of refugees as a paradigmatic means to assist them.[11] The UNHCR has contributed to building hundreds of camps over the decades. New camps continue to sprout up, despite renowned scholars and even the UNHCR[12] – its own *Handbook for Emergencies* advises against large, planned camps – expressing since the 1980s, in texts and policies, what was already evident on the ground. The majority of refugees choose to self-settle in urban centres, camps become long-term and appear to cause more problems than solutions for both refugees and direct local hosts (fig. 2.2).[13,14]

The reasons why containment strategies prevail – albeit with small modifications over time – above other policies are the primary focus of numerous refugee camp studies.[15] Some causes are the international community's geopolitical interests and mistrust in African governments – largely a post-colonial hangover, the large number of refugees, the overlapping long-term conflicts and the humanitarian system's biases triggered by lack of contextualised knowledge. Some of these biases include, for example, that displacement is temporary – contradicted by increasing refugee flows and long-lasting displacement[16] – and that refugees are a smooth fabric with no agency and not enough skill that needs to be contained and controlled to be assisted. Some scholars defend the idea that encampments are maintained because they justify the humanitarian aid system's work. The humanitarian system takes over host states' responsibilities through the camps, releasing them from the so-called refugee

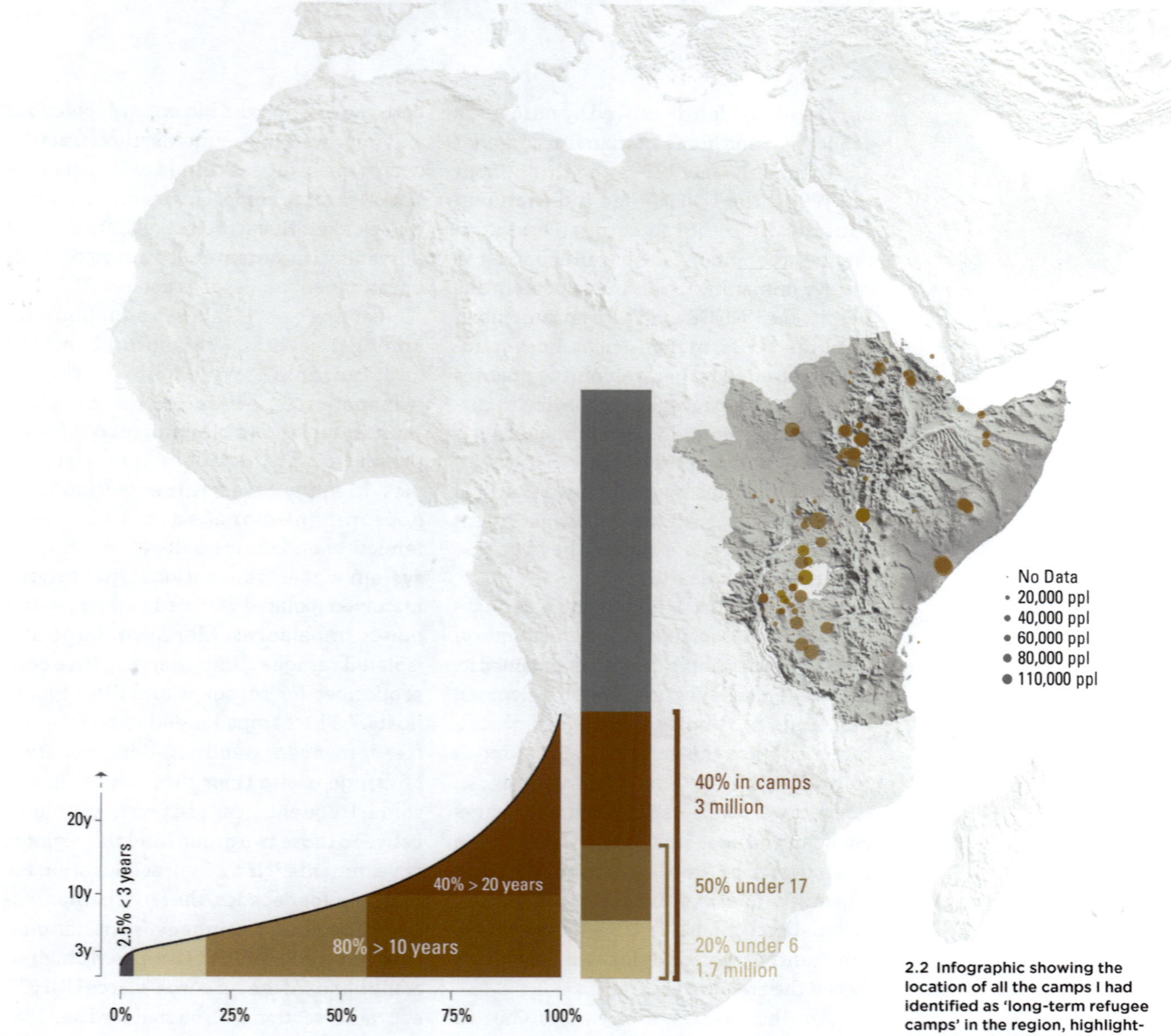

2.2

2.2 Infographic showing the location of all the camps I had identified as 'long-term refugee camps' in the region, highlighting that most UNHCR-registered refugees are in exile for more than 10 years, and only 40% of them settle in camps. Data sources: Nicholas Crawford, John Cosgrave, Simone Haysom and Nadine Walicki. 'Protracted Displacement: Uncertain Paths to Self-Reliance in Exile'. HPG Commissioned Report, Humanitarian Policy Group and Overseas Development Institute, London, 2015.© Amorós Elorduy.

burden – a burden disproved by numerous economists and humanitarian researchers.[17]

During the late 1980s and throughout the 1990s, the UNHCR-led international community imposed refugee encampment as a condition for African countries to receive humanitarian and development aid. Despite the UNHCR's push for encampment, until the 1990s, many African host countries promoted rather welcoming policies to neighbouring refugees according to customary practices and 'solidarity' between formerly colonised peoples.[18] However, as host countries began to have political and economic problems and displacement spanned years and decades, they became encumbered and fatigued.

Some countries fought the establishment of large, isolated, planned camps on their soil. For example, Malawi maintained its pre-existent policies until 1987. It welcomed hundreds of thousands of Mozambican refugees since the early 1980s, peaking at 1.2 million in 1990.[19] Initially, Mozambican refugees were encouraged to settle spontaneously, and refugee integration was evolving well, covered by the Malawian government. However, due to intricate national and international affairs, in 1986–7, the country reluctantly acceded to foreign aid, which forced the creation of camps.

Another example of this is Guinea (Conakry). Between 1989 and 1999, the West African country welcomed half a million Liberian and Sierra Leonean refugees with an open self-settlement approach, and accepted humanitarian aid solely if the UNHCR directed it to reinforce its national infrastructure where refugees freely chose to settle. This strategy strengthened relationships between existing and incoming populations and improved the country's infrastructure where the refugees settled, which usually was close to the borders where infrastructure was weaker. Nevertheless, eventually, the humanitarian system ended up imposing its encampment model of assistance.[20]

Guinea's and Malawi's situations are amongst several,[21] including Zambia[22] and Tanzania,[23] which illustrate how transnational powers and international humanitarian aid transformed Africa's pre-existing refugee assistance strategies. In many cases, this evolution from government-managed policies that tended to encourage self-settlement to a system where transnational institutions managed isolated planned camps caused power imbalances. Moreover, large and isolated refugee camps had negative consequences for refugees and direct local hosts.[24] The camps tended to reduce the freedom, agency and self-determination of refugees and their direct local hosts, which frequently caused power struggles between those two groups and the regional governments.[25] If we look at education for example, for decades, the large camps isolated the young refugees from national education programmes. Camps left children at the hands of the resource-scarce UNHCR education section with its standardised low-quality programmes and monitoring.[26]

As the humanitarian–development divide narrows, information and technology become more accessible[27] and the UNHCR acknowledges the protracted nature of refugee situations, refugee assistance is enjoying a longer-term vision. This elongated vision seems to be positive, as it matches the reality on the ground. Most of the refugee camps established in East Africa have not been dismantled and have become long term. However, despite efforts to move away from isolated and temporary planned camps into alternatives to camps and assistance in urban areas, the humanitarian system continues to rely on physical containment globally.[28] Even if aiming to equalise relationships with direct local hosts and hiding under different labels, spatial containment strategies continue.

The step from policy into practice is not bringing a structural change to encampment strategies. Under different labels, the containment and isolation of refugees into specifically designed zones continues. That is due in significant part to the inertia of host governments and humanitarian and international actors. Yet, I believe, it is also due to the unbalanced relevance given to advocacy efforts and politics rather than utilising more spatial knowledge. While the information is there, in the everyday running of the camps, policies do not tap into it. Having, and using, the physical information about these settlements and understanding how they change over time and how they affect camp inhabitants – especially young children and their support networks – can improve refugee assistance theory and practice. The use of contextualised knowledge can inform decisions in long-term camps and new interventions. That is what I have tried to achieve, on a small scale, and what I explain in the following sections.

In this chapter, I first describe Nakivale, Kyangwali, Kyaka II, Kakuma, Kiziba, Kigeme and Mugombwa refugee camps, how they were first established and what are they becoming, underlining how their architectures affect young children. For some, it is the first published account of their history. I then dissect and reassemble their spaces on regional, country and landscape scales to understand patterns and similar behaviours. I explain six spatial characteristics of all seven settlements which influence their evolution and affect the young refugees living in them: three interactive characteristics – growing heterogeneity and complexity, co-functioning/interconnectedness and ever becoming – and three static ones – porosity, land scarcity and poor soil, and isolation and proximity to the border. I then discuss what impact this situated knowledge has for refugee early childhood development (ECD) and refugee assistance in the region (fig. 2.3).

Complex, heterogeneous and ever-evolving encampment territories—The East African Rift is a geographical area ranging from the Red Sea to the southern tip of Lake Malawi. Mountain ridges with densely populated fertile valleys as well as sandy hot and dry planes usually scarcely inhabited by nomadic pastoralists characterise the Rift. The UNHCR and host governments establish the camps close to the porous borders of the different nation states along the Rift in relatively underpopulated lands where it is usually challenging to live. However, owing to environmental pressures and the camps' economic and social opportunities, the population in and around them grows, putting pressure on the land use.

The three areas I describe in this book – Southwest Uganda, Northwest Kenya

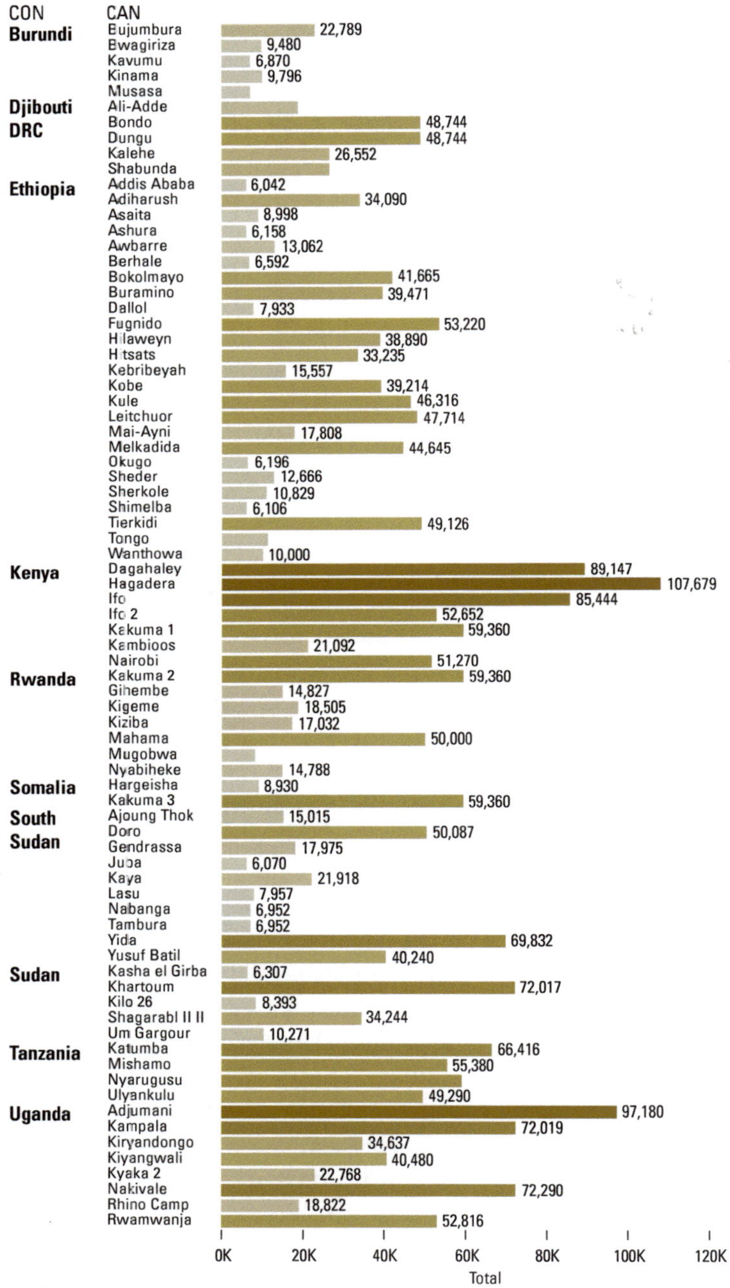
CON
CAN
Burundi
Bujumbura 22,789
Bwagiriza 9,480
Kavumu 6,870
Kinama 9,796
Musasa
Djibouti
Ali-Adde
DRC
Bondo 48,744
Dungu 48,744
Kalehe 26,552
Shabunda
Ethiopia
Addis Ababa 6,042
Adiharush 34,090
Asaita 8,998
Ashura 6,158
Awbarre 13,062
Berhale 6,592
Bokolmayo 41,665
Buramino 39,471
Dallol 7,933
Fugnido 53,220
Hilaweyn 38,890
Hitsats 33,235
Kebribeyah 15,557
Kobe 39,214
Kule 46,316
Leitchuor 47,714
Mai-Ayni 17,808
Melkadida 44,645
Okugo 6,196
Sheder 12,666
Sherkole 10,829
Shimelba 6,106
Tierkidi 49,126
Tongo
Wanthowa 10,000
Kenya
Dagahaley 89,147
Hagadera 107,679
Ifo 85,444
Ifo 2 52,652
Kakuma 1 59,360
Kambioos 21,092
Nairobi 51,270
Rwanda
Kakuma 2 59,360
Gihembe 14,827
Kigeme 18,505
Kiziba 17,032
Mahama 50,000
Mugobwa
Nyabiheke 14,788
Somalia
Hargeisha 8,930
Kakuma 3 59,360
South Sudan
Ajoung Thok 15,015
Doro 50,087
Gendrassa 17,975
Juba 6,070
Kaya 21,918
Lasu 7,957
Nabanga 6,952
Tambura 6,952
Yida 69,832
Yusuf Batil 40,240
Sudan
Kasha el Girba 6,307
Khartoum 72,017
Kilo 26 8,393
Shagarabl II II 34,244
Um Gargour 10,271
Tanzania
Katumba 66,416
Mishamo 55,380
Nyarugusu
Ulyankulu 49,290
Uganda
Adjumani 97,180
Kampala 72,019
Kiryandongo 34,637
Kiyangwali 40,480
Kyaka 2 22,768
Nakivale 72,290
Rhino Camp 18,822
Rwamwanja 52,816
0K
20K
40K
60K
80K
100K
120K
Total

2.3

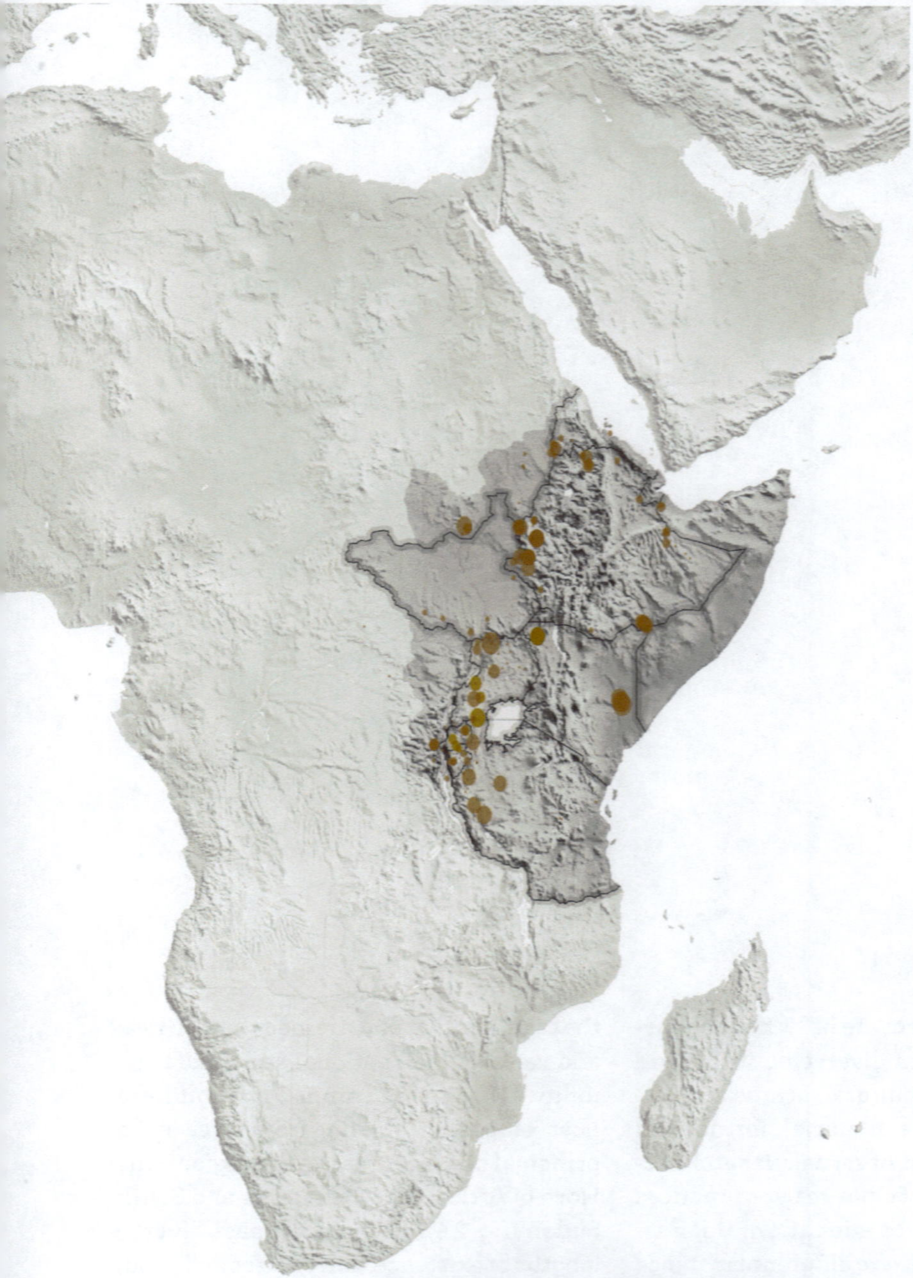

2.3 Map of East Africa (including the southern part of Sudan and Eastern Congo) with the 66 long-term camps I had identified in the region highlighting nation states' borders. The graphic shows the names of all 66 camps, their location and the number of refugees they hosted as of December 2016. © Amorós Elorduy.

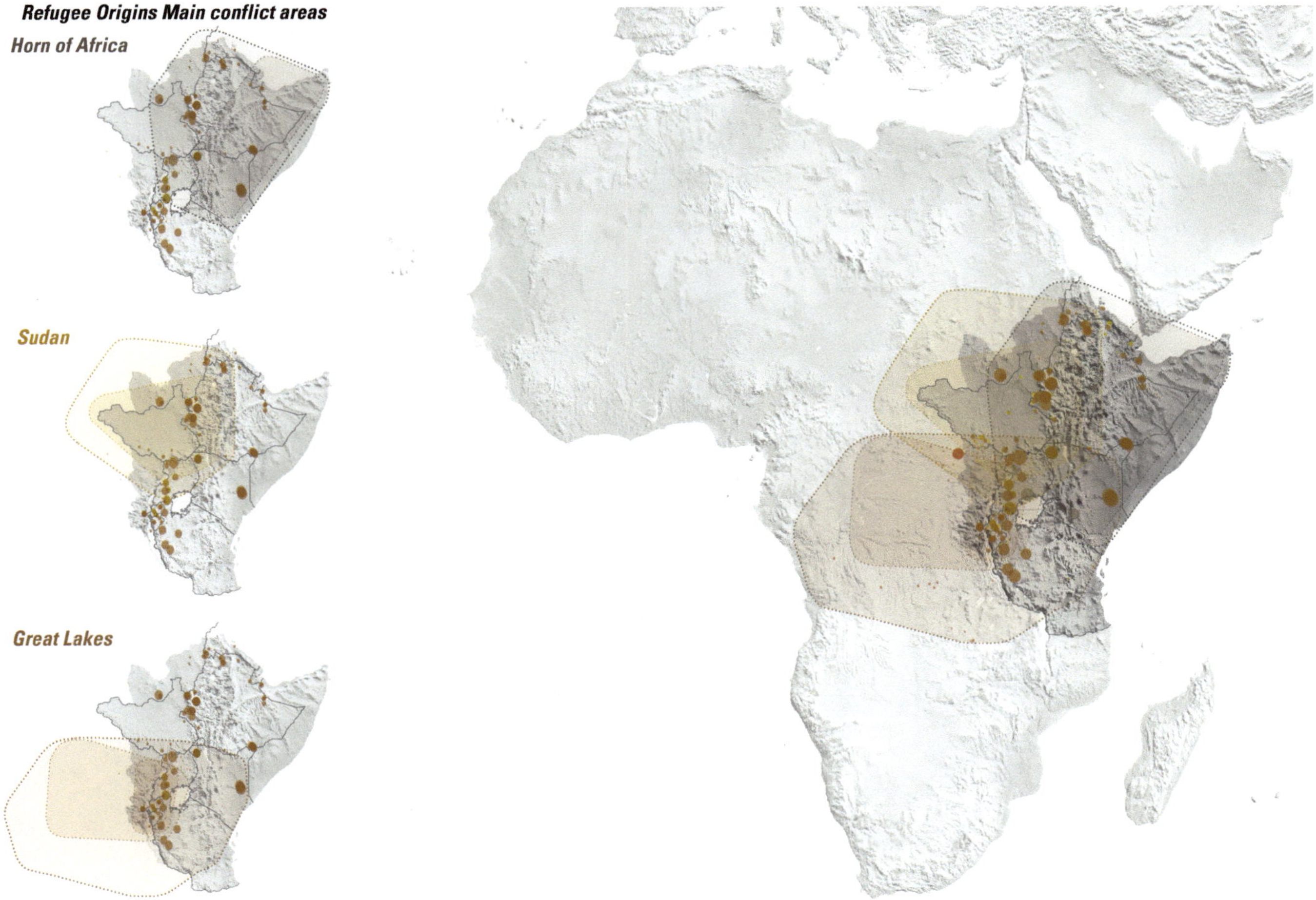

2.4

2.4 Maps of East Africa and the African continent showing the three main conflict areas that feed the refugee camps in East Africa: Horn of Africa, the Great Lakes region and South Sudan. © Amorós Elorduy.

and Rwanda – reflect the Rift's heterogeneity. They represent diverse conflicts and refugee policies; cultural, ethnic and linguistic abundance; material, formal and structural richness of vernacular architectures; and wealth of child-rearing practices and conceptions of education. Uganda, Kenya and Rwanda have different assistance policies, different relationships vis-à-vis the countries of origin of the refugees they host, the conflicts that constrained them to flee, and variable international and media visibility.[29] The seven camps I present here host refugees originating from three of the principal conflict areas in the region – the Horn of Africa, the Great Lakes and South Sudan (fig. 2.4). They encompass diverse lengths of existence, varied sizes and population densities, and different climates and geographies.

In this chapter, the possible refugee camp assemblage combinations in the region come to light. The description and analysis of the different camps elucidate how these environments came to be – or to become – and their effects on young children's learning. In Southwest Uganda, I present Nakivale (established in 1958), Kyangwali (created around 1964) and Kyaka II (established in 1983). All three are medium to large in terms of both the area covered and the population size, but they are low in population density. Located in subtropical forests, Kyaka II and Kyangwali are mainly inhabited by Eastern Democratic Republic of Congo (DRC) refugees, with some variation amongst their minority groups. Nakivale, the largest and oldest camp, is situated on a flooding savannah-like geography and hosts refugees from 11 different nationalities. In northern Kenya, I focus on Kakuma refugee camp (established in 1992). This camp hosts refugees from 11 nations, and it is placed in a desert area with seasonal floods. It has grown in four clearly defined phases which reflect conflict outbursts in the region. In Rwanda, I present the camps of Kiziba (established in 1996), Kigeme (established in 2005) and Mugombwa (established in 2014). All three camps host solely Eastern DRC refugees and are characterised by being small in terms of size and population. They occupy hilltops with steep slopes and have extremely high densities of inhabitation.[30]

Varied and changing learning environments—Long-term refugee camps are pluri-authored, polyrhythmic and ever-changing proto-urban assemblages that are learning environments for young children. What do I mean by that? East Africa's long-term refugee camps are cosmopolitan and cultivate socio-political and economic interactions, and within them, refugees and their direct local hosts continuously exercise their Lefebvrian 'right to the city'. However, they are not yet a polis, and as I explain in the chapter 'The urban turn: informality, co-modification and assemblage', I categorise them as proto-urban.

These settlements are the result of the relationships between numerous human and non-human actors. They all have different demographics, densities of habitation, surface areas occupied and socio-political contexts where they sit. Heterogeneity is the norm. They are in continuous evolution, as all seven camps I present will be different now than when I started their study. They are also composed of diverse rhythms: spatial rhythms, such as the grain and pattern of the homes and streets, the grid-like organisation of roads and residential areas and the spatial segregation of uses and different population groups; and temporal rhythms, such as the everyday human activities and the seasons with their floods, droughts and harvests.

A particularly relevant rhythm for this book is children's lifelong learning. Learning varies across ages, through the seasons and the daily activities according to access to direct content-based education and learning by experience. Learning also varies according to the environment where it is developed both directly and indirectly. At present, this influence is mostly negative.

I explore learning environments on diverse spatial scales. Let me provide some examples. On the regional scale, the fleeing routes and the geographic and climatic context of the camps affect young children's learning mostly indirectly. For instance, long fleeing routes means being further from conflict, but it also usually means different languages and culture in the host country. On the country scale, closeness to the borders causes insecurity, reducing children's chances of free play and increasing insecurity and potential kidnapping and conflict within the camp. On the landscape scale, the camp's boundaries have a relevant role. For example, the porous Ugandan camps and their position close to surrounding populations incentivise good relationships between both groups with common educational facilities that serve both refugees and direct local hosts. On the camp scale, some relevant variables are size, density, grain, outline and pattern, which architect Kevin Lynch has focused on in his studies about how the urban environment's conditions affect child psychology.[31] For example, the density of habitation and the growth patterns in the Rwandan camps provide ideal spaces for curiosity and imaginative play, which is relevant to indirect learning.[32]

On the building scale, I focus on three assemblages of learning environments: formal, non-formal and informal. The formal facilities – ECD centres – and the content-based education they provide are usually managed by non-governmental organisations (NGOs) and UN agencies, funded by international donors, built in somewhat permanent structures and with a set curriculum, grades and accreditation once completed.[33] These facilities do not meet all the needs of the refugees. Particularly in Southwest Uganda and Kakuma, refugees state that these centres are too few and located too far from where the children live. They are only open for a few hours in the morning, and they sometimes teach in a language that the children do not understand.[34] The refugees lead the non-formal initiatives that aim to bridge these educational gaps. Community groups, mother leaders, churches and madrassas, sometimes in liaison with smaller and local NGOs, create spaces and mobilise human resources towards young children's learning.[35] The most overlooked but most influential spaces for young children's learning are the informal learning settings: streets,[36] shared spaces,[37] homes[38] and WASH facilities. These environments and the activities developed in them are the principal influence on their emotional, social and physical development.[39] As John Dewey pointed out and literature in the learning environment field sustains, children extract skills, behaviours and attitudes and learn content within and through those informal learning environments.[40] These three categories resulted from the review of post-structural learning environment literature, specifically the works of architects Colin Ward,[41] Kevin Lynch[42] and Allison and Peter Smithson,[43] economist and education expert Philip Hall Coombs,[44] and various edited volumes.[45]

A constellation of refugee camp assemblages

Southwest Uganda: middle-sized, low-density, multi-ethnic camps and unmarked borders—Uganda began hosting refugees from neighbouring countries long before

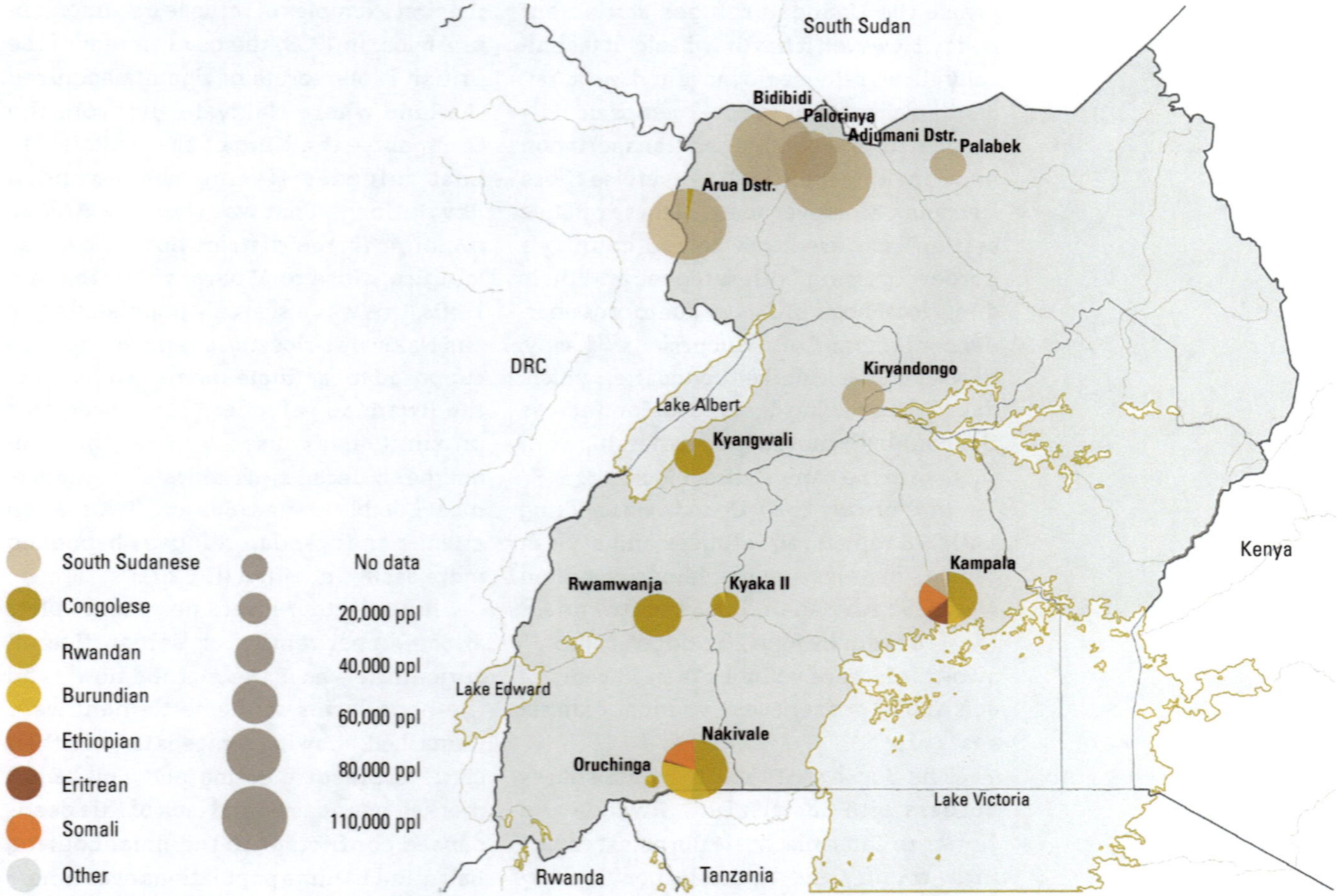

2.5

2.5 Map of Uganda showing the location of current refugee camps (or groups of camps), and their demographics. © Amorós Elorduy.

its independence from the British Empire, before the UNHCR started working in the continent.[46] From the mid-1950s, the British Empire began to house refugees – most of whom were Batutsi pastoralists from Rwanda – in planned settlements. These were close to Uganda's southern borders where land was available and where refugees could quickly return home. In these vast unmarked landscapes, refugees moved around, grazed their herds and were considered temporary residents. After Uganda's independence, the Office of the Prime Minister (OPM) and the UNHCR[47] continued the British policy of planned refugee settlements with some modifications.[48] They altered the pre-existing settlements, allocating a plot of land per refugee family for their self-sustainability, as later expressed in the Refugees Act 2006 (fig. 2.5).[49]

Currently, humanitarian relief workers, the media and even the refugees generally praise the Ugandan refugee settlement policy. However, it has drawbacks. It technically allows refugees to move and work. Yet, it still places them in rural camps usually isolated from economic and transportation hubs, making it difficult to exercise those freedoms. Moreover, many of these refugee settlements are close to the country's borders, putting both refugees and their direct local hosts in danger due to cross-border conflicts and rebel incursions.[50] Lastly, they tend to lack marked boundaries, which, due to the growing demand for land across the country[51] causes landownership conflicts with the camps' direct local hosts.[52]

In February 2020, Uganda was hosting 1,411,098 registered refugees and asylum seekers mainly from neighbouring nation states: South Sudan, DRC and Rwanda.[53] Most of them lived in 28 refugee camps.[54] Two-thirds were younger than 18 years of age, and 20 per cent were younger than six years of age.[55]

The Southwest region, which shares borders with Eastern DRC, Rwanda and Northern Tanzania, hosts the oldest camps in the country, and it is mostly populated by Eastern DR Congolese refugees.[56] Camps in the Southwest region provide more extensive pieces of land than those in the West Nile sub-region – an area historically more populated. The region's abrupt topography and multiple lakes create porous borders that facilitate the inconspicuous crossing of goods and people, including refugees and even rebels (fig. 2.6).

Nakivale: old, large and thinly spread on a dry borderland—Nakivale is the oldest settlement that I present here and one of the first examples of refugee encampment in Africa. In 1958, the government of the British Protectorate of Uganda acquired the land where Nakivale sits from the Omugabe – the King of the Ankole – to host refugees fleeing the Rwandan Revolution.[57] That was then the Ankole region,[58] in the district now known as Isingiro, close to Mbarara.[59] In the late 1950s, this was a scarcely populated area, and Nakivale's closeness to the border was supposed to facilitate the return home of the Rwandan refugees.[60] However, this proximity has caused troubles throughout the six decades of Nakivale's existence, most notably in the 1980s and 1990s, when attacks on Rwandan refugees happened more easily and often (fig. 2.7).[61]

Initially, there were no specific plots allocated per family for 'self-sufficient' agriculture – as is the method now – and the boundaries of the settlement were unmarked, allowing refugees to graze their cattle on the surrounding land. This lack of marked boundaries and lack of title deeds caused conflicts with the neighbouring Bairu and Bahima populations over time.[62]

At the end of February 2020, Nakivale housed 127,951 refugees and asylum seekers in 185 square kilometres on the shores of Lake Nakivale.[63] The settlement is made up of 79 villages divided into three zones: Juru, Base Camp and Rubondo.[64] In Base Camp – the oldest, most central and populated zone – refugees have named its different villages. Names such as Little Congo, Kigali, Mogadishu and Sudan – according to the people that inhabit them – now appear in the reports and plans of the UNHCR and the various

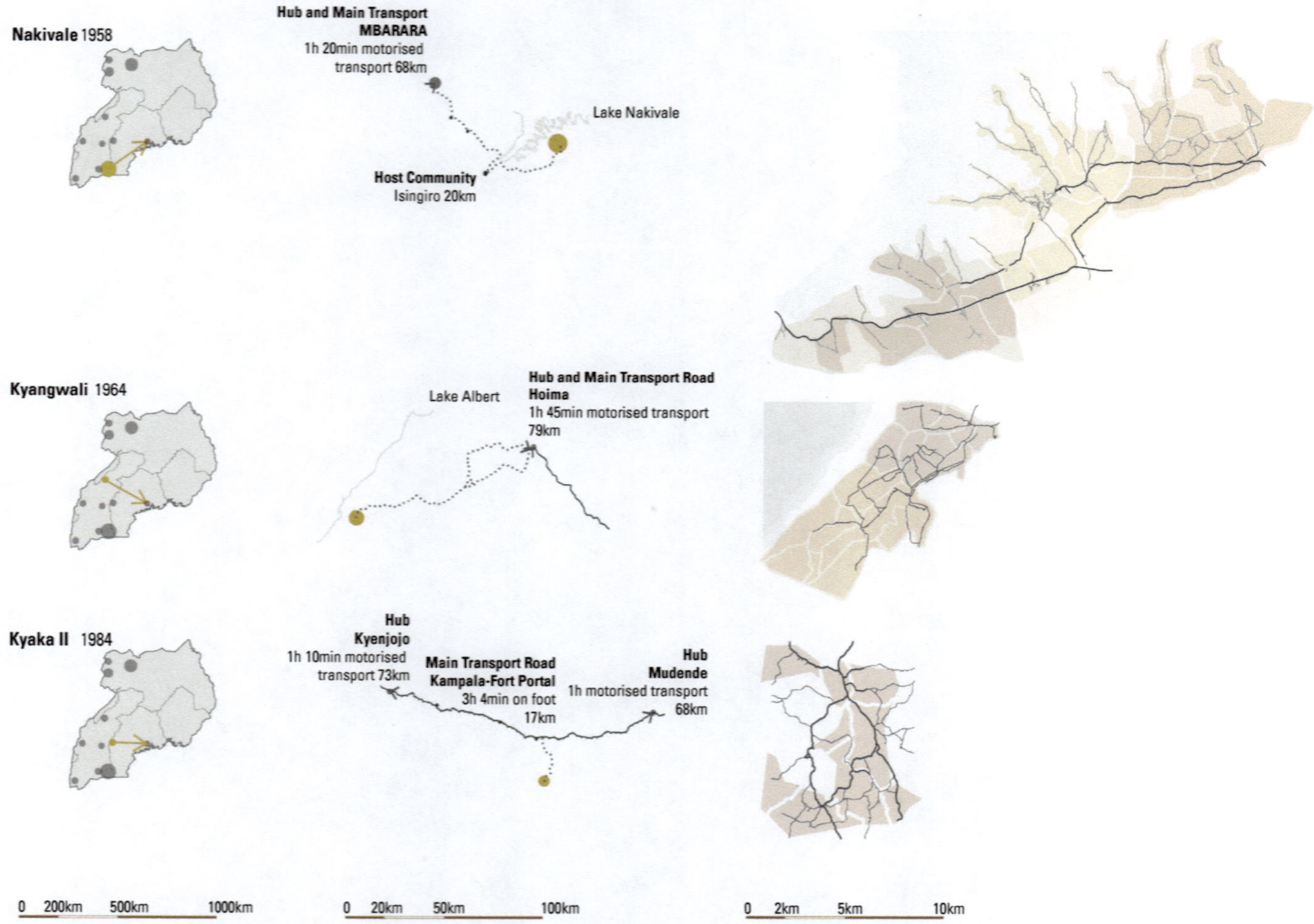

2.6

2.6 Maps and diagrams of the country, the landscape and the camp scales of Nakivale, Kyangwali and Kyaka II refugee camps. These maps show the relative position of the camps in respect to Kampala and the country's borders (country scale), nearest population hubs and main transportation arteries (landscape scale) and the different zoning and circulation arteries (camp scale). © Amorós Elorduy.

NGOs that implement humanitarian work in the camp.

In terms of formal and non-formal learning environments, since 2009, when the implementation of ECD programmes began in the camp, the number of formal ECD centres has grown exponentially.[65] In 2016, 13 formal ECD centres served around 2,627 children,[66] and 38 non-formal ECD centres served around 4,508 children. These facilities served around half of the 15,331 children who were aged between three and six years living in the camp at the time.[67]

Regarding informal learning environments and specifically WASH facilities, the soil of Nakivale is not adequate for latrines or wells. So, the refugees – who are the ones building the toilets in the Ugandan

Nakivale
1958

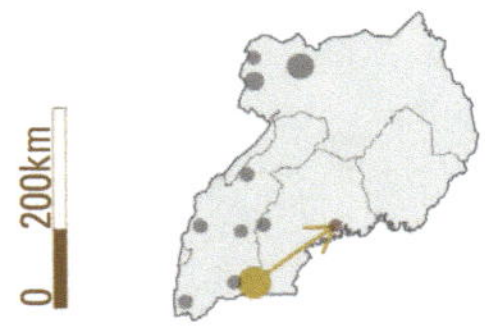

Total ECD:	52
Total Children registered:	7,186
% of children 3–6 y/o in ECD:	30%

2.7

2.7 Maps and diagrams of Nakivale on the Rift, country, landscape and camp scales. On the camp scale, the maps show the location of visited formal and non-formal early childhood development (ECD) centres and also three different villages, their grain, density, pattern of habitation and location of one formal or non-formal learning environments. The villages I have chosen are representative of the three zones that compose Nakivale refugee camp: Ruhoko village in Rubondo zone, Kigali and Kashojwa villages in Base Camp zone and Isanja village in Juru zone. © Amorós Elorduy.

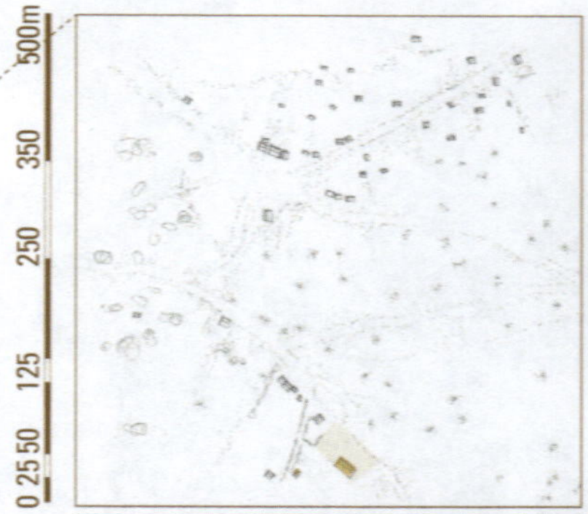

Rukoko Village in Rubondo Zone
Density of population: 500 ppl/sqkm

Ruhoko ECD
Total children registered: 263
2 classrooms 6 x 8 (under construction)
2 caregivers
Density: 2.7 children/sqm

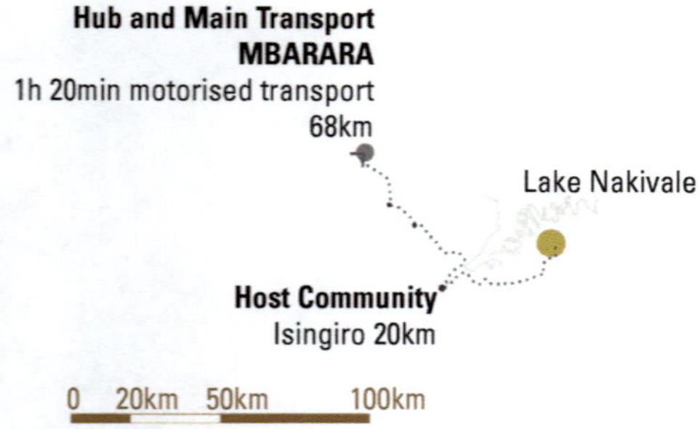

Kigali and Kashojwa Villages in Base Camp Zone
Density of population: 8000 ppl/sqkm

Kashojwa ECD
Total children registered: 221
2 classrooms 6 x 8 (especially designed and playground)
2 caregivers
Density: 2.3 children/sqm

Isanja Village in Juru Zone
Density of population: 1000 ppl/sqkm

Isanja Baptist ECD
Total children registered: 240 (I only saw 60)
1 classroom (church) 4 x 8mts
Density: 1.8 children/sqm
(If 240 pupils, 7.5 children/sqmts)

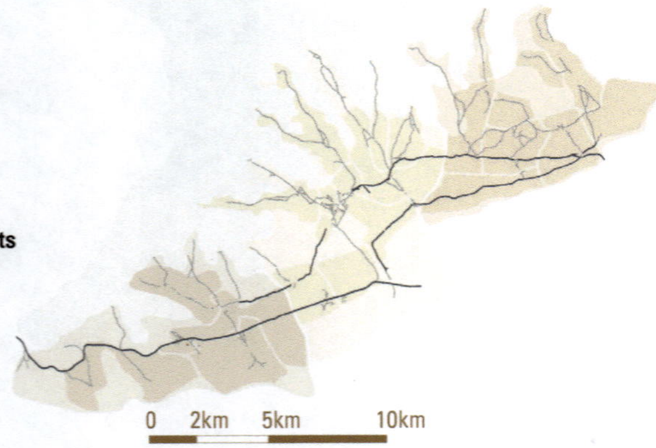

2.8

2.8 From top to bottom and left to right: Nakivale's main road at Juru zone, the road passing through Base Camp zone and at paths at Rubondo zone. August 2016. © Amorós Elorduy.

camps – resort to building latrines on termite mounds when possible.

The rhythm of everyday life varies amongst the 79 different villages. The diversity of population densities, longevity and location affects the distances that refugees must travel to get to the ECD centres, essential services and shops. Access to basic services is especially complicated in the newest and most remote Rubondo zone, which suffers from population fluctuations and considerable distances from outside transportation and market hubs (fig. 2.8).[68]

Kyangwali: elastic and porous on a jungle-like border lake—After Uganda's independence, the government established six new refugee settlements in the Southwest.[69] These initially hosted the Rwandan Batutsi escaping the Rwandan Revolution[70] and Eastern DR Congolese of diverse ethnicities escaping violence following the assassination of Patrice Lumumba in 1961.[71] The Ugandan government established the Kyangwali refugee camp in 1964[72] at the shores of Lake Albert – a natural border with Eastern DRC and 89 kilometres from the town of Hoima in Western Uganda.[73] From 1994 to 1995, most of the Rwandans repatriated,[74] leaving the camp almost empty until 1997 when a new wave of Eastern DR Congolese arrived due to the First Congo War (fig. 2.9).[75]

The current 89 square kilometres intended for the refugees in Kyangwali – not consistently demarcated until 1967[76] – hosted 120,626 refugees in February 2020,[77] mostly from Eastern DRC.[78] Almost 24,000 of those were children younger than six years of age.

Kyangwali has an undulated geography, fertile soil and generous rainy seasons, which are very favourable factors for agriculture. Its right soil conditions, porous unmarked borders and fluctuations in refugee population sometimes lead to land conflicts between the camp inhabitants and the growing numbers of surrounding settlers.[79]

The camp consists of 16 villages each with between 10 and 20 blocks of homes.[80] Refugees arrive in waves, and those define village creation and organisation, separating refugees usually by origin.[81] The camp has a central commercial area close to its administrative centre in Kasonga village and several small trading areas at each village centre.[82]

In terms of formal and non-formal learning environments, in 2016, the camp had 11 formal and 6 non-formal ECD centres – around one per village.[83] A total of 2,200 children, 27 per cent of the 7,900 ECD-aged children, attended these centres. Regarding informal learning environments, specifically common areas and streets, the situation at the buffer zones has changed radically in the last four years (2016–2020). In 2016, Kyangwali had a third of its February 2020 population, going from 36,713 to 120,626 mainly during 2018 and 2019. The density of habitation in 2016 was relatively low, especially in the 'buffer' villages of Mukunyu and Malembo that were almost unoccupied.[84] In terms of WASH facilities, the towns in the Kasonga area have more boreholes and access to health points than the newer villages of the Rwenyawawa zone with scarcer points and taps, which are close to the trading centres and health points (fig. 2.10).[85]

Kyangwali
1964

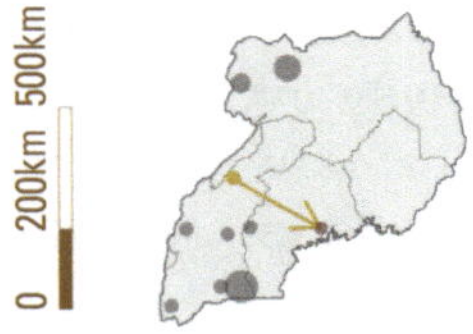

Total ECD:	17
Total children registered:	2,207
% of children 3–6 y/o in ECD:	25%

2.9 Maps and diagrams of Kyangwali on the Rift, country, landscape and camp scales. On the camp scale, the maps show the location of visited formal and non-formal ECD centres and also two different villages, their grain, density, pattern of habitation and location of one formal or non-formal learning environments. The villages I have chosen are representative of the two zones that compose Kyangwali: Nugurue in zone A and Malembo in zone B. © Amorós Elorduy.

2.9

Ngurue Village
Density of population: 300 ppl/sqkm
Ngurue (shared with PS)
Total children registered: 143

1 tent 4 x 10
2 caregivers
Density: 3.5 children/sqm

Hub and Main Transport Road Hoima
1h 45min motorised transport
79km

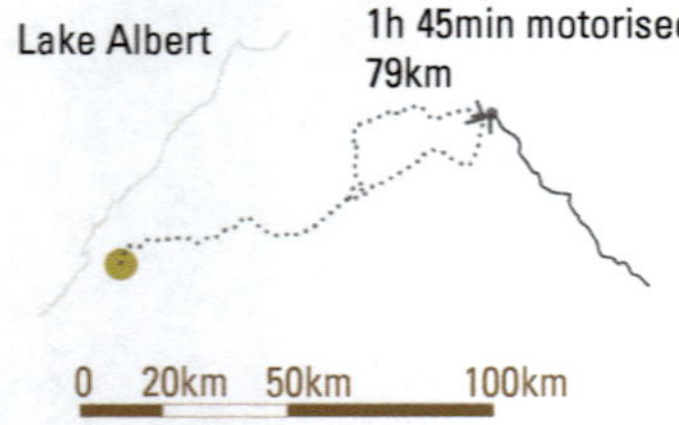

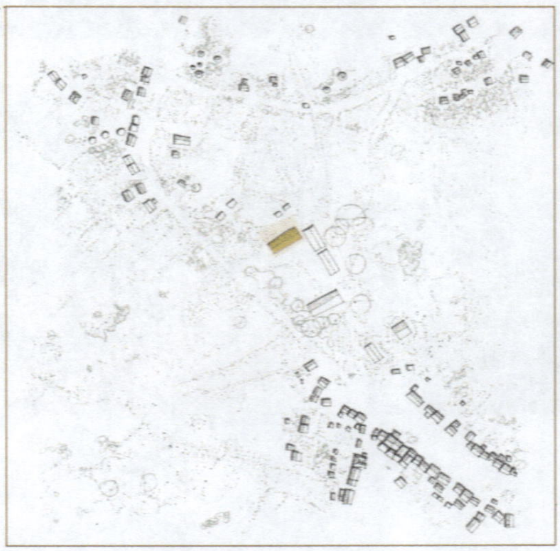

Malembo Village
Density of population: 600ppl/sqkm
Nyamiganda (shared with PS)
Total children registered: 214
2 classrooms
6 x 8mts (half walls)
2 caregivers
Density: 2.2 children/sqm

2.10

2.10 Kyangwali refugee camp.
Top: main road at Kasonga on zone A. Bottom left: path in Ngurue zone A. Bottom right: main road at Rwenyawawa zone B. August 2016. © Amorós Elorduy.

Kyaka II: a pluri-nuclear, spider-like growth over ridges and valleys—The Ugandan government established Kyaka II in May 1983 in the Kyenjojo District as Banyarwanda people – both economic migrants who had arrived throughout the century and Batutsi refugees from the 1960s who had previously avoided the planned camps – were forcibly moved into camps under Milton Obote.[86] Most of the Batutsi refugees repatriated in 1994. From 1996 onwards, Kyaka II began to host Rwandan Bahutu, Burundians, Eastern DR Congolese and a small number of Ethiopian and Somali refugees. Between 2005 and 2006, Kyaka II tripled its population from 5,000 to more than 17,000 inhabitants. The increase was due to the transfer of refugees from Kyaka I which closed in 2005, and to a significant influx of Eastern DRC refugees caused by a guerrilla conflict in the region.[87] It again quadrupled its population from 2018 to 2020 due to conflict and the Ebola epidemic in North Kivu in Eastern DRC (fig. 2.11).

In February 2020, the camp was hosting 123,086 refugees,[88] mainly from Eastern DRC. Twenty-five per cent of those were children younger than six years of age.[89] Kyaka II is located in the Kyegegwa District and is 81.5 square kilometres in size.[90] In 2016, it had nine zones[91] and 26 villages, with an average of 731 people per village.[92]

In terms of formal and non-formal learning environments, in 2016, Kyaka II had 30 formal and non-formal ECD centres attended by 2,819 children, which was 43 per cent of the settlement's total population of young children aged between three and six years.[93] The humanitarian system leads and funds the formal centres, while Ugandan nationals, and coalitions of nationals and refugees run private non-formal initiatives. Regarding the informal learning environments, in terms of WASH, water in the settlement depends on rainwater harvesting and water trucking. The distances between water points vary from 50 to 2,000 metres,[94] and 78 per cent of the families have access to private latrines. In terms of homes and commercial trading centres, Kyaka II suffers considerable fluctuations, affecting the diverse areas with some established and well-developed trading centres and other zones that are relatively poor and desolate (fig. 2.12).

2.11

Kyaka II

1984

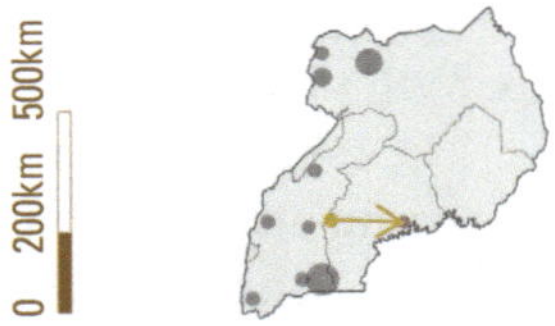

Total ECD: 30
Total children registered: 2,819
% of children 3–6 y/o in ECD: 43%

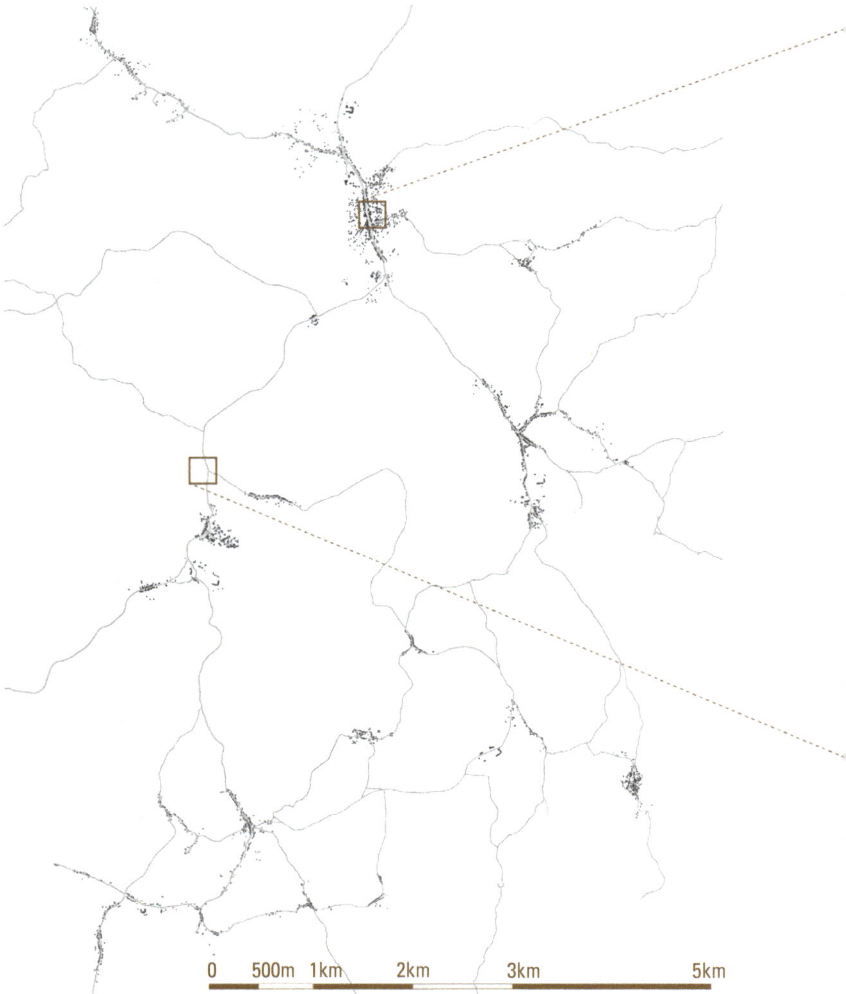

2.11 Maps and diagrams of Kyaka II on the Rift, country, landscape and camp scales. On the camp scale, the maps show the location of visited formal and non-formal ECD centres and also two different villages, their grain, density, pattern of habitation and location of one formal or non-formal learning environments. The villages I have chosen are representative of the two main types of urban grain present in the camp: the trading centre type represented by Bukere village and the farmland type represented by Bujubuli village. © Amorós Elorduy.

Bukere Village
Density of population: 600 ppl/sqkm

Grace Orphans
Total children registered: 176
3 classrooms
4 x 8 (under construction)
6 caregivers
Density: 1.8 children/sqm

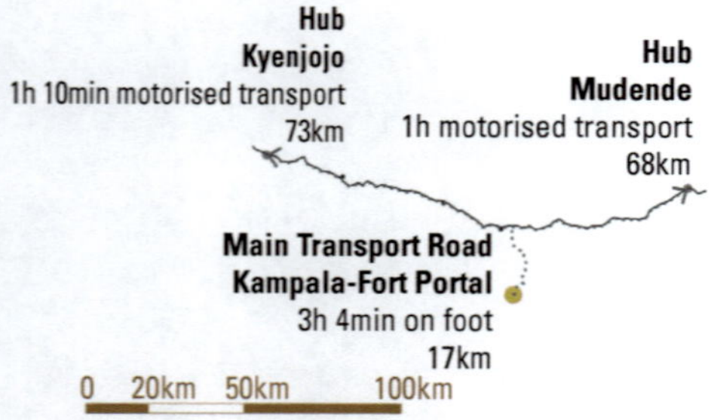

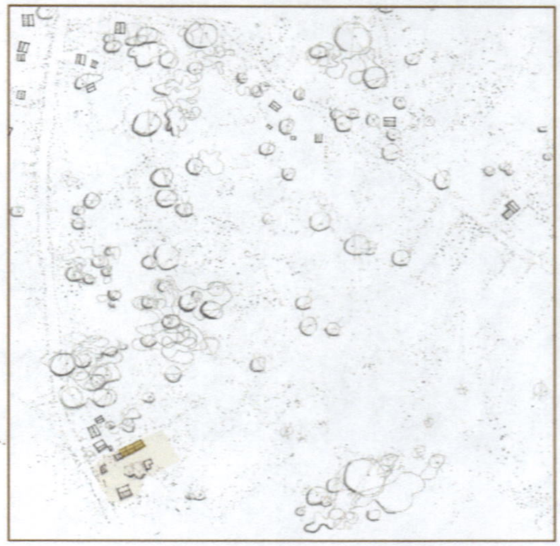

Bujubuli Village
Density of population: 400 ppl/sqkm

Saint John Nursery
Total children registered: 99
(I only saw 60)
3 classroom (church) 3 x 4mts
Density: 1.8 children/sqm
(If 240 pupils, 7.5 children/sqmts)

2.12

2.12 Kyaka II refugee camp. Top: road at SweSwe Zone. Bottom left: path through the fields, Alfajiri village in Bujubuli zone. Bottom right: the main path connecting Buliti with Bukere zones. August 2016. © Amorós Elorduy.

Northeast Kenya: a multi-ethnic, phased, and increasingly grid-like camp on desert plains—In the early 1990s with the growing conflicts in Somalia[95] and South Sudan,[96] Kenya began hosting large numbers of refugees. From 1992 to 1993 UNHCR supported the country in the creation of nineteen refugee camps.[97] The Kenyan government – like its Ugandan neighbour – inherited its refugee assistance policies from the British Empire. These policies were, and are still, based on spatial segregation, allegedly to govern refugees and reduce conflict, and to some degree also related to the refugees' kinship ties and their different times and points of entry into Kenya (fig. 2.13).[98]

Initially, two different encampment strategies took place in Kenya. One was the large planned rural camps – Kakuma, Hagadera, Ifo, Dagahaley and Liboi – sizable in population and surface, placed in desert areas close to Kenya's northern borders, and isolated from any political or economic activities. The other was the constellation of multiple coastal camps, relatively small and placed within or around bustling urban areas and on the trade routes along the coast. Initially, the government placed most of the Nuer and Dinka Sudanese in the northwest camp of Kakuma and Thika and Ruiru camps close to Nairobi. The coastal camps[99] and the large camps up north in Mandera[100] and Garissa Counties[101] hosted most of the heterogeneous Somali refugees.[102]

The coastal camps' informal growth and the refugees' lobbying to be resettled to third countries caused friction with their local hosts and the Kenyan government. Consequently, the government closed these camps and either repatriated or resettled refugees to the vast rural camps between 1995 and 1997.[103] In addition, in 1995, the Kakuma and Dadaab camps re-accommodated refugees from the unplanned ones close to the Somali border such as Liboi.[104] These movements contributed to the cosmopolitanism in Kakuma and the camps in the Dadaab complex.

At the end of February 2020, Kenya hosted 492,802 refugees in five rural camps: the three surviving Dadaab camps, still running after the Kenyan government forced repatriation of the Somali refugees[105] and resettlement to Kakuma and Kalobeyei in 2017.[106]

Due to the barren landscape around them and their crucial location, among other factors, these camps have become the leading commercial hubs in their areas. They connect Northeast Kenya with southern Somalia, and northern Kenya with South Sudan and Uganda.[107] The rural camps segregate refugees by origin and ethnicity and also separate administrators from refugees in their master plans. The compounds of the UNHCR and their implementing partners (NGOs) are located away from the refugees in permanent buildings surrounded by sturdy fences, barbed wire and guards.[108]

The discrepancy between the planning guidelines outlined by the UNHCR's Emergency Handbook[109] and the practical measures that the UNHCR implements in the Kenyan context is glaringly obvious. Planners disregard refugees' necessary participation and consultation and the importance of maintaining former traditional settlement patterns and relationships – issues that the handbook highlights.[110] The five oldest rural camps

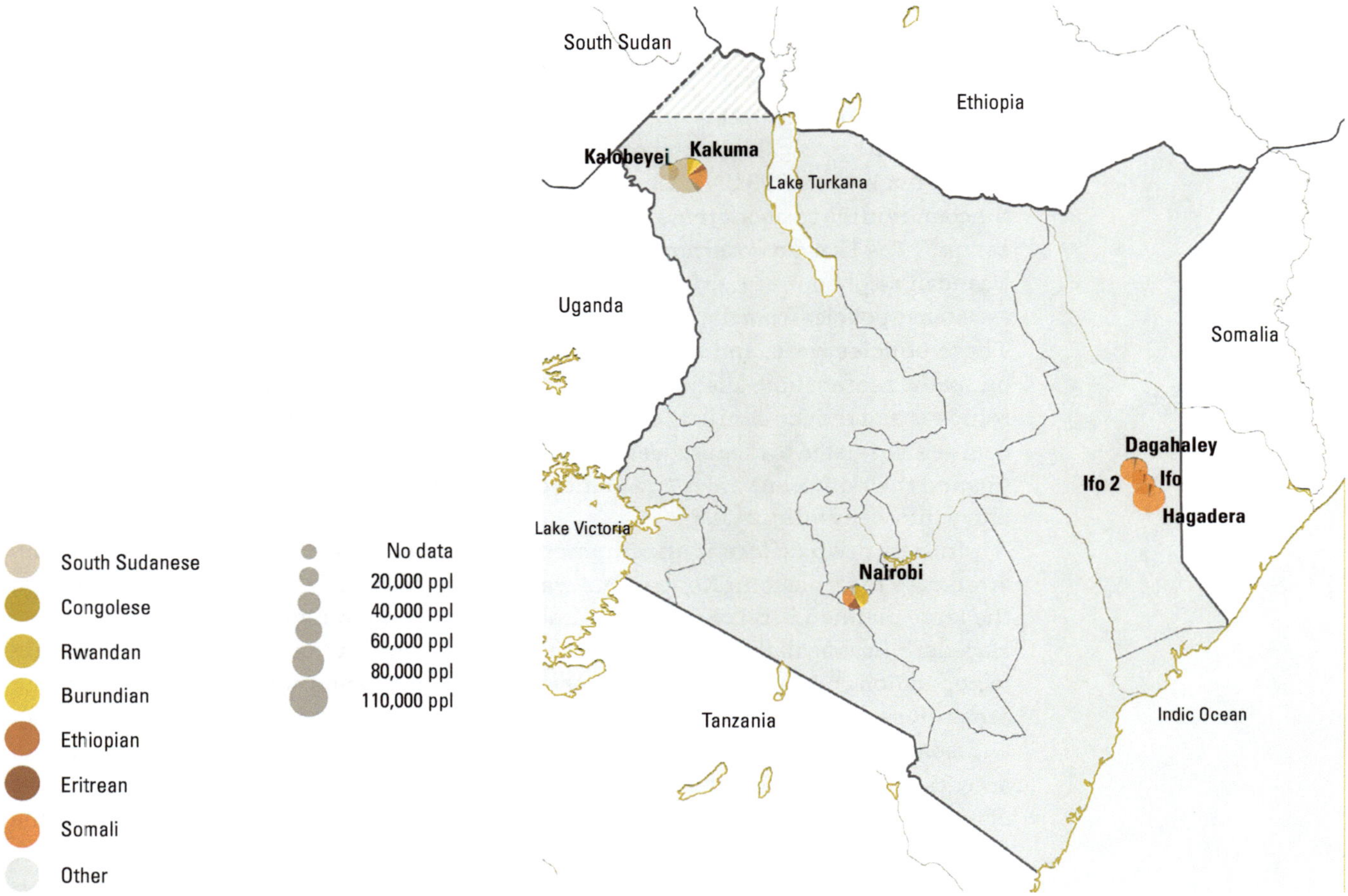

2.13

2.13 Map of Kenya showing the location of refugee camps (or groups of camps) and their demographics. © Amorós Elorduy.

were planned remotely – in Nairobi at best – making participation and contextualisation challenging. Besides, in their designs, humanitarian planners prioritise the perceived security and protection of the humanitarian workers and the efficiency of the humanitarian 'emergency' over the livelihoods, local integration and everyday life of refugees and their direct local hosts.[111]

This book focuses on Turkana County, home of Kakuma refugee camp. The mountain ridges of the East African Rift's eastern and western branches embrace the county and separate it from Uganda, South Sudan and the Gambella region in Ethiopia. The county is a vast, arid depression, with a hot and dry climate prone to severe and frequent droughts and brief violent storms that cause flash flooding of the dry riverbeds that cross the plains south-eastwards. The area is unfavourable for rain-fed agriculture, with livestock being the main traditional

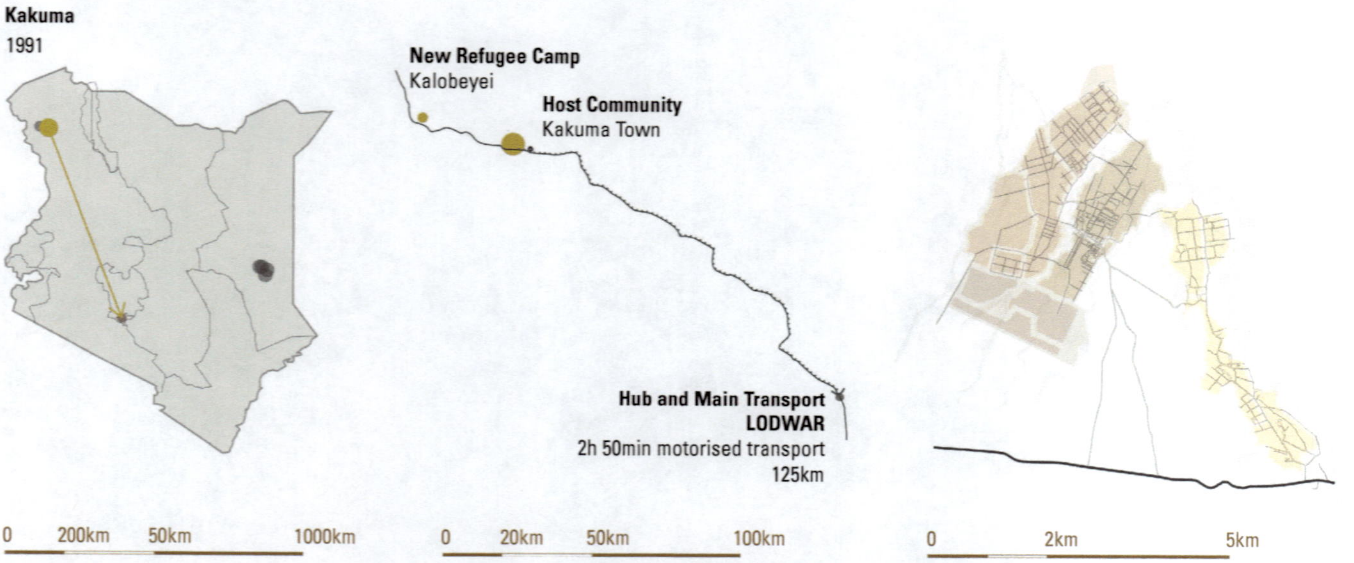

2.14

2.14 Maps and diagrams of the country, landscape and camp scales of Kakuma. These maps show the relative position of the camp in respect to Nairobi and the country's borders (country scale), nearest population hubs and main transportation arteries (landscape scale) and the different zoning and circulation arteries (camp scale). © Amorós Elorduy.

activity for most of the Turkana, the semi-nomadic pastoralists who have settled in the area for generations (fig. 2.14).[112]

Kakuma: from organic and dense to a planned low-density grid—The UNHCR and the Kenyan government established Kakuma refugee camp in July 1992[113] to house 10,000 Sudanese refugees[114] in an area separated from Kakuma town by the seasonal River Tarach.[115] However, the size and population of the camp have grown since its creation, reflecting the region's conflicts, especially those in nearby South Sudan.[116] At the end of February 2020, Kakuma housed 194,914 refugees from 11 nation states[117] and consisted of phases I, II, III and IV that covered approximately 12 square kilometres (fig. 2.15).[118]

The large population, in addition to the increasing drought, is draining the water and other resources around Kakuma. Lack of water is damaging the Turkana's livelihoods and putting a strain on their relationship with the refugees.[119] Conflict also erupts amongst refugees, due mostly to politically and ethnically triggered violence. Sometimes, these disputes mirror the larger-scale clashes that take place in the refugees' countries of origin.[120]

Kakuma grows in phases through expansion grids filled with new refugees and their shelters over time and is criss-crossed by dry riverbeds that flash flood seasonally. The camp's coarse urban grain has certain areas reserved for housing and others earmarked for services. The oldest, Kakuma phase I, has the highest population density and an organic structure of small intricate streets lined with tall, thorny fences separating the densely built residential compounds. Here, distances between

2.15

2.15 Kakuma refugee camp.
Top: Kakuma phase I main commercial road. Bottom left: road in Kakuma phase III. Bottom right: secondary path at Kakuma phase I. September 2016.
© Amorós Elorduy.

2.16 Kakuma refugee camp. Bottom left: Map of Kakuma showing the areas that flood during the rainy season. Top and bottom right: Photographs of the seasonal rivers/flood-prone areas called 'lagga' between Kakuma phases I and II. September 2016. © Amorós Elorduy.

2.16

2.17 **Kakuma**
1991

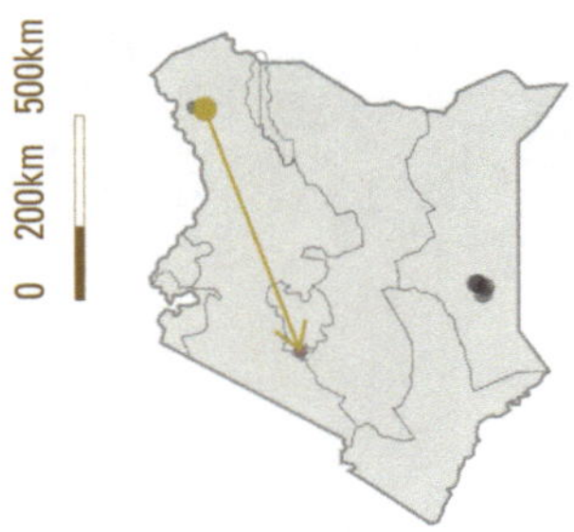

Total ECD: 12
Total children registered: 11,495
% of children 3–6 y/o in ECD: 35%

2.17 Maps and diagrams of Kakuma on the Rift, country, landscape and camp scales. On the camp scale, the maps show the location of visited formal and non-formal ECD centres and also three different zones, their grain, density, pattern of habitation and location of one formal or non-formal learning environments. The areas I have chosen are representative of Kakuma phases I, II and III. © Amorós Elorduy.

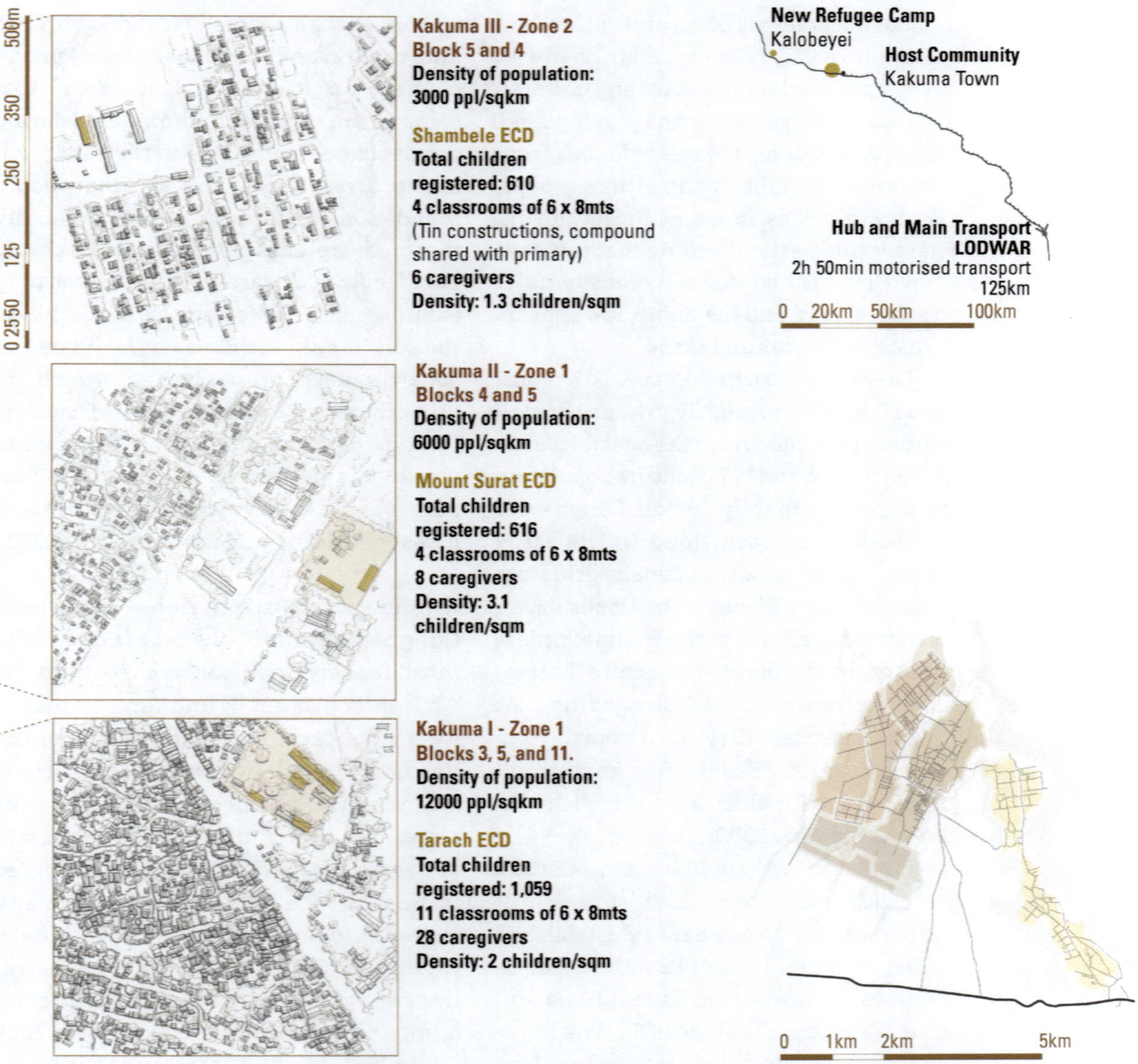
0 25 50 125 250 350 500m
Kakuma III - Zone 2
Block 5 and 4
Density of population:
3000 ppl/sqkm
Shambele ECD
Total children
registered: 610
4 classrooms of 6 x 8mts
(Tin constructions, compound
shared with primary)
6 caregivers
Density: 1.3 children/sqm
Kakuma II - Zone 1
Blocks 4 and 5
Density of population:
6000 ppl/sqkm
Mount Surat ECD
Total children
registered: 616
4 classrooms of 6 x 8mts
8 caregivers
Density: 3.1
children/sqm
Kakuma I - Zone 1
Blocks 3, 5, and 11.
Density of population:
12000 ppl/sqkm
Tarach ECD
Total children
registered: 1,059
11 classrooms of 6 x 8mts
28 caregivers
Density: 2 children/sqm
New Refugee Camp
Kalobeyei
Host Community
Kakuma Town
Hub and Main Transport
LODWAR
2h 50min motorised transport
125km
0 20km 50km 100km
0 1km 2km 5km

homes and services are relatively short. Kakuma phase I has some longitudinal commercial roads, busy with the noise and dust of fast motorbikes and trucks bringing in goods under messy heaps of electric cables passing overhead. These roads are filled with buyers, pedestrians, bicycles and children running to the school or the playing field. This phase accommodates refugees from different nationalities and ethnic groups, mainly Ethiopians, Eritreans and Rwandans. There is one particular zone that refugees named 'Hong Kong' due to its density, noise and messiness, and the name now appears in NGOs' accounts and maps.

The Kenyan government opened Kakuma phase II in 1998, primarily to house Somali refugees relocated from the coastal camps (closed in 1996 and 1997), and its population is still predominantly Somali. *Lagga* – dry riverbeds that flash flood in the rainy season – separate its mid-density grid from Kakuma phases III and I. The floods have a considerable effect on the foundationless mud houses and the infrastructure that seasonally becomes severely damaged (fig. 2.16).

Kakuma phase III resulted from the consolidation in 2009[121] of the first iterations of phases III and IV, which were established in 1999 and the early 2000s, respectively.[122] The current Kakuma phase III has a low-density grid, with wide, open and dusty roads. It is similar to Kakuma phase IV established in 2014 for a new influx of South Sudanese refugees. It has hosted Burundians and vulnerable Somalis since 2015. The latter came from the attempted dismantling of the Dadaab complex in 2017.[123] Kakuma phases II, III and IV feel drier and dustier than Kakuma phase I, since they have much less vegetation, wider roads and a lower population density. Distances to schools and water points are longer in these newer phases.

There are 12 formal ECD centres across all of Kakuma's phases,[124] several churches and madrassas per phase, two Furaha centres[125] and four Waldorf initiatives[126] that some young refugee children attend during out-of-school hours. Due to the sandy soil and recurrent floods, several of the school's foundations suffer from a lack of stability that creates cracks and destroys the poorly built facilities. Regarding informal learning environments, particularly WASH facilities, the soil in Kakuma does not facilitate the construction of proper latrines, which are primarily family owned. In terms of housing, this type of soil also makes it challenging to prepare the mud blocks needed to construct homes and compromises structural stability, especially in flood-prone areas (fig. 2.17).

Rwanda: small-sized, dense and steep Congolese camps—Rwanda is one of the most densely populated countries on the African continent,[127] and land availability is a concern. The vast majority of the Rwandan population still lives in rural areas. Scattered homes surrounded by their respective agricultural plots are sparsely and somewhat homogeneously distributed throughout the hills, leaving valleys and wetlands for agriculture.[128] The hills have traditionally constituted an administrative and social unit that pulls together the homes dispersed on their slopes (fig. 2.18).

In 1996, in the aftermath of the genocide, as refugee encampment began in Rwanda, the government (primarily funded by the UNHCR) approved and started the

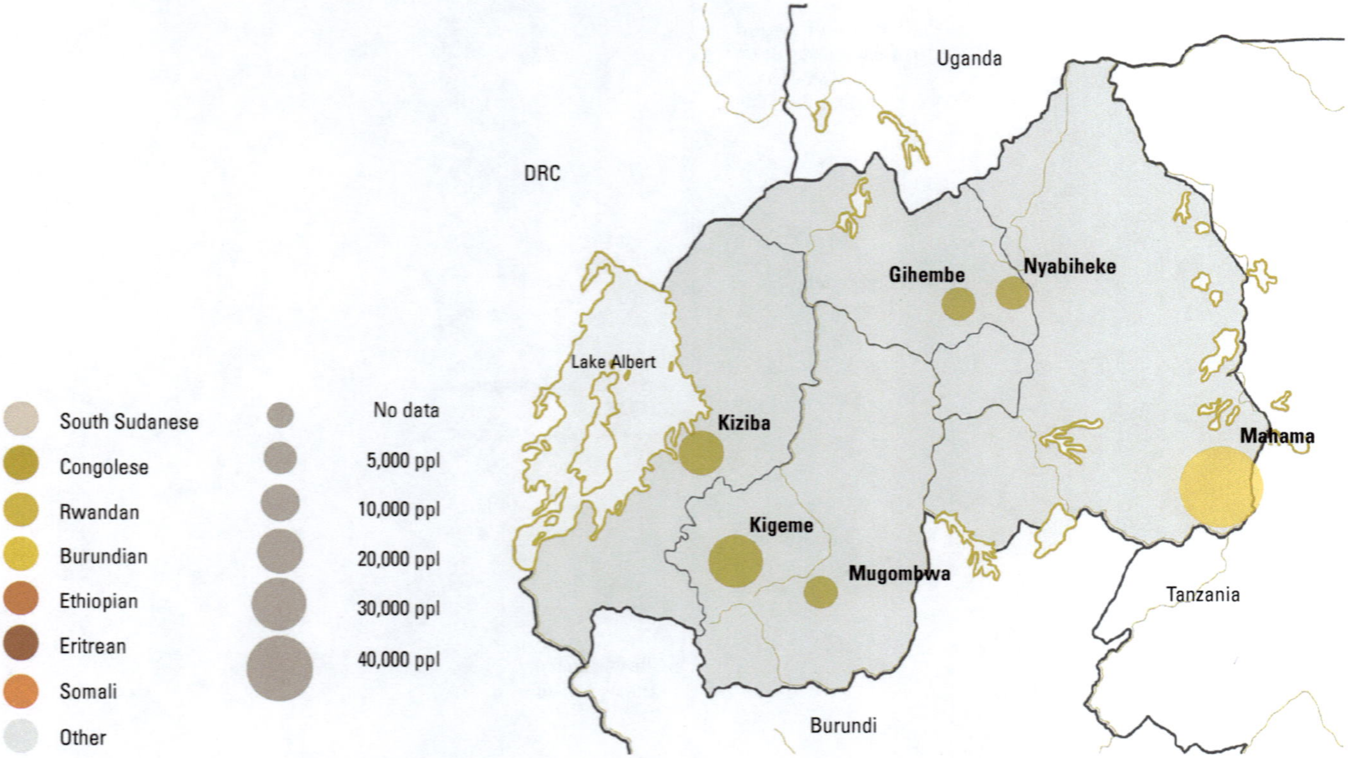

2.18

2.18 Map of Rwanda showing the location of refugee camps and their demographics. © Amorós Elorduy.

Policy of Regrouped Settlement Sites in the Rural Areas of Rwanda,[129] widely known as the Imidugudu Policy.[130] *Imidugudu* means 'villages' in Kinyarwanda. This policy was a villagisation strategy similar to those implemented by the World Bank during the 1960s and 1970s in other African countries with no great success.[131] The government initially presented this policy as an emergency strategy to resettle all the returnees that reached the already overpopulated country.[132] The involvement of UNHCR in the Imidugudu Policy probably influenced the spatiality of the Congolese refugee camps in the country that perched on top of hills are the size of a small- to medium-sized village with a similar organisation to a planned *imidugudu*.[133] One of the main differences between both settlement patterns is their materiality. Until 2013, the main driver behind the camps' materiality was their supposed temporariness.[134]

At the end of February 2020, there were 149,289 refugees in Rwanda living in six camps.[135] Most refugees in the country come from Eastern DRC and Burundi. Those who do not manage to go to Kigali, are housed in camps, five established for Congolese and one for Burundians. Most refugees – especially the Congolese – speak

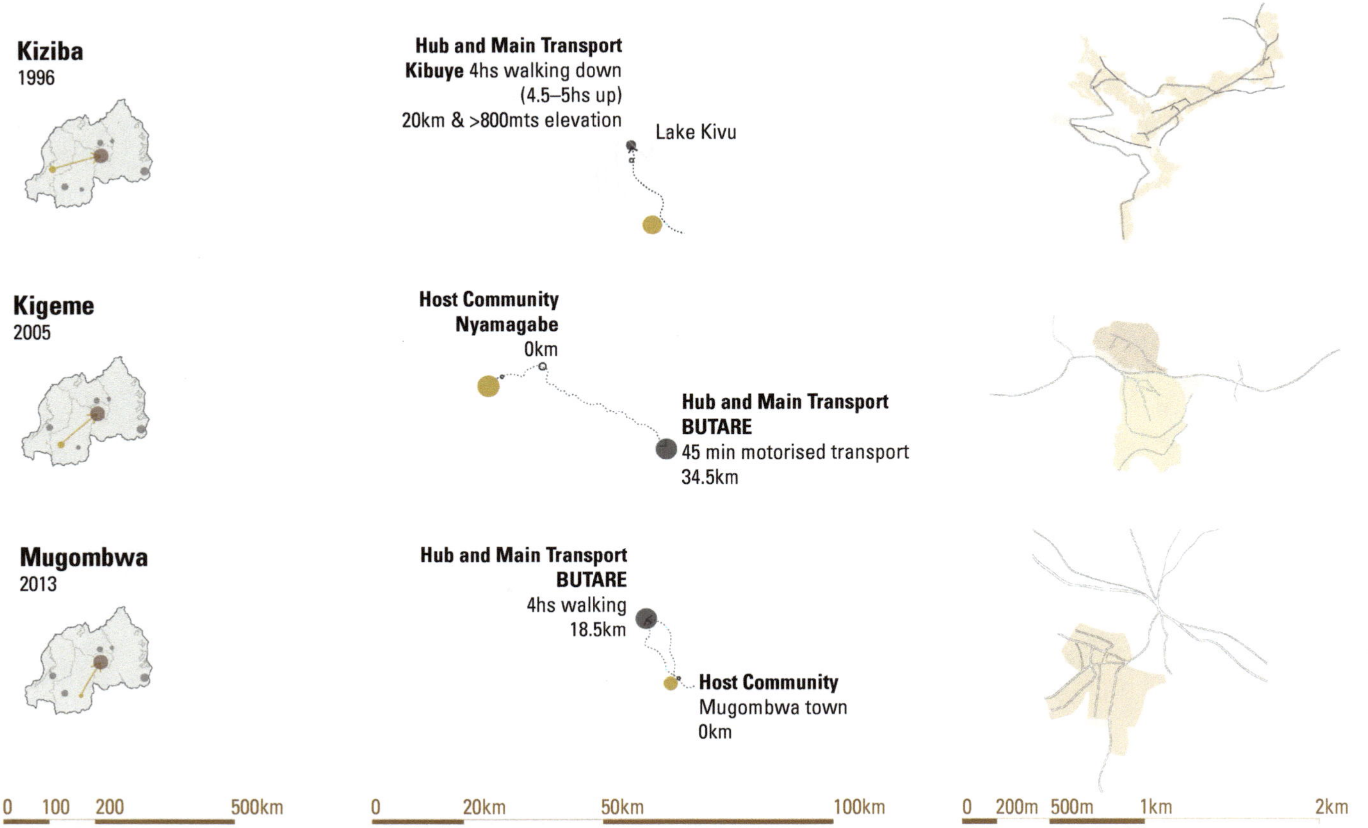

2.19

2.19 Maps and diagrams of the country, the landscape and the camp scales of Kiziba, Kigeme and Mugombwa in Rwanda. These maps show the relative position of the camps in respect to Kigali and the country's borders (country scale), nearest population hubs and main transportation arteries (landscape scale) and the different zoning and circulation arteries (camp scale). © Amorós Elorduy.

Kinyarwanda, the local language, and are ethnically and historically tied to their host country. Approximately 16 per cent of all the refugees in the country are children younger than six years of age,[136] and more than 54 per cent of the camps' populations are younger than 17 years of age. These children spend most of their time out of school roaming the streets – school usually lasts for four hours in the morning, and not all children attend. Rwanda is closely tied to the conflicts that push refugees from DRC and Burundi into its borders (fig. 2.19).[137]

Kiziba: along a ridge, isolated and negotiating expansion—The first significant registered influx of Eastern DRC refugees into Rwanda was related to the First Congo War, which lasted from 1996 to 1997.[138] These refugees were initially encamped in Umubano and Mudende refugee camps, close to Rwanda's north-western border town of Gisenyi. This location made the camps susceptible to border incursions. They were attacked several times until their relocation to the new camps of Kiziba in the Karongi District in December 1996,

2.20

2.20 Kiziba refugee camp. Top: kitchen constructions. Bottom left: children playing between houses. Bottom right: overview of the camp. September 2015. © Amorós Elorduy.

and Gihembe close to the central town of Byumba in December 1997 (fig. 2.20).[139]

Kiziba is the densest and most isolated of the camps in Rwanda. In February 2020, it hosted 17,043 refugees in 28 hectares, with a higher density than Manila, the world's densest city. It lies on a ridge, a two-hour walk from Kibuye town, which sits 500 metres below, on the shores of Lake Kivu, a natural border with Eastern DRC. The main initial buildings were the administrative hub, the health centre and the market. These facilities grow along the hillcrest, on a path that runs longitudinally southwards through the camp. Kiziba's shelters crowd the sides of this main path, and as the

2.21

Kiziba

1996

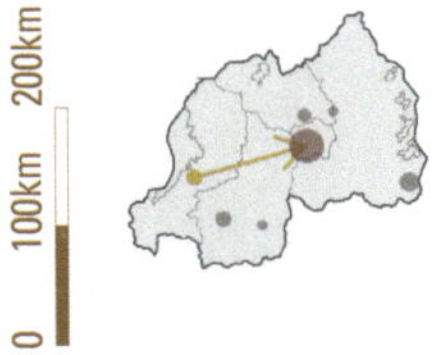

Total ECD: 10
Total children registered: 841
% of children 3–6 y/o in ECD: 24%

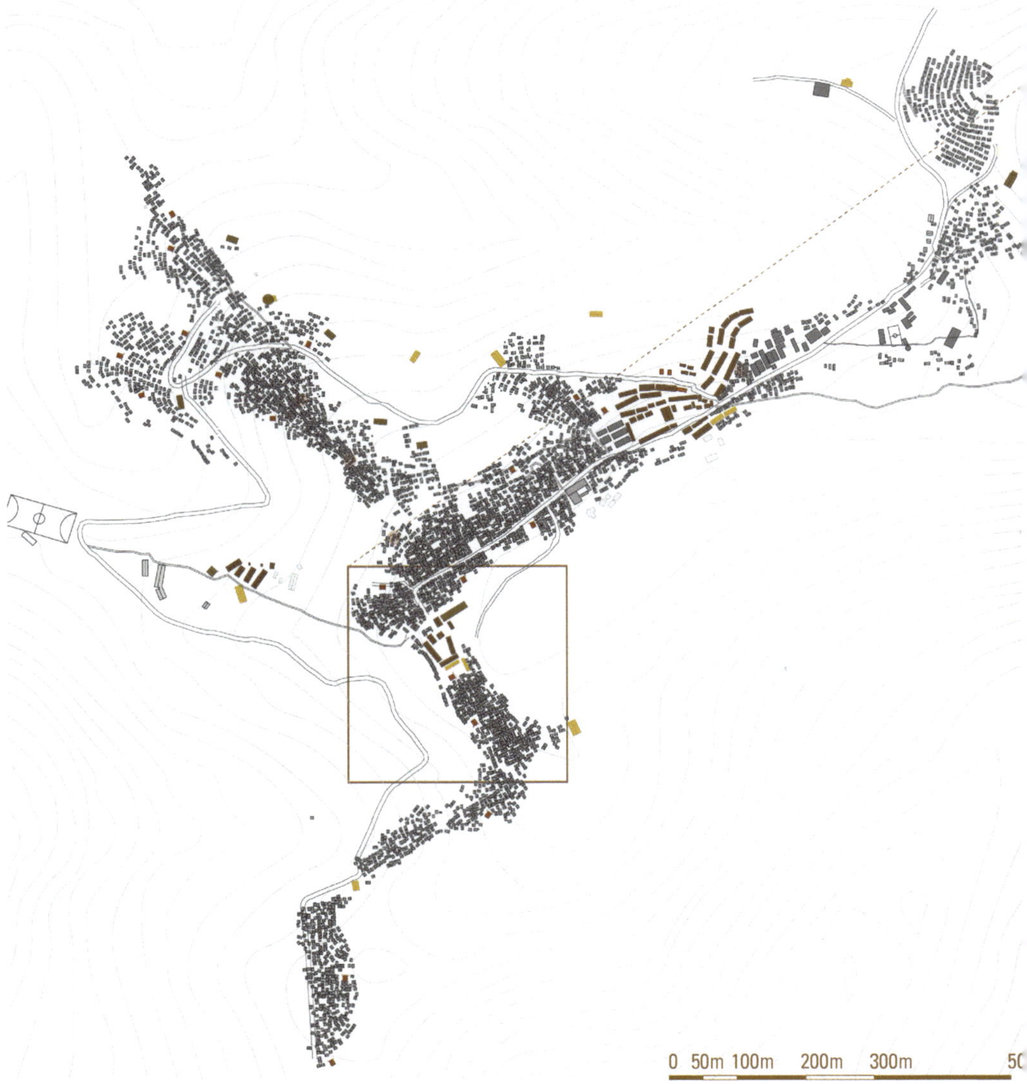

2.21 Maps of Kiziba on the Rift, country, landscape and camp scales. On the camp scale, the maps show the location of visited formal and non-formal ECD centres and also the quarter level showing its grain, density, pattern of habitation and location of one formal learning environment. © Amorós Elorduy.

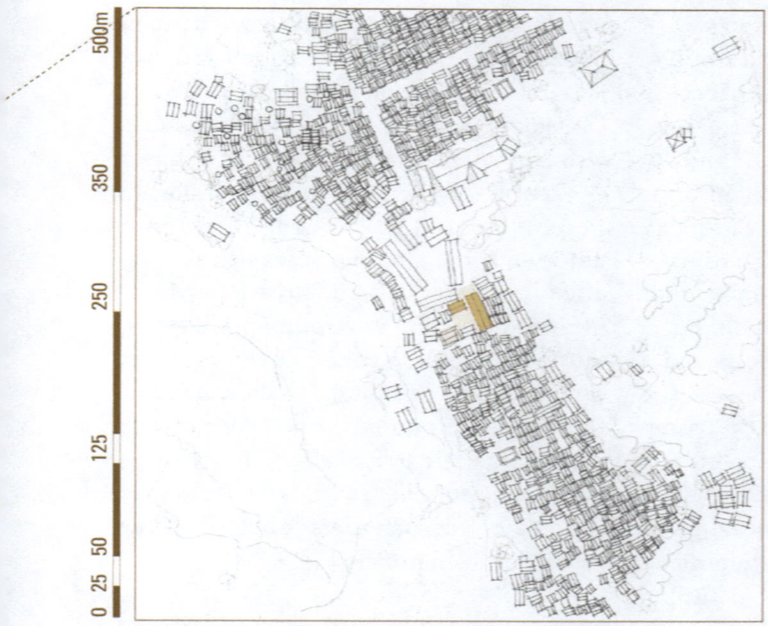

Kiziba (quarters: 2, 3, 4, 5, and 6)
Density of population: 61,600 ppl/sqkm

Maternelle quarter two
Total children registered: 400 (in two shifts am/pm)
6 classrooms of 5 x 8 mts
Density: 1.6 children/sqm

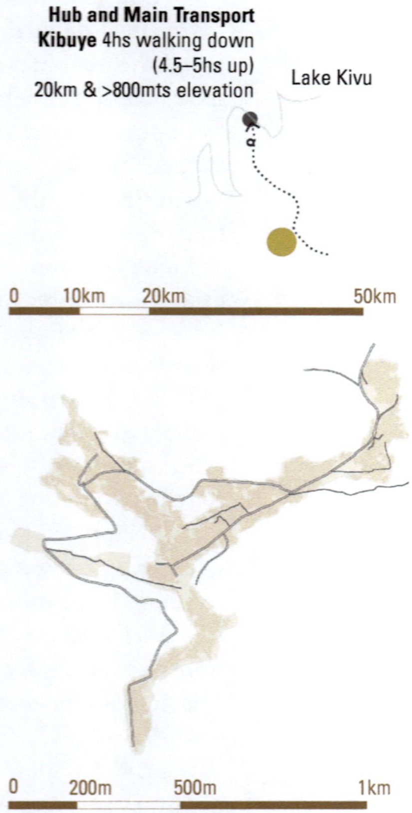

land gets ever-steeper further downhill, the habitation density decreases slightly.

For many years, Kiziba was one of the roughest and most marginalised of the Rwandan camps. Young people were abusing substances and causing trouble, mostly due to isolation and a lack of access to opportunities, such as further education and work.[140] At the end of 2017 and the beginning of 2018, the reduction of funds from donor countries due to the European 'refugee crisis' and the Burundian refugee emergency affecting the region brought important policy and resource changes. A first-shock reduction of rations and a halt to third-country resettlement – due mainly to the regulations of the US Trump administration – had devastating effects for the population and caused riots.[141] The country's policies changed and aligned with the newly signed Comprehensive Refugee Response Framework (CRRF).[142] The Strategy for Economic Inclusion of Refugees and the change from in-kind to cash hand-outs were two of the most significant alterations,[143] followed by the adoption of the CRRF with its own national strategy in 2020.[144] As a result, the atmosphere in the camp has improved significantly. More homes of Rwandan nationals are beginning to appear closer to the camp and on the two roads that lead to it.[145] Camp management and the NGOs have built a new primary school and a higher education institution within the camp, and refugees are improving their homes to more permanent materials with the cash hand-outs and the recent access to start-up funding.[146] This change in policies has also triggered entrepreneurship with burgeoning small business and new NGOs focused on direct cash exchanges, start-up training and crowdfunding.[147]

In terms of formal and non-formal learning environments, in 2016, Kiziba had 10 non-formal ECD initiatives that were run in churches built by refugees and their direct local hosts. These non-formal ECD initiatives served 661 children. At the time, the camp also had two formal ECD centres, in quarters 2 and 4, which assisted 372 children. In total, around 20 per cent of children between three and five years of age were attending some ECD initiative. In terms of informal learning environments, mainly WASH facilities, Kiziba has the bleakest scenario of all the camps that I analyse in this book, with one latrine hole for every 45 inhabitants, and practically no functioning public showers. The 12-square-metre homes are overcrowded, on average hosting six or seven family members (fig. 2.21).

Kigeme: two hills, unplanned and planned conjoined—In 2005, the government created two new camps to host refugees fleeing Burundi's long civil war: Nyabiheke and Kigeme. Most of these Burundian refugees repatriated between 2008 and 2009. This movement left Kigeme almost entirely dismantled, and it changed Nyabiheke's demographics to DR Congolese refugees driven into the country by rebel clashes in Eastern DRC.[148] In March 2012, a new guerrilla war brought thousands of new Eastern DR Congolese into Rwanda,[149] repopulating and expanding Kigeme at the end of 2012 (fig. 2.22).[150]

The road that connects Butare[151] with Bukavu passing through the Nyungwe forest[152] splits Kigeme across two hilltops.

2.22

2.22 Kigeme refugee camp. Top: general view of shelters at Kigeme B. Bottom left: vegetable patch at Kigeme B. Bottom right: path in Kigeme A. September 2015. © Amorós Elorduy.

Kigeme A, on the northern hill, was the original camp established in 2005 with virtually no humanitarian planning. Between 2012 and 2013, a UNHCR planner guided the plan of Kigeme B built on the southern hilltop.

In February 2020, Kigeme hosted 19,845 refugees in eight quarters spread over 34 hectares. The camp is close to the town of Nyamagabe, around a 30-minute walk, and to Kigeme's district hospital, about a five-minute walk.[153] The camp's location contributes to a thriving black market, with currency flowing into the encamped families and influencing the built environment.

In terms of early learning environments, the camp has two formal ECD centres, one

Kigeme

2005

Total formal ECD:	2
Total non-formal ECD:	94
Total children registered:	1,810
% of children 3–6 y/o in ECD:	45%

2.23 Maps and diagrams of Kigeme on the Rift, country, landscape and camp scales. On the camp scale, the maps show the location of visited formal and non-formal ECD centres and also the quarter level showing its grain, density, pattern of habitation and location of one formal learning environment in the camp. © Amorós Elorduy.

2.23

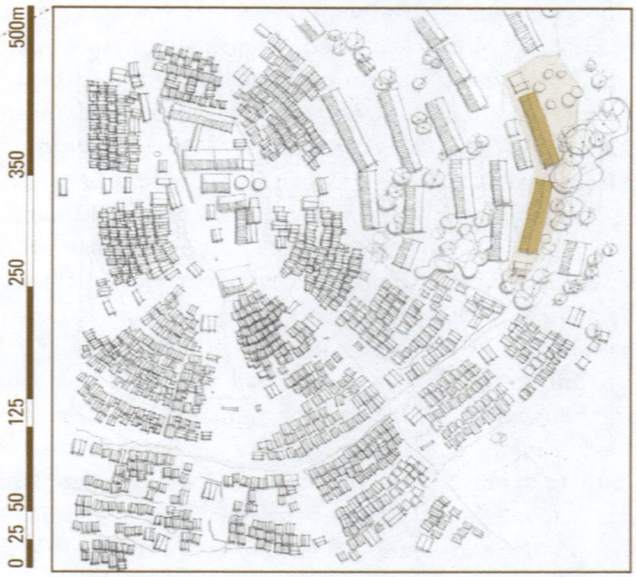

Kigeme B Quarters: 3, 4, 5, and 6

Density of population: 59,850 ppl/sqkm

Kigeme ECD centre

Total children registered: 400
8 classroom (church) 6 x 8mts
Density: 1 children/sqm

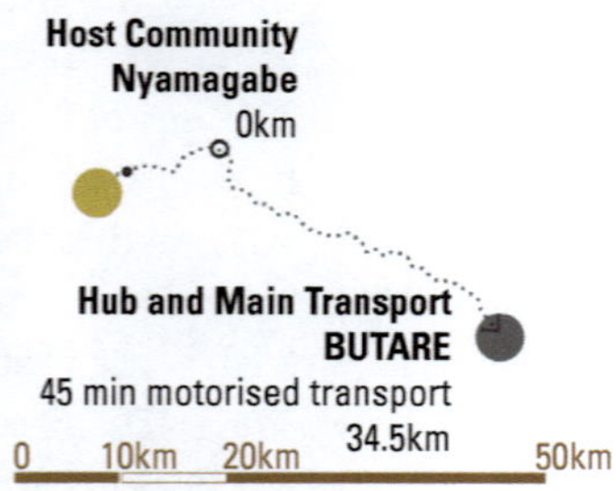

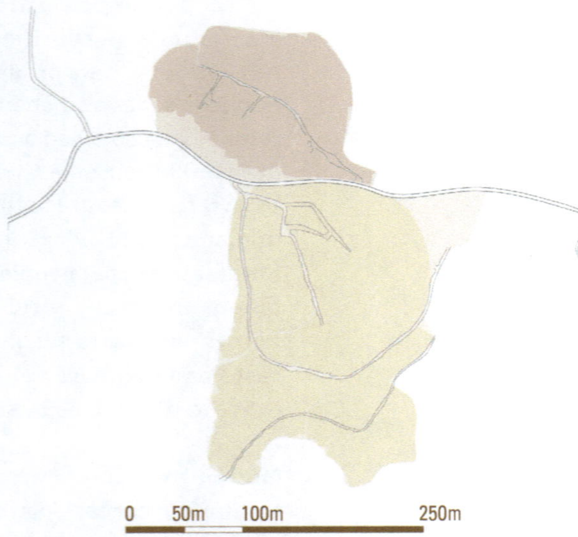

on each side of the road, serving 398 children. In addition, in 2016, Kigeme had 74 non-formal home-based ECD (HBECD) initiatives serving 1,222 children. The HBECD initiatives have taken place in Kigeme since 2012 and in Mugombwa since 2014. These initiatives are composed of groups of 10 mothers who each serve around 15 children aged three to five years from 8:00am to 11:00am, with some material support from the NGOs. The ECD centres and the HBECD help around 38 per cent of children who are of ECD age.[154]

In terms of informal learning environments – specifically, WASH facilities – Kigeme only provides refugees with public latrines and showers. Only certain refugees encroached on neighbouring land have built their own latrines. In Kigeme B, WASH facilities are better built than in the unplanned and older Kigeme A, which has fewer latrines per people and in worse conditions. In this camp, refugees extend their homes even up to second storeys in some cases, and they have more furnishings than those in the houses in Kiziba (fig. 2.23).[155]

Mugombwa: innovative planning yields similar outcomes—Eastern DR Congolese refugees kept entering Rwanda throughout the early 2010s. In October 2013, when the Nkamira transit centre, located close to Gisenyi, was unable to sustain the large numbers of incoming DRC refugees, the UNHCR created Mugombwa refugee camp, located 18 kilometres south-east from Butare in the southern province (fig. 2.24).[156]

Mugombwa is the smallest and newest of the DR Congolese camps in Rwanda. In February 2020, it hosted 10,420 refugees in eight quarters. The planning strategy in Mugombwa was to serve refugees and their direct local hosts simultaneously. This aim guided the choice of location and the camps' master planning. For the first time in Rwanda, a US architectural firm and a higher education institution were involved in planning the settlement.[157] Despite the new actors and goals, Mugombwa's morphology and materiality did not differ significantly from previous camp iterations. The most significant innovation in Mugombwa was having larger spaces between shelters – a move that a worker from the Cooperative for Assistance and Relief Everywhere (CARE) International had promoted.

Regarding formal and non-formal learning environments, Mugombwa is the only camp that I have included in this book, and the first camp in Rwanda, that planned for ECD since its establishment. The ECD centre sat at the camp's core and was highly commended by refugees and humanitarian workers. In terms of non-formal learning environments, in 2016, Mugombwa had 61 HBECD initiatives serving 739 children and one formal ECD centre serving 720 children. In total, these initiatives served almost half of the population of young children of ECD age. Mugombwa also shares its primary and secondary schools with the local people from Mugombwa town.

Regarding informal learning environments, particularly WASH facilities, the latrines and water access in Mugombwa, like those in the other DR Congolese camps, are communal. However, the lower density of habitation and the better planning allows for more latrines per capita than in the older camps, which in Mugombwa almost reaches the UNHCR standard of 20 people per hole.[158]

2.24

2.24 Mugombwa refugee camp. Top: Mugombwa's main road, the camp's centre and formal ECD centre. September 2017. Bottom left: east-facing shelters. Bottom right: west-facing shelters. September 2015. © Amorós Elorduy.

The larger in-between spaces facilitated the HBECD initiatives and the expansion of homes over time. Only four years after its establishment, some shelters were plastered, had iron sheet roofs and kitchens. Some years on, homes have improved pavements, walls and drainage, and many hold commercial activities (fig. 2.25).

Interactive and static spatial characteristics—Dissecting and reassembling the physical characteristics of the seven camps described above, I have found patterns on the regional, landscape and camp scales that might affect young children's learning. The three interactive and three static spatial characteristics, which I explain in

2.25

Mugombwa

2013

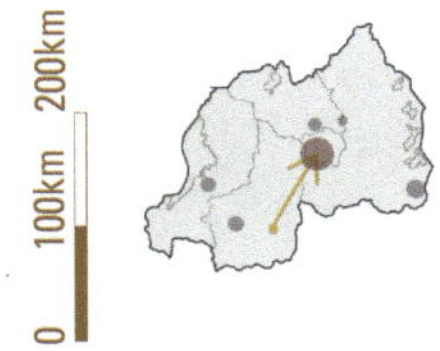

Total formal ECD:	1
Total non-formal ECD:	61
Total children registered:	1,515
% of children 3–6 y/o in ECD:	83%

2.25 Maps and diagrams of Mugombwa on the Rift, country, landscape and camp scales. On the camp scale, the maps show the location of visited formal and non-formal ECD centres and also the quarter level showing its grain, density, pattern of habitation and location of one formal learning environment. © Amorós Elorduy.

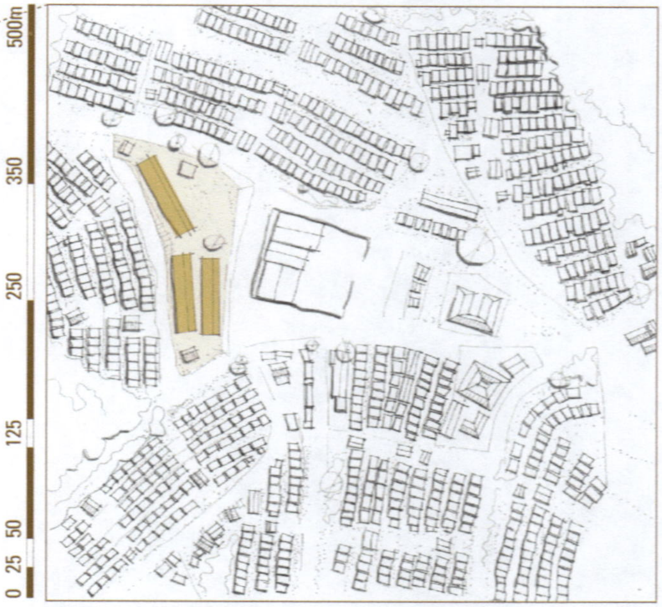

Mugombwa (all quarters)
Density of population: 38066 ppl/sqkm

Mugombwa ECD centre
Total children registered: 600 (in two shifts am/pm)
12 classrooms of 6 x 8mts
Density: 0.52 children/sqm

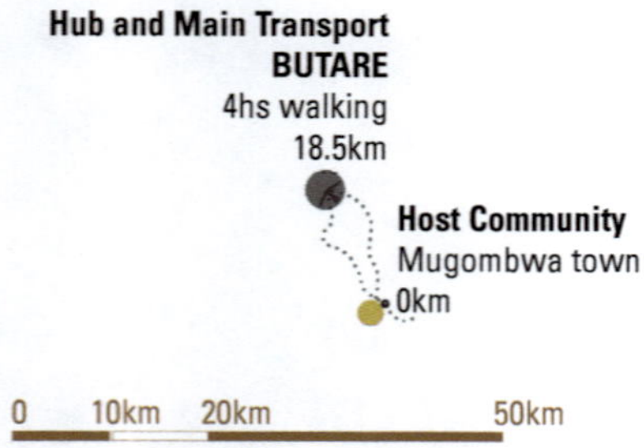

2.26 Location within East Africa, detailed maps and dates of establishment of my seven case studies: Nakivale (est. 1958), Kyangwali (est. 1964) and Kyaka II (est. 1983) in Southwest Uganda; Kakuma (est. 1992) in Northwest Kenya; and Kiziba (est. 1997), Kigeme (est. 2005) and Mugombwa (est. 2013) in Rwanda. © Amorós Elorduy.

2.26

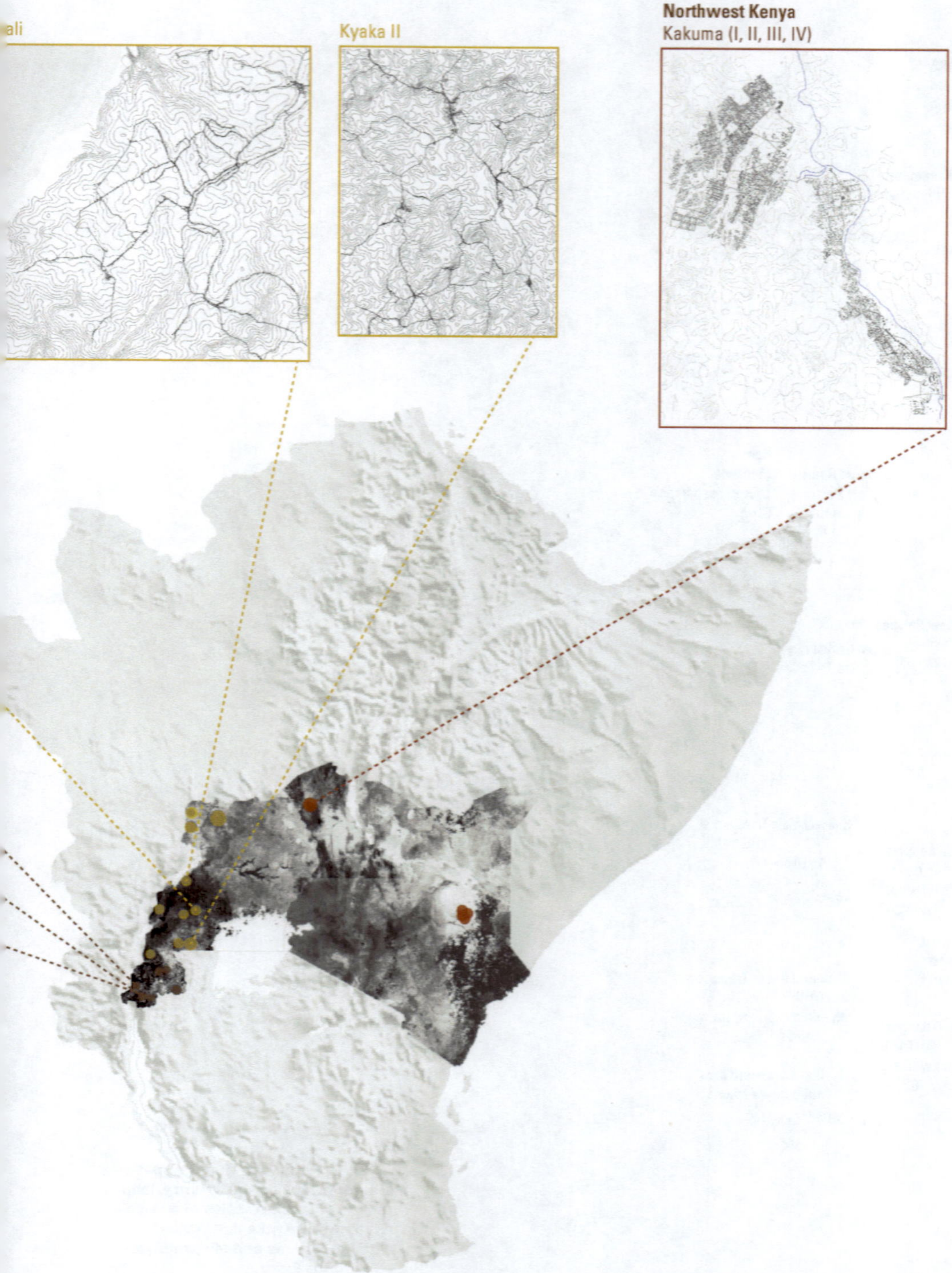
ali
Kyaka II
Northwest Kenya
Kakuma (I, II, III, IV)

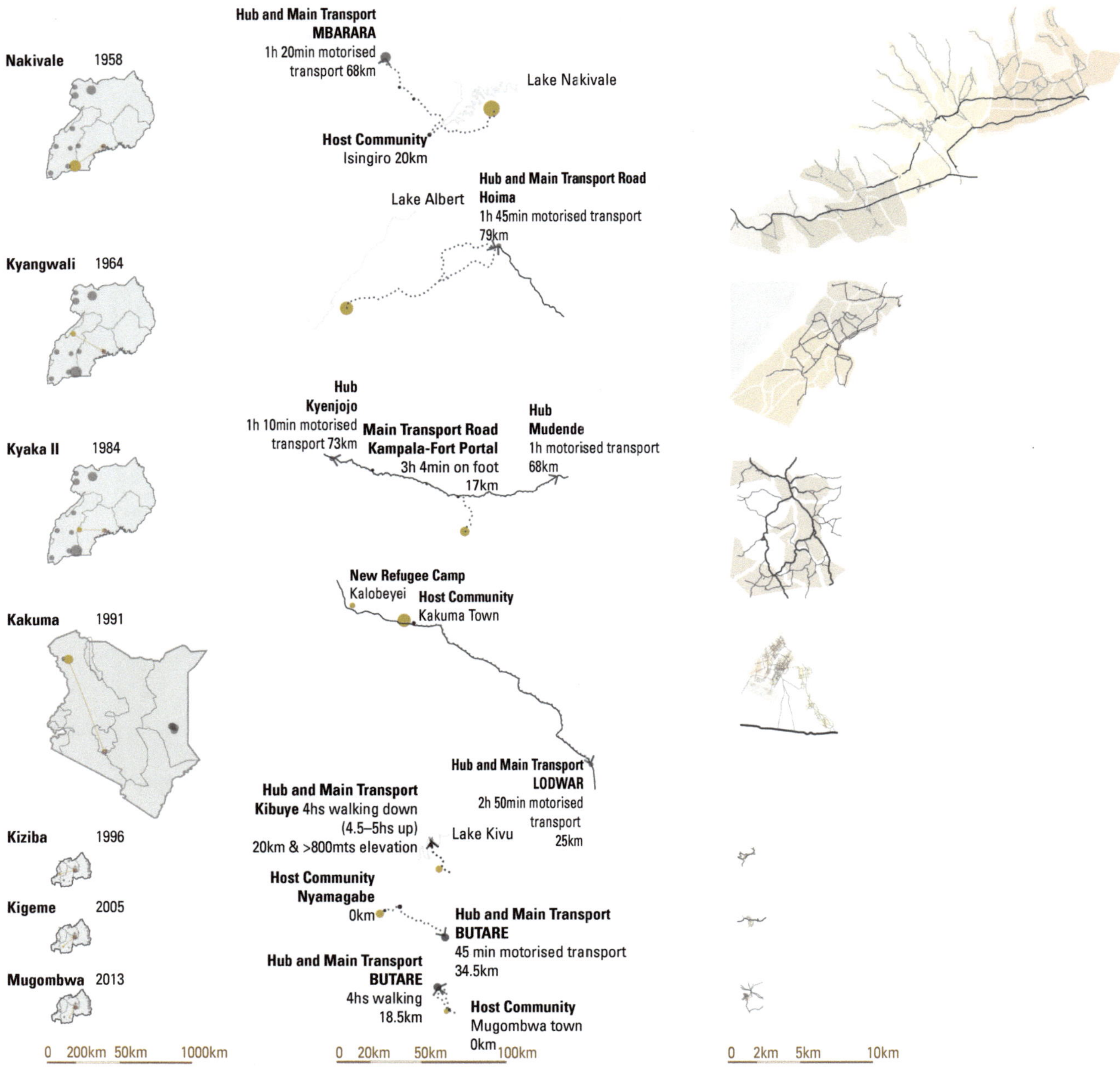

2.27

2.27 Diagram showing the spatial relationships on the country, landscape and camp scales of Nakivale, Kyangwali, Kyaka II, Kakuma, Kiziba, Kigeme and Mugombwa. © Amorós Elorduy.

the following pages, are shared by all seven camps and could help unveil their evolution and map their influence on camps' inhabitants. These six characteristics can help humanitarians, academics and host governments speculate on the potential development of other camps in Eastern Africa and better plan alternatives in order to improve young children's learning (fig. 2.26).

Interactive spatial characteristics

***Growing heterogeneity and complexity*—** Long-term camps are heterogeneous assemblages gaining complexity on a variety of temporal and spatial scales simultaneously. In these camps, refugees' child-rearing practices are multiple, and so are the host countries and the refugee policies that govern them, and the climates and geographical features where they stand (fig. 2.27). Their sizes and population densities are many and varied. For example, in Rwanda, the Congolese camps are the size of a small town, have high population densities and are placed on the steep slopes of volcanic hills, sometimes reaching the 40 per cent slope.[159] In contrast, the Southwest Ugandan camps occupy relatively large pieces of undulated and loosely planned land. They are conglomerates of fine-grain residential and agricultural uses sparsely populated, with an average 1.2-acre plot per family,[160] while Kakuma in Kenya is designed like a grid on a dry plain with a coarse grain of segregated uses, ethnicities and classes.

Heterogeneity is ubiquitous, even within the same country. For example, in the case of Uganda, the old, multi-ethnic and increasingly dry Nakivale has good soil for grazing cattle, but it is not suitable for agriculture and the construction of latrines and wells. In contrast, Kyangwali and Kyaka II benefit from a hilly topography with fertile soil and abundant rain – ideal conditions for agriculture and enough clay and grass to favour sturdy constructions.

Heterogeneity affects young children's learning both negatively and positively. A clear illustration of its adverse effects is evident in Tarach ECD centre in Kakuma phase I where UNICEF's standards devised in Geneva govern the schedule, curricula and class division. Its crumbling buildings reflect the impact that three decades can have on a mud construction over sandy soil. The classroom decorations suggest the origins and training that their caregivers. The children who attend Tarach represent the different cultures, stories and languages of the area's inhabitants. However, UNICEF's global standards fail to account for climatic, material, spatial, cultural and language variation.[161] In Tarach, the primary language spoken is Arabic, which means that the Congolese children who attend the centre feel marginalised.[162] The standards do not contemplate child-friendly designs[163] either, with one example of this being the windows, which are small and placed high up. The global standards and the short-term consultants that usually build centres such as Tarach ECD often seem unable to pre-empt certain variables. In Tarach, the unstable sandy soil and the years of use of a building thought to be for the short term are often the cause of broken toilets, cracked walls and

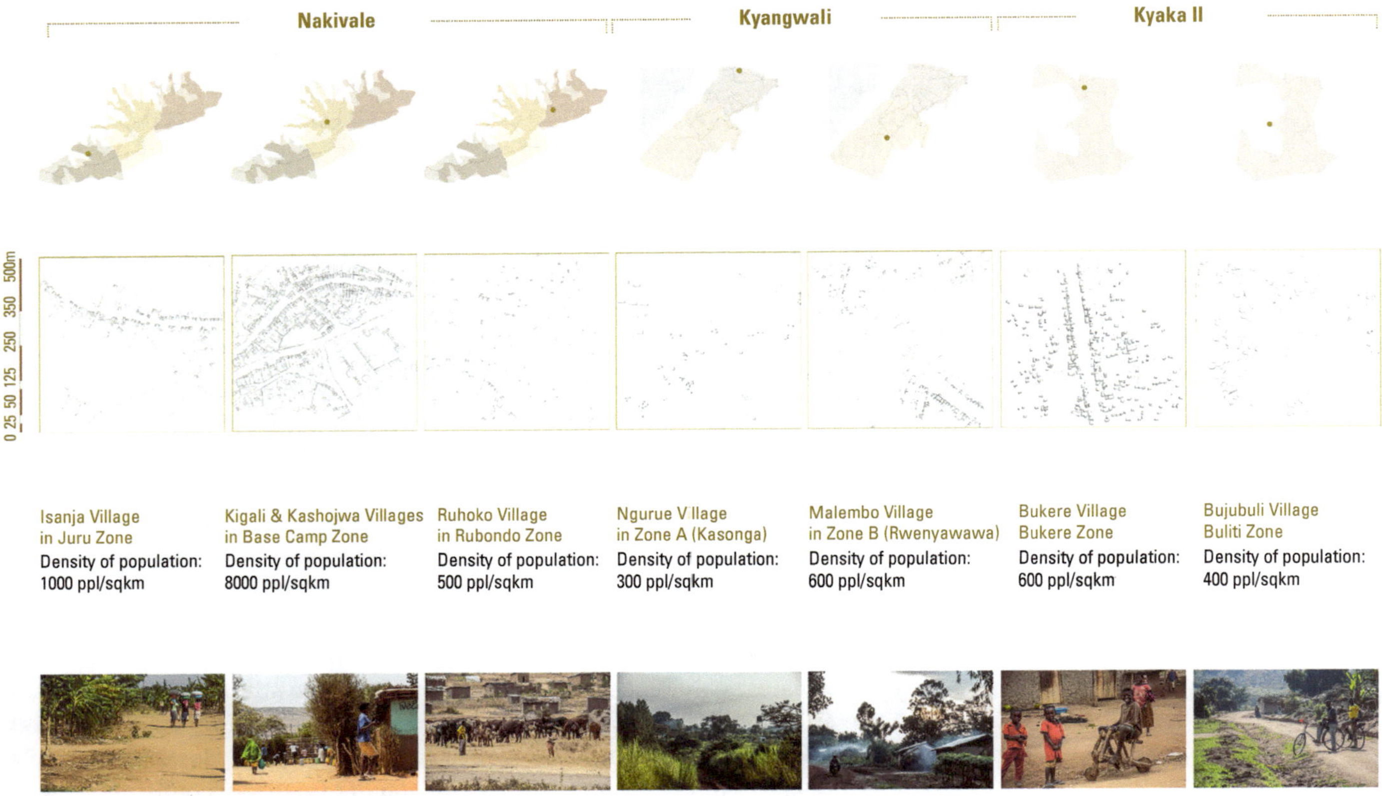

2.28 Infographic showing the variability within the camp scale across my seven case studies (the diverse villages and quarters). Specifically it shows: three villages at Nakivale portraying the camp's three zones (Ruhoko village in Rubondo zone, the encounter of Kigali and Kashojwa villages in Base Camp zone, and Isanja in Juru zone); two villages at Kyangwali, Ngurue in zone A and Malembo in zone B; two villages at Kyaka II, Bukere trading centre in Bukere zone and Bujubuli in Buliti zone; three zones at Kakuma, one per phase; the encounter of four quarters in Kiziba, quarters 2, 4, 5 and 8; the encounter of four quarters in Kigeme, quarters 3, 4, 5 and 6; and the centre of Mugombwa covering portions of all quarters except quarters 7 and 8. © Amorós Elorduy.

rusted playground equipment. The example of Tarach applies to most ECD centres in Kakuma.

According to the refugees, one positive effect of complexity for ECD is cosmopolitanism. Notably, in larger camps such as Kakuma and Nakivale, the richness of people's origins, language and cultures enhance social interactions, openness and children's learning through experience.[164]

The intricacy of the long-term camps affects their legibility, with repercussions on their funding and management. The more complex the camp and the conflicts that feed it, the more difficult it is for the structuralist, hierarchic and under-sourced humanitarian system to gather information and to identify specific problems with straightforward solutions – their usual modus operandi. Kim Dovey[165] and James Scott[166] explain in their reflections of top-down outlooks on social structures the downsides of this type of 'seeing like a state'. They focus on matters of invisibility, legibility and interpretation. Applied to the East African refugee camps, complexity and the state-like standpoint of the humanitarian system/host government assemblage

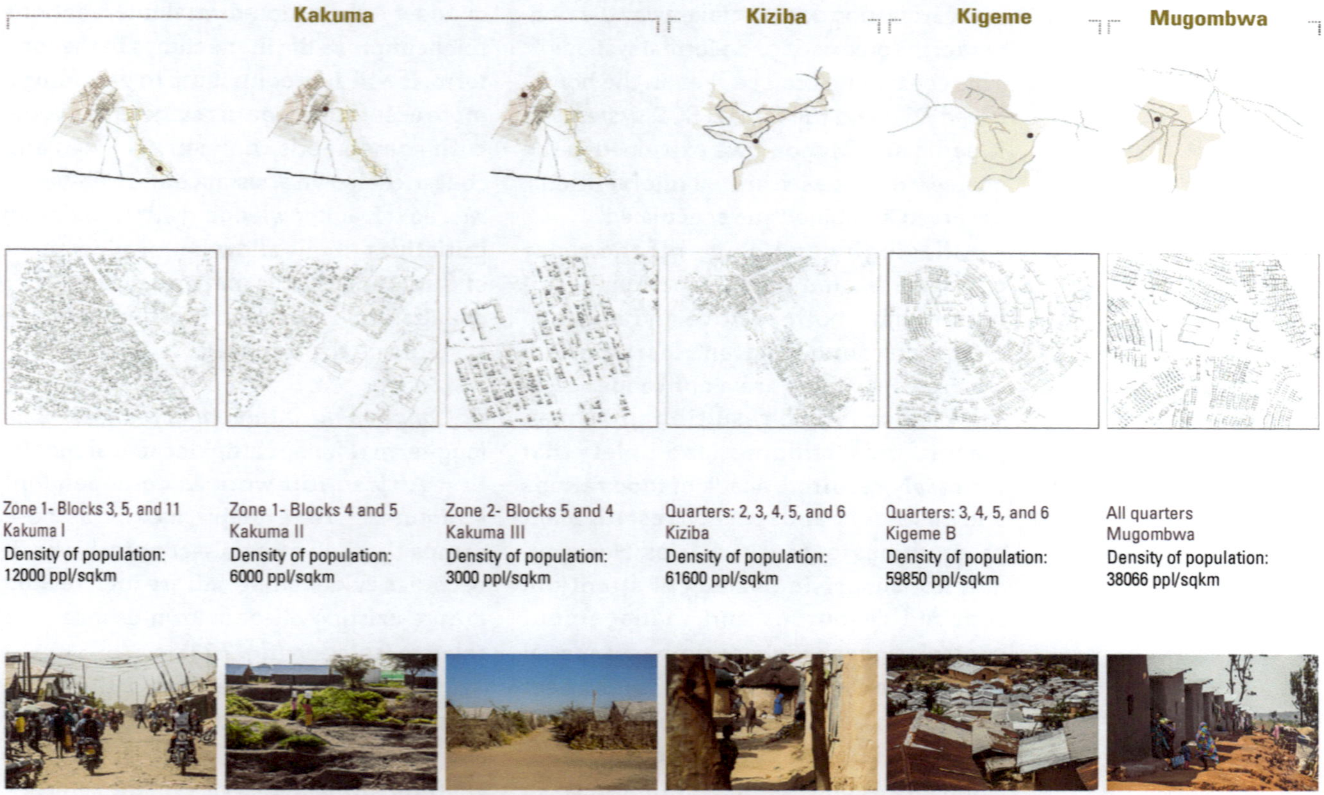

obligate the largely under-sourced and understaffed managers to create generalised and simplified assumptions to make the camps more 'legible' to the outsiders and more easy to run. This top-down approach and the lack of contextualised information leads to generalising views, and it discourages donors, governments and academics trying to understand the camps.

In an effort to count refugees, achieve Education for All goals[167] and improve the lives of children living in encampment, the humanitarian efforts try to counterpoint the complexity of the long-term camps. The appearance of formal ECD centres in the early 2010s contributed to the camps legibility. The formal learning avenues add up to the usually more invisible non-formal and informal efforts that refugees and direct local hosts had been running for years or decades. Formal centres literally put ECD on maps, reports, funding appeals, NGO programming and national regulations by creating a building specifically and only for one thing: young children's learning.

Hence, formal ECD centres benefit the ECD effort and will continue to do so, as long as standardisation does not take away the richness of the preexisting non-formal systems.[168] This coexistence can be seen in the home-based ECD and the formal ECD systems in Kigeme and Mugombwa explained in the chapter 'Refugee-led spatial interventions: observed, imagined and speculated'.

Illegibility and being off the radar of the media and the international community have both positive and negative effects on young children's learning. The adverse outcomes are a consequence of the lack of funds, resulting in broken playgrounds, buildings and toilets that are rarely repaired; a lack of food rations and hand-outs; and reduced resettlement programmes to third countries. However, and not surprisingly, lack of attention, reduced resources and management control trigger a higher number of spatial interventions led by refugees and direct local hosts, including non-formal learning facilities. The Southwest Ugandan camps are a good example, as their relaxed humanitarian control promotes the creation of numerous and varied non-formal learning initiatives. These improve the learning scenario for young children, being more culturally relevant, nearby and for smaller groups.[169]

Currently, many of the non-formal interventions go unaccounted for in humanitarian discourses of refugee education, contributing to the widespread assumption of refugees solely as victims, dependent and uneducated. In fact, as Sarah Dryden-Peterson points out, this lack of focus on refugee-led initiatives has been going on since the 1960s. Mapping – and hence making legible and visible to the outsider – these non-formal interventions might improve life in the camps in the long term. It will also contribute to providing a more accurate image of refugees as people with some needs that can also lead and co-lead their own assistance and well-being. Moreover, acknowledging all the existing initiatives might allow better placement of funds and efforts and enhance further collaborations between the humanitarian system and the refugees.

Co-functioning/interconnectedness—The long-term refugee camps located along the East African Rift work as co-dependent structures.[170] For example, looking at these camps through a social-economic lens, it becomes evident that[171] all are interrelated to a pre-existing village or town, despite their relative isolation (fig. 2.28).

Camps can create benefits for their local counterparts, which usually undergo urban and economic growth, and their inhabitants profit from the services in the camps.[172] For example, in Kigeme, Mugombwa and the Southwest Ugandan settlements, camp services usually serve both refugees and their equally isolated and marginalised direct local hosts,[173] bridging differences and strengthening their relationships. Hence, their interactions tend to be symbiotic, mutually beneficial and equitable,[174] opening up options for the young refugees. Healthy relationships between refugees and direct local hosts can affect young children's learning positively. They can increase children's access to essential goods and social services, provide economic opportunities for their parents[175] and improve refugees' social recognition in the host country.

Yet, camps can also create conflict between inhabitants and their neighbours. This tends to arise due to land ownership (explained in the following section) and unequal aid distribution, when the refugees reap benefits from humanitarian funds and services while their hosts, who are also marginalised and impoverished, do not.[176] For example, in the case of the formal ECD centres in Kyaka II, refugees received scholarships but Ugandan nationals did not, causing tension between both groups. In Kakuma, it is even worse, as ECD centres are only for refugees. Conflict reduces children's free-play options and increases their insecurity, affecting their learning through experience[177] and their access to goods and services.

An example of the interconnectedness of the camps with a vast network of actors is the correlation between camp life and that in the countries of origin. Both Peteet[178] and Sanyal[179] observed connection to origin in the Middle Eastern camps. This relationship is evident in East Africa on the refugee-led constructions – both homes and commercial facilities – in the patterns of school attendance and religious temples.

Interconnectedness can be observed between different groups of refugees living in the same camp, enhancing children's openness to other cultures and strengthening their socio-emotional and language development, such as in Kakuma and Nakivale. However, these multiple origins can also create violent encounters. In such cases, children are forbidden to play freely on the streets. They can suffer abuse, kidnapping and violence in the common areas and on the camps' outskirts, with repercussions on their physical and psychological development and preventing further learning. A clear example of this is Kakuma's streets and common areas. Kakuma can be insecure due partly to the poor relationship with neighbouring Turkana[180] and partly to conflicts between the different refugees within the camp. In Kakuma, unlike in the other camps that I describe in this book, there is a night curfew to control insecurity.

Bonds exist even between the host and the origin country. For example, the same host country may apply different policies for different refugee origins. That is the case of Burundian refugees and DRC refugees in Rwanda, who receive very different treatment and funding.[181] Furthermore, conflicts and alliances in the region mutate over time. On occasions, these conflicts implicate the host country, with repercussions for the refugees. This intricacy can cause insecurity for the easily locatable encamped refugees,[182] pressing some of them to travel as far as 2,000 kilometres – as is the case for many refugees encamped in Kakuma and Nakivale – to find safety away from their neighbouring countries.[183]

Co-dependency and interconnectedness can also be observed between the camps' morphologies and the landscape within which they reside. For example, in Rwanda, the Congolese camps are small clusters of dwellings located on hilltops that replicate the *imidugudu*–hill[184] relationship present in other village formations in the country. These camps work like a rhizome.[185] Once they reach a maximum surface area and population size, a new one sprouts up on another hilltop. These camps' relatively small size benefits young children's access to formal ECD facilities, since their location is usually less than a kilometre from any given household.

In contrast, the camps in Southwest Uganda follow a fractal growth along the ridges and valleys that criss-cross the topography. This growth behaviour involves an increase in the distance to essential services, including ECD facilities. Still, these sparsely populated camps and their porosity are positive for young children, as they enhance co-dependent relationships between direct local hosts and refugees and among refugees. They increase the number of non-formal ECD initiatives, facilitate refugees' access to arable land – improving child nutrition – and tend to reduce overcrowding at home. Finally, in Northwest Kenya, the camps spread like oil stains on flat, arid and mostly valueless land, their growth eventually interrupted by dry riverbeds that seasonally flash flood, destroying everything in their path.[186] The long distances hamper young children's access to services and ECD centres. The wide-open and unprotected streets – especially in its most recent phases – make parents wary, constraining children to play within their home compounds.

Interconnectedness can also be observed on larger spatial (regional) and temporal (years) scales, for example looking at the refugees' choice of fleeing routes and destinations. Regional political affairs, a family's economy and personal motivations, and the potential opportunities in a given camp influence these selections. Refugees' choice of route and final location might affect young children's learning. Most refugees in the East African Rift tend to seek asylum within their neighbouring countries, which are usually relatively poor, landlocked and have conflicts of their own bringing negative implications.[187] On the flip side, short distances to flee reduce risks during the journey, and once there, the languages and cultural upbringings at the formal ECD centres tend to be more similar between refugees, host countries' caregivers and their national ECD regulations

Ever becoming—Analysing refugee camps over a short period, they seem static. Only the daily and maybe the seasonal changes might become apparent. However, when observing them over several years or decades, their ever-becoming character becomes apparent. One example of this is the substantial population and land cover fluctuations that many camps suffer, especially those close to the borders such as Kyangwali, Nakivale and Kakuma. For example, Kyaka II almost emptied in 1994. It then trebled its population – 5,000 to 17,000 inhabitants – between 2005 and 2007, and then quadrupled it – 32,656 to 123,086 inhabitants – from early 2018 to early 2020.

These fluctuations in population prevent proper planning and funding, obstructing formal refugee education and aid hand-outs, creating instability in the camps and triggering issues such as epidemics. Formal ECD centres at areas sensitive to fluctuations tend to be transitional tented structures, even after months or years of the camp's establishment. The areas of Mukunyu in Kyangwali, Ruhoko in Nakivale and phases III and IV in Kakuma all had these temporary ECD centres in 2016.

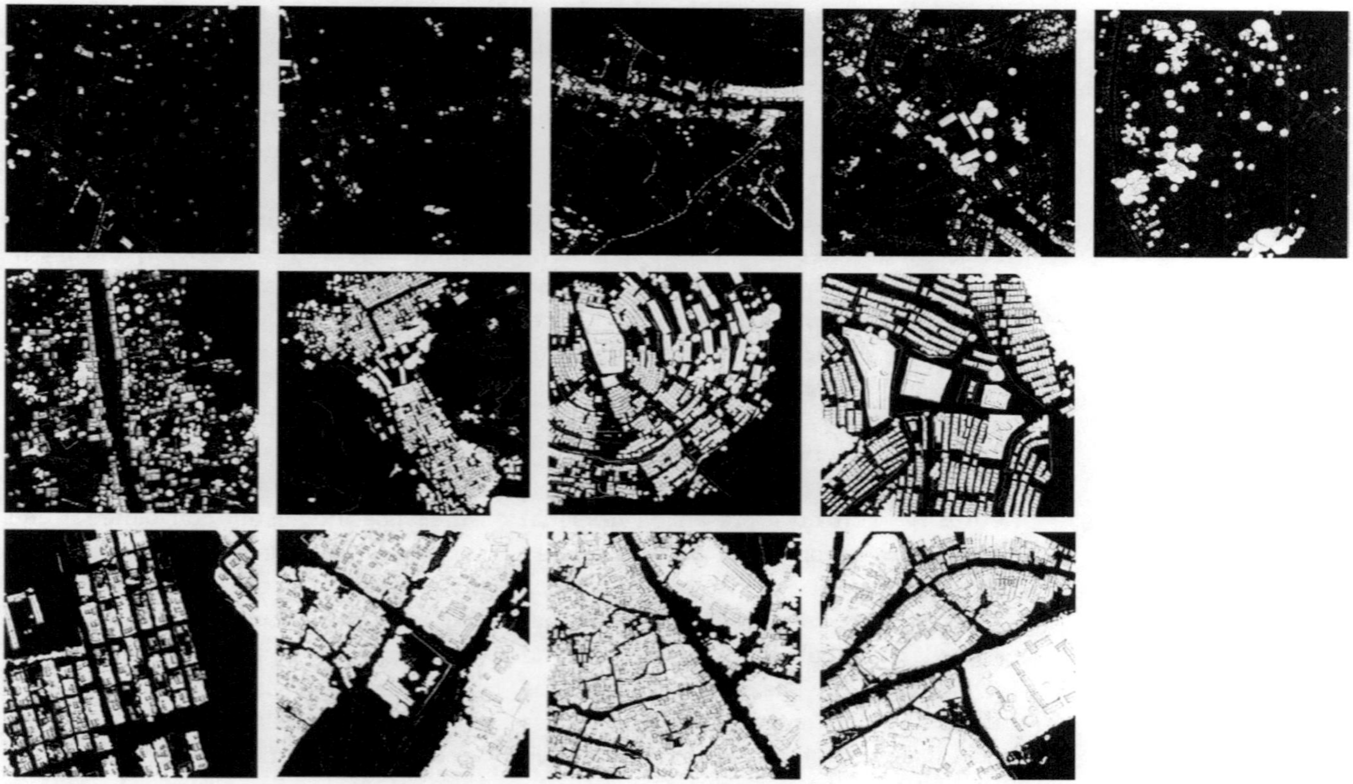

2.29

2.29 Diagram of the open areas and the porosity of different villages in my seven case studies. From top to bottom and left to right (organised from most to least permeable): Ruhoko (Nakivale), Ngurue (Kyangwali), Isanja (Nakivale), Malembo (Kyangwali), Buliti (Kyaka II), Bukere (Kyaka II), Kiziba, Kigeme, Mugombwa, Kakuma phase III, Kakuma phase II, Kakuma phase I and Base Camp (Nakivale). © Amorós Elorduy.

The unpredictability of these areas pushes the resource-scarce education cluster to invest only in very transitional and relatively cheap tented facilities. The hampered planning in these 'buffer' zones is also reflected in the scarcity of water taps, WASH facilities and the poor condition of the roads. These scantily planned facilities affect young children's learning and physical development mostly negatively, obstructing their access to proper content-based education and their learning through experience.[188]

Another example of the camps' ever-becoming status is their material malleability, which varies from camp to camp, within them and over time depending on many human and non-human actors, especially the agency of refugees and direct local hosts. The resource-scarce and less controlled camps tend to be more malleable, as the refugees and their local hosts have more agency to change the camps' spaces on the building scale. This malleability allows refugees to create and modify the spaces where children learn and spend most of their time: the homes, streets, open areas, community schools and religious temples. In Kiziba, as humanitarian resources decrease and with them the humanitarian authoritarian control and the international attention, refugees negotiate with their direct local hosts and create religious temples, mills and family homes on the outskirts of the camps, modifying the camps' boundaries. Both refugees and their direct local hosts use these temples as non-formal ECD initiatives on weekdays. These negotiated interventions benefit young children with direct content-based learning and learning through experience, since they strengthen relationships with the direct local hosts.

Static characteristics

Porosity—Porosity is present on all spatial scales. The nation states' borders located along the East African Rift are very porous, allowing for the relatively easy movement of goods and people, including refugees and rebels (fig. 2.29). The camps' borders are also porous; no fences or hard boundaries exist in any of the camps at which I have worked. These two levels of porosity, in addition to the camps' relative closeness to national borders, increase potential incursions and attacks. Raids cause insecurity, with the abduction of both children and adults. The camps at Kiziba, Kyangwali and Kakuma all have records of such situations.[189] Insecurity might cause physical and psychological trauma to children, and even when not directly affected, parents might prevent them from playing on the street, causing them to lose out on potential socio-emotional, physical and intellectual gains.

However, porosity at landscape and camp levels can be positive for young children's learning. The highly porous and sparsely populated camps in Southwest Uganda allow children to create shortcuts through the landscape and play freely in the bushes and fields. In Rwanda, the unfenced homes and intricate streets facilitate the occupation of interstices for games and for community-organised learning activities, enhancing children's curiosity and opportunities for free play.

The case of Kakuma is particularly interesting in that it presents different levels of porosity, depending on the viewer – a reminder of the importance of contextualisation and the need for more and richer situated bits of knowledge. In Kakuma phase I, the fenced homes and convoluted streets may appear quite hermetic to a stranger in the area. Yet, they are secure and beneficial to the local young children who know everybody in the neighbourhood. This duplicity strengthens young children's sense of community, safety and free-play options. In contrast, Kakuma phases II and III gain in visual porosity for strangers due to their open gridded roads, which become impermeable for young children due to their long distances and other risks. Parents living in these areas prevent children from venturing outside their home compounds. In these phases, the double-faced porosity has the opposite effects on young children's learning compared to Kakuma's initial phase.[190]

In general, a high porosity at the camp and building levels coupled with high population densities enhance children's curiosity and learning-by-experience options. It may also encourage community activities and interactions with neighbours, friends and the environment around them.

Land scarcity and poor soil—It seems that most of the conflicts that push refugees to flee their homes and many of the disputes within and around the camps are related to land, its scarcity and related resources.[191] Tensions arise from the moment when governments and humanitarian agencies try to find land to establish a camp, raising issues of citizen rights and representation. Governmental power and geopolitics play a role. Particularly in East Africa, colonisation and lack of representation of certain groups – minorities and marginalised ethnic groups – affect access to land and recognition of rights.[192]

Land issues also arise during the life of a camp. Growing and fluctuating populations and unmarked boundaries tend to trigger these types of conflicts. For example, in the 1980s, due to land shortages and political turmoil in Uganda, many people – primarily Bahima pastoralists – moved to the surroundings of Nakivale. In mid-1994, many of the camp's refugees repatriated to Rwanda, and the surrounding settlers moved within the camp's unmarked limits to graze their herds or settle. Later that same year, when new Rwandan refugees arrived, friction and conflict took place. A similar situation is recurrent in Kyangwali and Kyaka II.[193] These types of disputes, which vary from camp to camp, significantly affect young children's mobility and security, preventing play and hence obstructing their learning by experience.[194]

Another dimension related to land, which I have found mostly on the camp and building scales, is the poor soil and the lack of land that hamper the building of proper constructions, especially latrines. In fact, WASH is an endemic problem in all the camps that I present in this book. For example, the sandy, unstable soil in Nakivale and Kakuma makes digging pits for the latrines difficult, especially for child-led families. In Nakivale, to circumvent this problem, refugees have resorted to building latrines on top of empty termite mounds due to their sturdiness. However, this practice prevents access for many young children and people with disabilities. In the Rwandan cases, the lack of land makes it unviable to have private WASH facilities – both latrines and showers – which consequently are public, scarce, overcrowded, dirty, unsafe and not child-friendly.[195] Hence, most children choose to excuse themselves in the bush on the outskirts of the camp, which presents opportunities for abuse and accidents.[196]

Finally, it is extremely rare that refugees can use the camps' land for profit as many aid plans assume. In a few best-case scenarios, the area is available and fertile, such as in Kyangwali and Kyaka II. Yet, even in such cases, not all refugees are agriculturalists, and even when they are, they tend to lack the tools, seeds and markets to place their produce. In most cases, the land is not fertile – such as in Nakivale and Kakuma – or big enough – such as in the Rwandan cases. I have hardly seen any refugees who can make agricultural profits or live off the land lent to them.

As a consequence of the lack of agricultural profits and scant aid hand-outs, a large number of young children suffer from malnutrition.[197] Undernourishment affects children's brain and physical development and consequently their learning abilities, social interactions and socio-emotional development.[198]

Finally, the extreme lack of land – Kiziba in 2019 reached a density of around 65,000 people per square kilometre[199] – combined with decades-long displacement makes overcrowding at the camp, the home and the ECD initiatives a real problem for young children's learning. Congestion affects children negatively, especially in homes and sleeping areas, making these environments noisy and lacking privacy and enough space. These home environments impact the physical integrity and the cognitive development of the young children and affect their lifelong learning.[200]

Isolation and proximity to the border—Isolation on the country and landscape scales increases the cost of goods and information affecting the refugees' access to food, building materials and jobs for income generation.[201] Lack of construction materials is reflected in inadequate housing, WASH and even educational facilities, affecting young children's learning. The distances to major hubs also affect access to secondary and higher education and to proper health care.[202]

Moreover, being close to borders increases insecurity, the chances of raids in the camps and the likelihood of child abductions. This insecurity jeopardises refugee children's rights to life and physical security under the Convention on the Rights of the Child.[203] According to the UNHCR's and OAU's guidelines, refugee camps should not be located close to a border,[204] which has loosely translated as a minimum of 50 kilometres from the border.[205] Nevertheless, a standardised set measurement does not ensure a safe distance. Security from border incursions depends on geographical barriers, the porosity of the country's borders and other variables particular to each environment. The politics involved in land use, host nation security concerns and other aspects relating to the site selection of a camp become obstacles to achieving a secure site far enough away from the border.[206]

Distance from the border is a clear example of how global standards, which are widespread in humanitarian practice, should be highly contingent on context, whether it be geographic, spatial, cultural, socio-economic or temporal. A post-structural and contextualised approach to the study of refugee assistance and its practice is needed. Kiziba, Nakivale, Kyangwali and Kakuma are all located close to a border. Governments and the UNHCR have established even newer camps closer than the 50-kilometre standard, such as Rwanda's Mahama – established in 2015 – and Kenya's Kalobeyei – established in 2016.[207]

Ever-changing, proto-urban, learning assemblages—The detailed maps of the long-term camps and their geographical and physical features provide an interesting and diverse picture of these settlements. Understanding the camps' interactive and static spatial characteristics – growing heterogeneity and complexity, co-functioning/interconnectedness, ever becoming, porosity, land scarcity and poor soils, and isolation and proximity to the border – and their effects on livelihoods and especially on young children shed light on how these camps grow/change. This information could make future refugee assistance strategies more adaptable and able to improve in ways that are beneficial to the people living there.

As I have explained, children extract some positive learnings from the long-term camps' built environments. They learn about openness from the cosmopolitan Nakivale and Kakuma. They develop their curiosity in the labyrinthic, dense and porous Rwandan camps and the old centres of Nakivale (Base Camp), Kakuma (phase I), Kyaka II and Kyangwali (trading centres). The increased presence of formal and non-formal ECD facilities raises awareness amongst parents, and desire amongst children, of attaining a formal education and of improving their living standards with better nutrition, health and cognitive stimulation from an early age.

However, currently, the long-term camps are in general poor learning environments for young children. Geopolitics, international and national policies, geography, socio-economics and the camps' interactive and static characteristics are generally hampering young children's direct content-based learning and learning through experience. The current scenario creates mostly dangerous and harmful environments for young children. The multi-scalar land scarcity and porosity, the ever-evolving conflicts and the locations of the camps create insecure environments that reduce children's access to health, education and essential goods, hindering their healthy physical and psychological development. Moreover, the humanitarian system one-size-fits-all policies and approaches to learning are unsuitable for the varied long-term camps. Language and cultural mishaps see many encamped children marginalised in the formal ECD centres. Finally, the lack of data on these complex and ambiguous long-term camps makes for an unappealing target to funders. Hence, ECD initiatives in the most complex and least researched camps are in extreme lack of funds.

Camps do not usually get dismantled but rather evolve. A percentage of encamped refugees will come and go, as happens in urban settlements. The camps' borders will increasingly blur, triggered by sophisticated negotiations between the strained humanitarian system, the host government, the local authorities, the surrounding communities and the refugees. As the population grows in and around the camps, land scarcity and poor soils will probably become more problematic.

Gradually the camps will become more urban. If that is the envisioned future, humanitarian assistance should perhaps become more like acupuncture and less like major surgery to address specific problems. Moreover, projects and programmes should be accompanied with ongoing advocacy efforts to bring refugee rights to the same level as those for other humans.

For example, as Rwanda signed the CRRF,[208] which emphasises the social and economic inclusion of refugees in national systems, the country is pushing refugees not only to become self-reliant but to eventually leave the camps.[209] This change from what was a highly paternalistic approach to a self-help approach is due not only to the

CRRF but also to the decrease in humanitarian funding, the acknowledgment of the long-term camp problematic and the protracted conflict in DRC, as well as the tight ethnic and cultural ties between Rwanda and its refugees. Could there be a possibility of shifting these camps into actual villages? As self-building is already taking place, what would be required to achieve other types of autonomy? Could these camps also become attractive to locals and, with time, rather than a refugee settlement become just another *umudugudu*?

Further questions arise. Are the camps' six spatial characteristics present in other long-term camps and newer settlements? If so, could we envision the routes that these newly built camps such as Mahama, Kalobeyei and Bidi-bidi[210] will take? Would having this knowledge help in defining real alternatives to camps that improve young children's lifelong learning?

There is value in studying long-term camps as a phenomenon in themselves, different from the generalising 'refugee camp'. Detailed spatial information through the lens of time has the potential to show evolutionary paths for other camps, shedding light on the impact of international visibility and funding into the lives of encamped refugees and their direct local hosts, and elucidating some of the macro and micro politics involved in forced migration in different geographical areas. Humanitarians, governments, international institutions, academics and researchers, citizens and neighbours need to see long-term refugee camps in a holistic light and understand the complexity of interactions between human and non-human actors in these settlements. If long-term camps are considered real human settlements, rich and complex, they will be treated with the respect, dignity and care – in their design and maintenance – that any human-made settlement where millions of lives develop deserves. They will be treated as a place of human – not just humanitarian – relevance.

Notes

1. Niane, *Africa from the Twelfth to the Sixteenth Century*; Ogot, *Africa from the Sixteenth to the Eighteenth Century*.
2. The United Nations General Assembly, 'Convention relating to the status of refugees'.
3. Niane, *Africa from the Twelfth to the Sixteenth Century*; Ogot, *Africa from the Sixteenth to the Eighteenth Century*.
4. Slaughter and Crisp, 'New issues in refugee research'.
5. Harrell-Bond, *Imposing Aid*; Harrell-Bond, 'UNHCR – Are refugee camps good for children?'.
6. Harrell-Bond, 2–3.
7. Scott, *Seeing Like a State*; Harrell-Bond, 'UNHCR – Are refugee camps good for children?'.
8. Daley, 'Refugees and underdevelopment in Africa', 205; Kaiser, 'Structural adjustment and the fragile nation', 1996, 227–37; Kayizzi-Mugerwa and Levin, 'Adjustment and poverty', 1994.
9. Harrell-Bond, 'UNHCR – Are refugee camps good for children?'.
10. The Convention Relating to the Status of Refugees, signed in 1951 alongside the creation of the UNHCR, was to coordinate action and ease refugee assistance allocation, initially just for European refugees. The subsequent 1967 Protocol helped to define the term 'refugee', which became globally accepted, including in Africa, even before the signature in 1969 of the Convention Governing the Specific Aspects of Refugee Problems in Africa. The UNHCR first became involved in the continent in July 1957, when refugee camps started to dot its geography. Camps became prevalent during the 1990s as they substituted other pre-existing means of refugee assistance. The United Nations General Assembly, 'Convention relating to the status of refugees'; Loescher, 'International recognition of refugees'; UNHCR, OAU 'Convention

governing the specific aspects of refugee problems in Africa'; Loescher, 'The emerging independence of the UNHCR under Auguste Lindt'; Kibreab, *African Refugees*; Stein and Clark, 'Refugee integration'.
11. Betts, Loescher and Milner, *The United Nations High Commissioner for Refugees (UNHCR)*.
12. Chapter 12 ('Site selection, planning and shelter') of the UNHCR *Handbook for Emergencies* states: 'Avoid high population density in settlements and in shelters; Avoid very large emergency settlements; refugee camps should normally be considered as a last resort; Involve refugees in all phases of settlement and shelter planning and construction', UNHCR, *Handbook for Emergencies*, 134. In the four editions of the *Handbook for Emergencies*, the first one, published in 1982, questions the effectiveness of encamping refugees and is wary of imposing such a settlement pattern: '... as a general principle, the response should draw to the extent possible on local resources, materials and methods, and should, for example, avoid regimented refugee camps. Solutions that can be readily implemented with existing resources and simple technologies should be sought', UNHCR, *Handbook for Emergencies*, 6.
13. Harrell-Bond, 'Camps: Literature review', 1998.
14. Harrell-Bond, *Imposing Aid*; Feldman et al., 'The failure of self-reliance', 2013.
15. The works of Lacey Gale and Wim Van Damme in West Africa and Roger Zetter in Malawi present three good illustrations of this shift in assistance strategies. Gale, 'The invisible refugee camp', 2008; Van Damme, 'Do refugees belong in camps?', 1995; Zetter, 'Incorporation and exclusion', 1995.
16. UNHCR, 'Population statistics'; Crawford, Cosgrave and Mosel, '10 Things to know'.
17. Crisp, 'Forced displacement in Africa', 2010; Gottwald, 'Burden sharing and refugee protection'; Kreibaum, 'Their suffering, our burden?', 2016; Rutinwa, 'Beyond durable solutions', 1996.
18. Niane, *Africa from the Twelfth to the Sixteenth Century*.
19. At the time, this signified 15 per cent of Malawi's population, which was one of the highest refugee/host ratios in the world. Zetter, 'Incorporation and exclusion', 1995, 1654.
20. Van Damme, 'Do refugees belong in camps?', 1995, 361.
21. Marie and Shimo, 'Zambia initiative', 2002.
22. Bakewell, 'Repatriation and self-settled refugees in Zambia', 2000.
23. Turner, 'The barriers of innocence'; Landau, 'The humanitarian hangover', 2002; Rutinwa, 'The Tanzanian government's response', 1996.
24. Harrell-Bond, *Imposing Aid*.
25. Malkki, 'The rooting of peoples', 1992; Holzer, *The Concerned Women of Buduburam*.
26. Dryden-Peterson, 'Refugee education: The crossroads of globalization', 477.
27. Thanks to the Internet and new technologies, it is easier to access information about the camps through remote sensing, big data, satellite imagery and open-source repositories.
28. Ever since the publication of the Alternatives to Camps policy in 2014, many new 'camps' have been built. In East Africa, two key examples are Mahama in Rwanda and Kalobeyei in Northwest Kenya.
29. The camps of Dadaab and, to a certain degree, Kakuma in Northwest Kenya attract a good deal of attention from mainstream publications and academia alike. At the same time, the Rwandan or the Southwest Ugandan settlements are studied only sporadically, with the majority of relevant works developed around two decades ago.
30. In 2016, Nakivale and Kakuma surpassed 100,000 inhabitants. Kyaka II, the smallest camp in Uganda, housed around 40,000 people. The biggest of the Congolese camps in Rwanda – Kigeme – had around 20,000 people. The densities of the Congolese camps in Rwanda were around 30,000–60,000 people per square kilometre, while the Southwest Ugandan camps had around 300–600 people per square kilometre. For more information, see: UNHCR, 'UNHCR Rwanda monthly population statistics'; MIDIMAR, 'Rwanda Ministry of Disaster Management and Refugees'; UNHCR and Office of the Prime Minister Uganda, Uganda Refugee Response Portal.
31. Lynch, 'The form of cities', 1954; Lynch and Banerjee, *Growing Up in Cities*.
32. Montessori, *The Absorbent Mind*; Dewey, 'Experience and education', 1986.
33. Amorós Elorduy, 'Learning in and through the long-term refugee camps in the East African Rift'.
34. ECD centres activities run for four hours a day. In most case studies, the activities were held in the morning from 8:00am until 11:00am or midday.
35. Amoros Elorduy, 'Learning in and through the long-term refugee camps in the East African Rift'.
36. Ward and Fyson, *Streetwork: The Exploding School*; Hart et al., *Cities for Children*; Nallari, 'The meaning, experience, and value of

"common space"'; Karsten and Van Vliet, 'Children in the city'.
37. Rasmussen, 'Place for children', 2004; Chawla and Malone, 'Neighbourhood quality in children's eyes'.
38. Proshansky and Fabian, 'The development of place identity in the child'; Walter and Wrester, 'Early childhood development'; Bronfenbrenner, 'Contexts of child rearing: Problems and prospects'; Gottfried and Gottfried, 'Home environment and cognitive development in young children of middle-socioeconomic-status families'; Halldén, 'Children's views of family, home and house'.
39. Amorós Elorduy, 'Learning in and through the long-term refugee camps'.
40. Halldén, 'Children's views of family'; Chawla and Malone, 'Neighbourhood quality in children's eyes'; Matthews, 'The street as liminal space'; Zeiher, 'Shaping daily life in urban environments'; Ward, 'The child in the city', 1978.
41. Ward; Ward and Fyson, *Streetwork: The Exploding School*.
42. Lynch, *The Image of the City*; Lynch and Banerjee, *Growing Up in Cities*.
43. Smithson and Smithson, *Ordinariness and Light*, 45–6.
44. In the 1960s, Coombs acknowledged the importance of the learning that happened outside formal schooling facilities. He introduced the notions of non-formal and informal lifelong learning. Coombs and Ahmed, 'Attacking rural poverty'; Coombs, *World Educational Crisis*.
45. David and Weinstein, *Spaces for Children*; Christensen and O'Brien, *Children in the City*.
46. The British Uganda Protectorate became independent on 9 October 1962. The UNHCR began its operations in the country in the early 1960s. The first accounts of refugees in the country date from the Second World War when it hosted displaced Europeans until 1945. In 1955, Uganda started hosting Sudanese refugees and then those from neighbouring countries struggling for independence, including: Kenyans during the Mau Mau struggle, Rwandese escaping the 1959 Rwandan revolution, DR Congolese in the aftermath of Lumumba's assassination in 1961 and a number of Ethiopians and Somalis during the war for the Ogaden. In that time, Uganda's internal violence, triggered by Milton Obote and Idi Amin, created forced migration out of the country to Sudan, Kenya, Tanzania and further afield. Mazrui, *Africa Since 1935*, 110; Lomo, Naggaga and Hovil, 'The phenomenon of forced migration in Uganda', 1:3.
47. The refugee camps' managers in Uganda are the UNHCR and the OPM. At each refugee camp, there is a Refugee Welfare Council (RWC) of refugee-elected representatives. The RWC is the equivalent of the local government system in Uganda, but it has no real power. Its members are a spokesperson in consultations, but for the most part, the refugees feel politically disempowered. Omata and Kaplan, 'Refugee livelihoods in Kampala', 6; Refugee Law Project, 'Refugees in Kyangwali settlement', 12.
48. The Cap 62, of the 1960 Control of Alien Refugees Act, constrained refugees' freedoms and human rights. In 2006, the Ugandan government published the Refugees Act 2006 and repealed the Cap 62 of the former Control of Alien Refugees Act. Government of Uganda, 'Uganda: Control of Alien Refugees Act'; Office of the Prime Minister of Uganda, The Refugees Act 2006.
49. Office of the Prime Minister of Uganda, para. 44.
50. UNHCR, *Handbook for Emergencies*. The emergency preparedness and response section, 16, 17, 19, 136 and 138.
51. The overall number of encamped refugees has increased since data began to be recorded in the early 1960s. Bagenda, Naggaga and Smith, 'Land problems in Nakivale settlement'.
52. Bagenda, Naggaga and Smith; Gardner, 'Beneath the surface'.
53. Nationalities include those from Sudan, South Sudan, Burundi, Rwanda, Ethiopia, Eritrea, Kenya, Somalia and the Eastern DRC region (including the district of Ituri in the Oriental province and the provinces of North and South Kivu). UNHCR Uganda, 'Statistical summary refugees and asylum seekers in Uganda'.
54. The UNHCR lacks consistency in naming and tracking refugee camps and refugee-hosting regions in Uganda, making mapping and keeping track of numbers difficult. The only refugee settlement in Western Uganda is Kyriandongo in the Kyriandongo District. The refugee settlements in Southwest Uganda, all of which were established more than three decades ago, are Nakivale and Oruchinga (Isingiro District), Kyaka II (Kyegegwa District), Rwamwanja (Kamwenge District) and Kyangwali (Hoima District). Sources: UNHCR and Office of the Prime Minister Uganda, Uganda Refugee Response Portal.
55. UNHCR Uganda, 'Statistical summary refugees and asylum seekers in Uganda'.
56. A total of 236,406 Congolese refugees were hosted in settlements in Southwest and Western Uganda in 2016. UNHCR Uganda.

57. By 1963, the Rwandan revolution, also known as *Muyaga*, caused the exile of around 130,000 of the 420,000 Tutsi who fled Rwanda for the then Belgian Congo, Burundi, Tanganyika and Uganda. During that period, 78,000 refugees fled into Uganda (contested figure). Prunier, *The Rwanda Crisis, 1959–1994*, 41–54 and 62–3.
58. The Ankole sub-region used to be the Ankole Kingdom before Milton Obote abolished Uganda's kingdoms in 1967. The *Banyankole* are the region's main population. Their language, the *Runyankole*, is very similar to *Kinyarwanda*, the language of the *Banyarwanda*. The *Bairu* are sedentary agriculturalists, and the *Bahima* are pastoralists; both are ethnonyms of the *Banyankole*. Bagenda, Naggaga and Smith, 'Land problems in Nakivale settlement'; Niane, *Africa from the Twelfth to the Sixteenth Century*.
59. Most authors state that Nakivale camp was created in 1960. However, Nakivale was established in 1958 and 'officially recognized as a refugee settlement in 1960 through the Uganda Gazette General Notice No. 19', UNHCR Uganda, 'Nakivale fact sheet'. There are also conflicting sources on where the settlement is placed. It is located in the Isingiro District – not in the Mbarara District as it is often said to be – in Uganda's Western region and in the Ankole sub-region. Winter, 'Uganda – Creating a refugee crisis', 1983; Bagenda, Naggaga and Smith, 'Land problems in Nakivale settlement'.
60. Currently, the need to assist refugees and settle them away from borders is widely recognised. It is a security issue for both the direct local hosts and the refugees due to abductions and rebel incursions. UNHCR, *Handbook for Emergencies*. The emergency preparedness and response section, 16, 17, 19, 136 and 138.
61. Especially in the 1980s and 1990s, many refugees were scared of the possibility of attacks from across the Rwandan border. Winter, 'Uganda – Creating a refugee crisis', 1983.
62. Bagenda, Naggaga and Smith, 'Land problems in Nakivale settlement'.
63. Despite several contradictory sources about the surface area of Nakivale camp, spatial analysis confirms that in 2016, it was 185 square kilometres as stated by the UNHCR. UNHCR Uganda, 'Nakivale fact sheet'.
64. My calculations and those of UNHCR Uganda show that the average population per village in 2016 was 800–1,300 inhabitants. The Base Camp's villages were close to the 1,300 population mark and Rubondo's around the 800 population mark. From the 79 villages that form Nakivale, 63 were populated solely by refugees, two by both refugees and Ugandans, and the other 14 by Ugandans only. These villages were clustered into 27 groups as follows. In the Juru zone, the villages were: Kahirimbi, Ngarama, Juru, Kakoma, Kankinji, Isanja and Soaza. In the Base Camp zone, the villages were: Kabahinda, Kiyaza, Nyarugugu, Sangano, Base Camp, Kigali, Kashojwa, Kiretwa, Kabazana, Kasasa and Misiera. In the Rubondo zone, the villages were: Mugenyi, Ruhoko, Kabwera, Nyakagando, Mirambira, Kyeibare, Kisura, Rwoma and Rubondo. Data collected from the UNHCR's Nakivale base map.
65. Education was included in the humanitarian cluster system in 2007 with the creation of the education cluster. The cluster began to incorporate ECD in 2009. UNHCR, 'Global strategy for settlement and shelter'; Anderson and Hodgkin, 'The creation and development of the global IASC education cluster'.
66. Data extracted from Windle Trust data sets of ECD attendance in Nakivale from 13 to 16 August 2016.
67. UNHCR Uganda, 'Statistical summary refugees and asylum seekers in Uganda'.
68. For example, the average distance children must walk to access a formal/non-formal ECD centre in Nakivale's Base Camp is 500 metres, whereas in Rubondo, it is 1,200 metres.
69. The six camps established between 1964 and 1966 include Kyangwali and Kyaka I. The dates of establishment of the Southwest Ugandan camps built before the 2000s are unclear, since the available sources contradict each other, and the UNHCR does not provide coherent dates for some of them, including Kyangwali and Kyaka II. I consider that Kyaka II was created in 1983 and Kyangwali in 1964 and was officially recognized and demarcated in 1967. Lubega, 'The coming of Rwandan refugees'; Matsiko, 'Museveni shocked at Kyangwali eviction'; Stein and Clark, 'Refugee integration'; UNHCR Uganda, 'Kyaka II fact sheet'.
70. Prunier, *The Rwanda Crisis, 1959–1994*.
71. DRC has suffered diverse conflicts since King Leopold II of Belgium largely destroyed the fabrics of the diverse Congo basin societies, creating huge internal displacements. The country's independence, in addition to geopolitical and economic interests, unleashed conflict, particularly after the assassination of Zaire's first Prime Minister, Patrice Lumumba, on 13 February 1961 and the subsequent government under Mobutu Sese Seko. Between 1960 and

1965, approximately 100,000 people were killed, and tens of thousands were forced into internal displacement or exiled to Congo Brazzaville, Central African Republic, Uganda, Rwanda, Sudan, Burundi, Tanzania, Angola and Zambia. Kibreab, 'Forced migration in the Great Lakes and Horn of Africa'; Mazrui, *Africa Since 1935*, 877–86.

72. This establishment date is contested. The most cited dates are 1964 and 1966. I use 1964 because the second wave of refugee camp establishment in the country was around those dates – right after the Rwanda Revolution and the assassination of Patrice Lumumba in DRC.
73. UNHCR and Office of the Prime Minister Uganda, Uganda Refugee Response Portal.
74. The Rwandan Batutsi genocide took place between 7 April and mid-July 1994. The end of the genocide happened when the Rwanda Patriotic Front (RPF), a rebel group formed mainly by former Batutsi refugees in Uganda, took power over the country. When that occurred, hundreds of thousands of Bahutu fled the country to Eastern DRC, Uganda, Burundi and Tanzania. The Batutsi who had been refugees in those countries returned to Rwanda. The RPF later formed a political party, which still rules the country today. Stearns, *Dancing in the Glory of Monsters*; Prunier, *The Rwanda Crisis, 1959–1994*.
75. Stearns, *Dancing in the Glory of Monsters* Prunier, *The Rwanda Crisis, 1959–1994*.
76. Refugee Law Project, 'Refugees in Kyangwali settlement'; Matsiko, 'Museveni shocked at Kyangwali eviction'.
77. In 2016–7, this camp hosted 36,713 refugees. This fast trebling in population is related to Kyangwali's close location to DRC's borders, as well as to renovated conflicts and an Ebola outbreak in Eastern DRC throughout 2019.
78. Over time, Kyangwali became a location for vulnerable South Sudanese as the long distance with the South Sudanese border provided more protection for those refugees. Currently, the majority of the refugees in Kyangwali are DR Congolese and South Sudanese. There are also Burundians, Ethiopians, Kenyans, Rwandans, Somalis and Sudanese. Refugee Law Project, 'Refugees in Kyangwali settlement', 4.
79. 'In 2013, more than 60,000 so-called encroachers, Ugandan nationals who settled on land earmarked for refugees, were forcibly evicted from the Kyangwali refugee settlement in central-western Uganda to make way for Congolese new arrivals'. Gardner, 'Beneath the surface', 3.
80. Data collected from Kyangwali's UNHCR office and contrasted with Kyangwali's base map and semi-structured interviews during the data collection fieldwork to the camp from 17 to 21 August 2016.
81. To ease administration, the OPM divided the villages of Kyangwali into area A (which has nine villages and the main administrative office) and area B (which encompasses seven villages and a second administrative office in Rwenyawawa). Kupfer, 'Accessibility and quality of education for refugees', 3. The villages in area A are: Malembo, Old Malembo, Mukunyu, Nyamiganda, Kentome, Kitoro and Kagoma. The villages in area B are: Nyampindu, Munsisa, Kinakyetaka, Mukarange, Kasonga, Kyebitaka, Ngurwe, Nyambogo and Kituti. Data collected from Kyangwali's UNHCR office and contrasted with Kyangwali's base map and semi-structured interviews during data collection fieldwork from 17 to 21 August 2016.
82. Kyangwali's trade centres have a 'couple dozen shops selling grains, imported goods, sodas, beer, and cigarettes. Regular trucks come from Hoima supplying these shops; in addition, traders from Hoima and as far away as Kampala and Arua come during harvest time to purchase the agricultural production of the refugees'. Refugee Law Project, 'Refugees in Kyangwali settlement', 5.
83. Counting both formal and non-formal ECD initiatives. Data collected from the offices of Kyangwali's Save the Children and Action Africa Help (AAH) and contrasted with semi-structured interviews during data collection fieldwork from 17 to 21 August 2016.
84. These are now occupied by recent arrivals of Eastern DRC refugees.
85. Data collected through the analysis of the existing map of the camp and confirmed through semi-structured interviews with AAH personnel on 19 August 2016.
86. Winter, 'Uganda – Creating a refugee crisis', 1983.
87. Skeels, 'March activities in the Kyaka II refugee settlement (0art 2)'; UNHCR Uganda, 'Kyaka II fact sheet', 2.
88. The camp grew fourfold since the time when fieldwork was conducted in 2016–7 when it hosted around 32,656. This steep increase was mainly due to DRC refugees escaping renovated conflict and an intense Ebola epidemic in 2019.
89. UNHCR Uganda, 'Statistical summary refugees and asylum seekers in Uganda'.
90. The main local hosts are the Batooro and the Bakiiga, which are ethnonyms of the traditional Tooro Kingdom, located between Lake Albert and Lake Edward. The Tooro Kingdom

is currently a subnational constitutional monarchy within Uganda. Their language is called Rutooro and it closely resembles Runyoro, spoken in the neighbouring kingdom of Bunyoro. Mazrui, *Africa Since 1935*; UNHCR Uganda, 'Kyaka II fact sheet'.

91. The nine zones in Kyaka II are Sweswe, Buliti, Bukere, Mukondo, Ntababiniga, Kakoni, Bwiriza, Byabakora and Kaborogota.
92. UNHCR Uganda, 'Kyaka II fact sheet'. Data collected from Kyaka II's UNHCR offices and contrasted with maps and semi-structured interviews during data collection fieldwork from 9 to 12 August 2016.
93. Data collected from UNHCR education section and population statistics and contrasted in the camp's field offices through semi-structured interviews with the NGO Windle Trust personnel on 10 August 2016.
94. In Kyaka II, there are '60 water sources: 31 shallow wells, 20 boreholes and nine protected wells or springs as well as a water dam at Sweswe and a 7,500 litres mini water treatment plant. There are also 34 rainwater-harvesting structures to boost water supply in the settlement'. UNHCR Uganda, 'Kyaka II fact sheet', 2.
95. For more information on the Somali conflict, see, for example: Loescher, 'The new cold war'; Kibreab, 'Forced Migration in the Great Lakes and Horn of Africa'; Pérouse de Montclos, 'Humanitarian aid, war, exodus, and reconstruction of identities', 2008; Hyndman, 'Geographies of displacement'.
96. For more information on the South Sudanese conflict, see, for example: Jansen, 'The refugee camp as warscape', 2016; Merkx, *Refugee Identities and Relief*; Martell, *First Raise a Flag*.
97. Kenya has built 29 camps from the late 1980s to date: Thika from an unknown date in the 1980s until March 1995; Liboi from September 1989 until 1995; Ruiru from 1991 until 1995; Walda from 1991 until April 1993; Mandera from 1991 until 1994; El wak from 1991 until 1994; Habaswein from 1991 until 1995; St Anne's from March 1991 until June 1997; Utange from May 1991 until April 1995; Majengo from August 1991 until December 1993; Ifo from September 1991 and ongoing; Hagadera from June 1992 and ongoing; Hatimi from July 1992 until June 1997; Kakuma from July 1992 and ongoing; Dagahaley from August 1992 and ongoing; Jomvu from January 1993 until June 1997; Swaleh Nguru from August 1993 until June 1997; Marafa from 1993 until December 1995; Ifo 2 from 2011 and ongoing; Kambioos from 2011 until April 2017; and Kalobeyei from August 2016 and ongoing. Pérouse de Montclos, 'Humanitarian aid, war, exodus, and reconstruction of identities', 2008, 292; UNHCR, 'Dadaab Refugee Camps, Kenya UNHCR Dadaab bi-weekly update'; UNHCR, 'Kalobeyei settlement'.
98. As Pérouse de Montclos explains, the same hosting and resettlement system contributed to the formation and crystallisation of many refugee identities. Pérouse de Montclos, 'Humanitarian aid, war, exodus, and reconstruction of identities', 2008.
99. These camps were Kwa Jombu, Hatimi, St Annes, Swaleh Nguru, New Majengo, Utange and Marafa close to Mombasa.
100. These camps were Banissa, Mandera, El Wak and Habaswei.
101. These camps were Hagadera, Ifo, Dagahaley and Liboi, now called the Dadaab camps.
102. The coastal camps concentrated most of the Somali ethnic 'minorities': Kwa Jombu hosted refugees from the Bajun Fishermen; Hatimi and St Annes hosted Bravani; Swaleh Nguru hosted mostly Benadiri; New Malengo hosted a mix of all the above-mentioned minorities; Utange hosted mostly Marehan and Marafa hosted mainly low cast Sabs and Bantu. The big rural camps hosted largely the major Ogadeni Clans such as the Darood, the Rahaweyn, the Hawiye and the Isaak. The Bantu settled both in the Dadaab's camps and in the coastal camps, and were later resettled to Kakuma where they had more security, since most inhabitants were Sudanese. Pérouse de Montclos, 'Humanitarian aid, war, exodus, and reconstruction of identities', 2008; Ayiemba, 'Refugees in post-conflict reconstruction'.
103. Hyndman, 'Geographies of displacement', 259, 261.
104. Hyndman, 193.
105. UNHCR Kenya, 'Dadaab refugee complex – UNHCR Kenya'.
106. Kalobeyei was established 15 kilometres west of Kakuma towards the Ugandan border in June 2016.
107. UNHCR Kenya, 'Dadaab refugee complex – UNHCR Kenya'.
108. Hyndman, 'Geographies of displacement', 199.
109. UNHCR, 'Emergency handbook. Camp planning standards. (Planned settlements)'; UNHCR, 'Refugee children: Guidelines on protection and care preface'.
110. According to data collected during fieldwork to Kakuma and from the literature, Kakuma

was mostly devised from Nairobi. However, this information is difficult to contrast because no organisation has information on who was involved in the planning of the camps in the 1990s. Not even the dates of establishment are clear in the sources. Pérouse de Montclos, 'Humanitarian aid, war, exodus, and reconstruction of identities', 2008; Ayiemba, 'Refugees in post-conflict reconstruction'.

111. Hyndman, 'Geographies of displacement'.
112. The Turkana people belong to the ethnic groups known as the Eastern Nilotes. Apart from grazing cattle, they carry out some subsistence farming in a number of irrigation schemes along the two major seasonal rivers, the Turkwel and Kerio. Ministry of Planning and National Development, 'Turkana district development plan (2002–2008)', 4.
113. This date is contested. According to the Department of Refugee Affairs (DRA) Commissioner (semi-structured interview on 5 September 2016), the camp was established in 1991. However, publications suggest conflicting dates of establishment. Some state July 1992, and others state 1991.
114. These Sudanese refugees arrived in Kakuma after almost a decade in the Ethiopian camps of Gambella where they had been arriving since 1983. Most of the refugees fled the fighting between the government of Sudan and the Sudanese People's Liberation Army (SPLA). Most of the refugees who arrived in Kakuma were supporters or combatants of the SPLA. They left Gambella camp after Mengistu Haile Mariam (president of Ethiopia who supported the SPLA) was ousted in 1991. The Ethiopian government of Meles Zenawit expelled the Sudanese refugees from the Gambella camps. Some of them were the so-called Lost Boys who arrived in Kenya after a long trek across southern Sudan. Many of these children had been recruited by the SPLA and arrived in Kakuma together. Jansen, 'The refugee camp as warscape', 2016, 431–8; Hyndman, 'Geographies of displacement', 231–4.
115. Kakuma town is located on the eastern side of the seasonal Tarach River along the Lodwar-Kakuma-Lokichoggio highway, 119 kilometres from Lodwar and 880 kilometres from Nairobi. Oka, 'Unlikely cities in the desert', 2011, 226.
116. 'In 2002 the refugees were about 84,000 and by May 2009 the number had dropped to 42,304'. Ayiemba, 'Refugees in post-conflict reconstruction', 8.
117. The refugees living in Kakuma are from Eastern DRC, Rwanda, Burundi, Uganda, South Sudan, Ethiopia, Somalia, Sudan, Eritrea, Congo Brazzaville and Malawi. UNHCR, 'Statistical summary refugees and asylum seekers in Kenya as of January 31st 2018'.
118. Data extracted from Kakuma's base map collected during fieldwork in Kakuma from 2 to 10 September 2016.
119. During my fieldwork trip to Kakuma from 2 to 10 September 2016, both refugees and NGO workers reported attacks by Turkanas on refugees. The Turkanas on the other hand complained about the help the refugees received and the curtailment of their pastoral routes. For example: 'These refugees are everywhere in our villages, collecting firewood, cutting trees, they are bathing and drawing water from Tarach River our only source of water, their children have taken over our schools and they do not respect us. Something must be done to reduce their numbers because they are [a] threat to our people'. Emuria, 'Clashes between refugees and host communities', 55.
120. Newhouse, 'More than mere survival', 2015, 2300–1; Crisp, 'A state of insecurity'.
121. According to the DRA Commissioner who I held a semi-structured interview with at the Kakuma DRA Office on 5 September 2016.
122. The embryonic Kakuma phases II and IV, which were then merged into the current Kakuma phase III, were established to cater for the Sudanese refugees in 1999. What is now Kakuma phase III began to host refugees from South Sudan, Eastern Congo, Ethiopia, Rwanda, Burundi, Congo, Eritrea (since 1994), Somalia (since 1997) and Darfur (since 2008). Oka, 'Coping with the refugee wait', 2014, 26; Ayiemba, 'Refugees in post-conflict reconstruction', 4.
123. I gathered this information from informal conversations during fieldwork done in Kakuma and Kalobeyei from 2 to 10 September 2016. For more information, see UNHCR, 'UNHCR welcomes Kenya statement'.
124. The 12 ECD centres are: Tarach, Gilo and Lake Turkana in Kakuma phase I; Mount Surat, Turkwell and Gambella in Kakuma phase II; Shambele, Nasibunda and Mount Songot in Kakuma phase III; and Hope, Peace and Eliyes in Kakuma phase IV. These data were collected during fieldwork done from 2 to 10 September 2016.

125. The two Furaha centres, placed in Kakuma phases III and IV, are a joint effort between the UNHCR, UNICEF and the NGOs in charge of education and child protection that began in 2016. They are fenced compounds that open after school to children of all ages and comprise a well-equipped playground, a referral centre – including counselling rooms – and toilets.
126. These are the first play-based ECD initiatives in the camp. They began in 2012 with the activities of the NGO Waldorf Kakuma Project programmes. The four Waldorf initiatives are based on the Western pedagogy of the same name, which uses art as a means of learning and expression. Currently, only the Kakuma phase IV initiative has its own space; the other three take place at the Mount Songot ECD and at two open areas in the protection and reception centres. Children come to the spaces for a few hours in the mornings and plant, paint, make clay models and take part in other manual activities.
127. The density of Rwanda in 2018 was 430 people per square kilometre.
128. Berlanda, 'Umujyi: Cities and human settlements in Rwanda'.
129. MININTER, 'Main orientations of the Policy of Regrouped Settlement Sites'.
130. The Imidugudu Policy has been criticised for forcing the regrouping of returnees and regular citizens into government planned *imidugudu*. Other known villagisation projects in Sub-Saharan Africa are Tanzania's (beginning in 1967), Ethiopia's (beginning in 1975) and Mozambique's (beginning in 1977). van Leeuwen, 'Rwanda's imidugudu programme', 2001, 625–30; Government of Rwanda and UNDP, '2014 National human development report'; Ministry of Infrastructure of Rwanda, 'Updated version of the national human settlement policy in Rwanda'.
131. See Chapter 1 and Harrell-Bond, 'UNHCR – Are refugee camps good for children?'.
132. Returnees mainly arrived in Rwanda in two waves: in 1994 and from 1996 to 1997. These waves coincided with the end of the genocide and the First and Second Congo Wars. The first returnees were the Batutsi refugees who had been hosted in Tanzania and Uganda, and they came back to Rwanda during the second half of 1994 after the Rwandan genocide. The second wave of returnees were Bahutu refugees who had been hosted in camps in Goma and Bukavu in Eastern DRC from mid-1994 when they escaped repression after the genocide. van Leeuwen, 'Rwanda's imidugudu programme', 2001; Hilhorst and van Leeuwen, 'Emergency and development', 2000.
133. The five Congolese refugee camps in Rwanda are: Kiziba, established in Rwanda's Western province in December 1996; Gihembe, established in the Northern province a year later; Nyabiheke, established in the Eastern province in April 2005; Kigeme, originally established in the Southern province in 2009 and reopened in 2012; and Mugombwa, established in the Southern province in February 2014. Data collected from semi-structured face-to-face interviews held with MIDIMAR representatives at camp level during fieldwork done in September 2015 and from UNHCR, 'UNHCR Rwanda monthly population statistics'.
134. In 2013, the strategy changed to some degree, and shelters were allowed more 'permanency', with elements such as iron sheeting roofs rather than tarpaulins. UNHCR, 'Global strategy for settlement and shelter'.
135. Apart from the five Congolese camps, a new camp, Mahama, was created in April 2015 to host Burundian refugees.
136. UNHCR, 'Population statistics'.
137. Stearns, *Mai-Mai Yakutumba*; Stearns, *Dancing in the Glory of Monsters*; Prunier, *From Genocide to Continental War*; Mamdani, *When Victims Become Killers*.
138. The First Congo War took place from December 1996 to May 1997. The Second Congo War began in August 1998 and officially ended in July 2003. However, conflict is still present in the country, especially in its border regions.
139. UNHCR and MIDIMAR, 'Economic inclusion of refugees in Rwanda', 19.
140. AVSI and InfoAid, 'Child protection KAP survey in Rwandan refugee camps'.
141. UNHCR, 'UNHCR calls for calm'; Human Rights Watch, 'Rwanda: A year on'.
142. UNHCR, 'Comprehensive refugee response framework'.
143. UNHCR, 'MIDIMAR–UNHCR joint strategy partners'; UNHCR and MIDIMAR, 'Economic inclusion of refugees in Rwanda'; UNHCR, 'Operational update – Rwanda 2017', 2.
144. UNHCR, 'Rwanda country refugee response plan 2019–2020'.
145. Data collected through observation and informal conversations with camp managers and NGO workers. Fieldwork trips developed

in Kiziba, Kigeme and Mugombwa from 30 August to 15 September, from 1 to 7 October and from 5 to 11 November 2017, respectively.

146. These data were collected through observation and informal conversations in Kiziba from 30 August to 15 September, from 1 to 7 October and from 5 to 11 November 2017.

147. Some examples are: start-up crowdfunding strategy run by the organisation Inkomoko, direct cash transfers run by the organisation Give Directly, product launches with organisations such as Inyenyeri (improved pellet stoves) and Bbox (solar energy mini grids).

148. MIDIMAR, 'Rwanda Ministry of Disaster Management and Refugees'.

149. For more information on the rebel group M23, see Stearns, *Mai-Mai Yakutumba*, 44–45.

150. MIDIMAR, 'Rwanda Ministry of Disaster Management and Refugees'.

151. Butare was the old Rwandan capital under Belgian colonial rule. It is also the seat of the National University of Rwanda and the National Ethnographic Museum.

152. Bukavu is the capital of South Kivu, an important transport hub and gateway to the resource rich Eastern DRC. The road that connects Bukavu with Kigali is key for the entry and exit of goods to and from Eastern DRC because the infrastructure and the roads in the DRC are in an extremely poor condition, and there are no real connections with the capital, Kinshasa.

153. My team at Active Social Architecture (ASA) studio designed and built Kigeme hospital's maternity ward.

154. HBECD facilities are explained in depth in Chapter 3.

155. Data collected through a multi-method qualitative approach, using mainly observation, in various visits and fieldwork to Kiziba and Kigeme from 11 to 14 September 2015 and from 30 August to 15 September, and from 1 to 7 October and from 5 to 11 November 2017, respectively. These data were also collected through my architectural work with humanitarian agencies in both camps from February 2011 to November 2014.

156. These data were collected from MIDIMAR. and contrasted with information from semi-structured, face-to-face interviews during fieldwork done in Rwanda from 4 September to 1 October 2015.

157. The internationally renowned architect Shigeru Ban had collaborated in the shelter design for Gihembe refugee camp in 1999. Ban, 'Paper emergency shelters for UNHCR'.

158. UNHCR, 'Operational update – Rwanda 2017', 6.

159. In 2016, Kiziba had a surface area of 28 hectares, Kigeme of 34 hectares and Mugombwa of 24 hectares. Kiziba and Kigeme had a density of 60,000 people per square kilometre

160. In 2016, Kyaka II had the lowest density with an average of 400 inhabitants per square kilometre, and Nakivale had the highest with 600 inhabitants per square kilometre. However, within Nakivale, there are big differences. The trading centres at Base Camp 1 and Base Camp 2 had an average density of 8,000 people per square metre, and the densest areas in Rubondo such as Ruhoko centre had an average density of 500 people per square kilometre.

161. Pence and Hix-Small, 'Global children in the shadow of the global child', 2007.

162. Bühmann and Trudell, 'Mother tongue matters'; Fafunwa, 'Education in the mother tongue', 1974.

163. Koralek and Mitchell, 'The schools we'd like'; Chiles, 'The classroom as an evolving landscape'; Dudek, *Kindergarten Architecture*.

164. Dewey, 'Experience and education'; Rasmussen, 'Place for children', 2004; Z eiher, 'Shaping daily life in urban environments'.

165. Dovey and King, 'Forms of informality', 2011.

166. Scott, *Seeing Like a State*.

167. UNESCO, 'The Dakar Framework for Action'.

168. Pence and Hix-Small, 'Global children in the shadow of the global child', 2007.

169. Data collected through a multi-method qualitative approach from the Rwandan case studies in September 2015 and from September to November 2017, from Southwest Ugandan case studies in August 2016 and from Kakuma in Kenya in September 2016.

170. Bonta and Protevi, *Deleuze and Geophilosophy*.

171. The two newest and best-connected camps I have studied are both in Rwanda, while in general, the East African camps I have studied are isolated: Nakivale is 44 kilometres from Mbarara, Kyangwali is 89 kilometres from Hoima, Kyaka II is 79 kilometres from Kyenjojo, Kiziba is 20 kilometres from Kibuye town and Kakuma is close to Kakuma town but 119 kilometres from Lodwar, the next nearest hub. Data collected through a multi-method qualitative approach during fieldwork in

September 2015, August and September 2016 and September to November 2017.

172. For example, Kakuma town's population increased from 5,000 in 1990 to 40,000 in 2000: 'Prior to 1991, Kakuma was a transport and regional market town primarily settled by Somali Isaak and Hawiye traders who dominated the pastoral exchange, provided retail and wholesale services to the local [Turkana] pastoral communities and lodging/boarding for drivers on the Kitale-Juba road'. Oka, 'Unlikely cities in the desert', 2011, 226.
173. Usually, shared benefits take the shape of transportation infrastructure, health and educational facilities and income-generating activities. UNHCR, Policy on alternatives to camps.
174. Data collected through a multi-method qualitative approach during fieldwork in the Rwandan case studies from 11 to 23 September 2015 and through a literature review: AVSI and InfoAid, 'Child protection KAP survey in Rwandan refugee camps'.
175. Omata and Kaplan, 'Refugee livelihoods in Kampala'.
176. Chambers, 'Hidden losers?', 1986; Chambers, 'Rural refugees in Africa', 1979, 388–9; Rithi, 'Conflict amongst refugees'.
177. Valentine and McKendrck, 'Children's outdoor play', 1997; Matthews, 'The street as liminal space'.
178. Peteet, *Landscape of Hope and Despair*.
179. Sanyal, 'Refugees and the city', 2012.
180. Some refugees with access to cash employ the Turkanas to collect and carry water and firewood for them and to clean their homes. According to refugees' and NGO workers' accounts, there have been instances when the Turkanas have raided their 'employer's' homes at night. The Turkanas see the refugees as a threat to their survival. They see refugees as responsible for their land eviction, the obstruction of their cattle grazing and the increasing lack of water and desertification of the landscape. Many Kakuma town residents benefit from the job opportunities created by the flow of funds into the camp. However, the Turkanas do not usually access those opportunities and despise the camp and their residents. These data were collected during fieldwork in Kakuma from 2 to 10 September 2016 and contrasted with the literature. Rithi, 'Conflict amongst refugees'; Emuria, 'Clashes between refugees and host communities'.
181. UNHCR Rwanda, 'Participatory assessment 2017'.
182. A good example of this is the Bahutu and Batutsi conflict that includes the nation states of Burundi, Rwanda, Uganda and DRC. The conflict has lasted for centuries. A couple of publications that explain part of this conflict and the Rwanda's involvement in the Congo Wars are: Stearns, *Dancing in the Glory of Monsters*; Prunier, *From Genocide to Continental War*; Mamdani, *When Victims Become Killers*.
183. For example, some of the inhabitants of Nakivale come from Somalia, and some of the inhabitants of Kakuma come from the areas of Rutsuru and Beni in Eastern DRC. For more information, see the interactive maps at the website. Amorós Elorduy, 'Mapping refugee spaces'.
184. Imidugudu means 'villages' in Kinyarwanda.
185. Guattari and Deleuze, *Rhizome*; Müller and Schurr, 'Assemblage thinking', 2016, 219.
186. Data collected through a multi-method qualitative approach, mainly using the spatial analysis of the maps that I made for the seven camps presented in this book and also collected from the Rwandan camps in September 2015 and from September to November 2017, from Southwest Ugandan settlements in August 2016 and from Kakuma in Kenya in September 2016.
187. As, for example, Uganda, Rwanda, Burundi, South Sudan or Ethiopia
188. Anecdotal data collected through architectural work in the Rwandan camps from 2011 until 2014, and qualitative data collected through fieldwork in September 2015, August and September 2016 and September to November 2017.
189. Rebels had in the past abducted children to employ them as child soldiers in the surrounding conflicts. Data collected through fieldwork in September 2015, August and September 2016 and September to November 2017 and contrasted with the literature. Muggah, *No Refuge*.
190. Data collected through the spatial analysis of the maps that I made for all the camps presented here and also collected during fieldwork in September 2015, August and September 2016 and September to November 2017.
191. These land disputes tend to be raised with the local authority, the Ugandan government or the UNHCR. They do not usually result in violence between the refugees and their

direct local hosts. Bagenda, Naggaga and Smith, 'Land problems in Nakivale settlement'; Matsiko, 'Museveni shocked at Kyangwali eviction'; Gardner, 'Beneath the surface'.

192. Emuria, 'Clashes between refugees and host communities'; Bagenda, Naggaga and Smith, 'Land problems in Nakivale settlement'; Rogge, 'Africa's resettlement strategies', 1981.
193. Bagenda, Naggaga and Smith, 'Land problems in Nakivale settlement'; Gardner, 'Beneath the surface'.
194. For land conflicts in Uganda's refugee camps, see: Basiime, '6 Injured as refugees clash with locals in Kyegegwa'; Mutegeki and Basiime, 'Refugee camp chief killed in land dispute'.
195. For example, Kiziba has an average of 45 people per latrine. None of the toilets are specifically designed for young children. Data collected during fieldwork in September 2015, August and September 2016 and September to November 2017 and through the spatial analysis of the maps that I developed.
196. Anecdotal data collected through architectural work in the Rwandan camps from 2011 until 2014, and qualitative data collected through a multi-method qualitative approach from the Rwandan case studies in September 2015 and from September to November 2017, from Southwest Ugandan case studies in August 2016 and from Kakuma in Kenya in September 2016.
197. AVSI and InfoAid, 'Child protection KAP survey in Rwandan refugee camps', xi, 21 and 48; UNHCR, 'Refugee children: Guidelines on protection and care preface', 1, 14, 23 and 71.
198. UNESCO, 'Strong foundations'; UNICEF, 'Building better brains'.
199. At the end of 2017, Nakivale covered 185 square kilometres and had a density of 650 people per square kilometre, Kyangwali covered 90 square kilometres and had a density of 484 people per square kilometre, and Kyaka II covered 81.5 square kilometres and had a density of 400 people per square kilometre. Kakuma covered a total of 18 square kilometres and had a density of 9,000 people per square kilometre. Kiziba covered 28 hectares and had a density of 61,600 people per square kilometre, Kigeme covered 34 hectares and had a density of 59,185 people per square kilometre and Mugombwa covered 24 hectares and had a density of 38,066 people per square kilometre.
200. Evans, 'The environment of childhood poverty', 2004; Evans and Saegert, 'Residential crowding in the context of inner city poverty', 7; Proshansky, Fabian, and Kaminoff, 'Place-identity', 1983; Gottfried and Gottfried, 'Home environment and cognitive development'.
201. Refugee Law Project, 'Refugees in Kyangwali settlement'.
202. Data collected through a multi-method qualitative approach from the Southwest Ugandan case studies from 7 to 29 August 2016.
203. United Nations, Convention on the Rights of the Child.
204. '. . . for reasons of security, countries of asylum shall, as far as possible, settle refugees at a reasonable distance from the frontier of their country of origin'. UNHCR, OAU Convention governing the specific aspects of refugee problems in Africa.
205. UNHCR, *Handbook for Emergencies*. The emergency preparedness and response section, 16, 17, 19, 136 and 138.
206. For example, in Rwanda, the proximity to the border, in conjunction with isolation and marginalisation, contributed to the attacks at the two camps of Umubano and Mudende from 1996 to 1997. Since then, there has been an effort to place the camps at a distance from the border. Nevertheless, Kiziba was still placed 20 kilometres from the Lake Kivu's shore (the natural border between Rwanda and Eastern DRC). Anecdotal evidence collected through my architectural work with humanitarian agencies in Rwanda from February 2011 until November 2014, and fieldwork in September 2015, August and September 2016 and September to November 2017.
207. Mahama does not even meet the minimum standards set by the international community. It sits at the border with Tanzania.
208. UNHCR, 'Comprehensive refugee response framework'.
209. UNHCR, 'Rwanda country refugee response plan 2019–2020'.
210. Mahama was established in April 2015 in Rwanda, Kalobeyei was established in July 2016 in Northwest Kenya and Bidi-bidi was established in 2017 in Northwest Uganda.

Refugee-led spatial interventions | observed, imagined and speculated

Long-term camps, a socio-political and humanitarian oxymoron, will not disappear or become thriving human settlements overnight.[1] Yet, they are slowly morphing towards urbanity through the action of many different human and non-human actors. The surreptitious spatial modifications led by the encamped refugees and their direct local hosts are central in this evolution. These changes ripple through impacting refugees, direct local hosts and the humanitarian system.

Over the last decade, the humanitarian relief assemblage has tried to change its encampment strategy in a bid to avoid the creation of more long-term camps (fig. 3.1). The United Nations High Commissioner for Refugees (UNHCR) has put forward policies and frameworks such as the Alternatives

3.1

3.1 Two neighbours at Kiziba refugee camp rebuilding an old shelter from scratch on land appropriated outside the camp through negotiations with direct local hosts. Kiziba refugee camp, September 2017. © Amorós Elorduy.

to Camps, which unfortunately still relies on the physical containment of refugees, the Refugee Protection and Solutions in Urban Areas[2] and the Comprehensive Refugee Response Framework (CRRF),[3] which emphasise refugees' inclusion in national systems. The humanitarian system is embracing, alas slowly, the long-term character of most refugee situations and acknowledging their challenges.[4]

However, the implementation of these policies is uneven across the globe. The UNHCR's position is highly political, placing donor agendas and international affairs before the well-being of refugees and direct local hosts. The UN agency also relies on governments and implementing partners to execute its policies. Moreover, these humanitarian strategies are overarching and general, usually based on partial data, with a blatant scarce representation of the voices of refugees, direct local hosts and the experiences in the least visible cases – such as those in East Africa. Hence, as these policies translate into action, they do not always achieve the intended goals.

Refugee studies have discussed extensively the power differentials that swing so fully in favour of donors and geopolitics.[5] They try to understand how hierarchies and powers became so fixed in place, as Deleuze and Guattari say, so 'territorialised' and 'stratified'.[6] Will having better spatial data and situated bits of knowledge help in contextualising policy and decentralising power?

The goal of this chapter is to understand if and how architecture might contribute in shifting the current power imbalances, even if slightly, by grounding and contextualising research and including new voices in a collective experiment and by bringing to the fore different types of existing, albeit fairly invisible, power and agency, including that of the built environment, parents, young children, students of architecture, artisans, refugees and their direct local hosts.

The power of place-making—The humanitarian approach to camp planning aims primarily to protect and preserve the lives of refugees, although, in need of speed and efficiency and owing to political agendas, it does so without their input. Hence, encampment strategies fail to address the reality of what will most certainly become a long-term settlement. The built environment experts, who are increasingly involved in the sustainability and efficiency of the new and the long-term refugee camps, still tend to adopt a technocratic bid. They are usually delivering what they think is 'neutral', technical expertise, unwittingly aligning with the power that subcontracts them.[7] Due to time and budget constraints, and usually short-term appointments, they tend to lack contextual knowledge and largely disregard the social, political and economic implications of the physical containment of refugees, not to mention the impacts of the camps' spaces on children. They miss opportunities and create oxymorons.

Yet, surprisingly to many, in the seven long-term camps that I present here, camp inhabitants are the main force reproducing the camps' built environments, contrary to the general belief that the humanitarian technicians are the main actors who shape

3.2

3.2 Commercial strip in Kakuma phase III. Kakuma refugee camp, September 2016. © Amorós Elorduy.

these settlements. The multi-scale analysis of the camps that I started in Chapter 2 brings to the fore the variety of forces shaping the lives of encamped refugees. As in many human settlements and urban areas around the world, different kinds of power exist. Some can only be observed when looking from diverse standpoints and considering different scales. As I unveil further in this chapter, these types of power might not look like 'traditional' power but are effective in shaping the built environment and the people who inhabit it.

Refugees and their hosts are paramount in the spatial reproduction of the long-term camps. Their role is vital, despite the inherent and often overwhelming 'traditional' power imbalance in refugee camps and the lack of representation of refugees and their direct local hosts in managerial decision making. Refugees create exceptionally contextualised spaces as they inch their way to achieve their goals, counterbalancing the bleak, often heartless, humanitarian camp designs (fig. 3.2).

In this chapter, I present my efforts to understand how continuous surreptitious change takes place in the East African long-term camps. I show the exploration – developed with a team of local architects, artisans and refugees – of potential ways of harnessing that silent force to improve young children's learning. Moreover, my goal here is to flip the traditional aid discourse. Rather than letting refugees participate in humanitarian-led spatial interventions, this chapter tests a potential refugee-led change with humanitarian technicians and other external actors as active participants. I aim to employ what Edgar Pieterse terms 'radical incrementalism':

'Surreptitious, sometimes overt, and multiple small revolutions that at unanticipated and unexpected moments galvanise into more profound ruptures that accelerate tectonic shifts of the underlying logics of domination.... A disposition and sensibility that believes in deliberate actions of social transformation but through a multiplicity of processes and imaginations, none of which assumes or asserts a primary significance over other struggles'.[8]

Moreover, in this speculative chapter, I explore how Lefebvre's 'transduction'[9] might trigger a Freirean conscientious[10] spatial change and might raise awareness of the role of place in young children's learning. This test will not resolve refugees' existential struggle or radically change the current poor learning environments in the camps into thriving 'schools without walls'.[11] However, it might provide a means to manage and tackle these problems by 'stumbling across what works and what does not'.[12]

In the first section of this chapter – Observed Quiet Encroachment and Everyday Life Practices – I describe existing refugee-led spatial appropriations. I categorise them according to how the humanitarian system responds to them: with unawareness, permissibility or encouragement. In the second section – Refugee-Imagined Radical Incrementalism – I present proposals that refugee respondents imagined and desired in order to improve young children's learning environments. For this purpose, I use the case of Kiziba refugee camp, and I categorise the utopic interventions as they focus on formal, non-formal and informal learning environments.[13] In the third section – Speculated Transversal Spatial Appropriations – I use participatory action research (PAR) to test 'transduction' in the improvement of young children's learning environments, explicitly focused on Kiziba and Kigeme refugee camps.[14] I also explore some of the ethics, risks, limitations and opportunities involved in the development of multi-authored and utopic spatial appropriations in these two Congolese refugee camps.

The dissection of the observed spatial appropriations, the analysis and representation of the imagined ones and the test of new spatial interventions bring to the fore the relationships between, and the agency of, the diverse groups of human and non-human actors that form the learning assemblages of the long-term camps.[15] It shows that encamped refugees and their direct local hosts are exercising their 'right to the city' daily: they are continuously modifying young children's learning environments through 'radical incrementalism'. However, and as AbdouMaliq Simone expresses well, with this approach:

'The point is not to suggest models or admire resilience. Rather, the point is to pursue the dogged work of trying to understand the implications of what people do, particularly as it is clear that residents, even in the desperate ways they may talk about their lives, usually think about them as more than survival alone. Yes, survival is the overwhelming preoccupation for many. But the pursuit of survival involves actions, relations, sentiments, and opportunities that are more than survival alone.... And thus the important work is perhaps simply to document these efforts on the part of the poor to give rise to a new moral universe, a sense of value, of potential, and of the unexpected to which people's attention, no matter how poor, is also paid'.[16]

Knowing who modifies the camps' spaces, and how and what young children learn from these, is timely, as new strategies for refugee assistance and refugee education are shaping up globally. In the long-term refugee camps in which I have worked, the humanitarian resources are dwindling and their traditionally top-down approaches to management are not meeting the increasingly interconnected and complex needs of the refugees and their direct local hosts. As policies and camp administrations adopt the CRRF[17] and become more open to refugees and direct local hosts agencies, the prevalent refugee-led spatial appropriations gain relevance. Understanding these spatial modifications and their effects on the camps' ecosystems can shed light on the potential future of refugee assistance and refugee early childhood development (ECD).

Extracting from urban theory—As I expressed earlier in this book, there is an extreme lack of pre-existing literature on space production in refugee camps, especially in East Africa. Yet, a recent 'urban turn' in refugee studies draws on urban theory literature to state the relevance of the built environment as a critical non-human actor in assistance strategies. In this urban theory literature, I identify four sets actors as spearheads of urban spatial transformations: international and national authorities, architects, universities and non-governmental organisations (NGOs), and local groups. Exceptionally significant for this chapter is the role of that last set of actors, described in the literature as covert, informal, survivalist, rebellious and inconspicuous.

The spatial actions of refugee camp inhabitants could be seen through survivalist lens, as expressed by Simone in the previous quotation or by James Scott in his *Weapons of the Weak: Everyday Forms of Peasant Resistance* published in 1985. Contrary to the 'rebellions which hold pride of place in the archival record'[18] that seek structural change against oppressive systems and where a cohesive community is identified, Scott emphasised the self-interest that drove 'non-spectacular forms of class struggle',[19] in fact, survival strategies:

'The ordinary weapons of relatively powerless groups: foot dragging, dissimulation, desertion, false compliance, pilfering, feigned ignorance, slander, arson, sabotage, and so on.... Everyday forms of resistance make no headlines. [However, it] is largely in this fashion that the peasantry makes its political presence felt.... For these reasons alone, it seems important to understand this quiet and anonymous welter of peasant action'.[20]

Another lens to look at this refugee-led transformation could be that of discreetness and anonymity, reflected in the work of sociologist Asef Bayat and his notion of 'quiet encroachment'[21]:

'The notion of "quiet encroachment" describes the silent, protracted and pervasive advancement of ordinary people on those who are propertied and powerful in a quest for survival and improvement of their lives. It is characterised by quiet, largely atomised, and prolonged mobilisation with episodic collective action – open and fleeting struggles without clear leadership, ideology, or structured organisation'.[22]

The post-structuralist look proposed by Bayat and other authors such as Roy and Caldeira aligns with one of the most important authors in refugee studies and proponent of situated knowledges: Barbara Harrell-Bond. She opposed the 'over-socialised' view of man, which wrongly assumes that once people are together, man's 'social nature' will quickly develop a social structure which will ensure the equitable and acceptable distribution of resources, no matter how limited those resources may be'.[23] Harrell-Bond stated that the over-socialised view of man tends to romanticise the struggles of the oppressed – including refugees and the urban poor – a superficial view of flat characters. In her response to Gaim Kibreab's critique about her work *Imposing Aid*, Harrell-Bond stated that it is also self-interest that drives many of the survival actions of refugees. She stated that refugees do not always develop a cohesive social structure of mutual help – something I have found as well in the seven camps that I portray in this book.

Before 2005, it was rare to find literature on refugee-led spatial interventions in long-term refugee camps, as refugee-led actions represented a challenge to the 'refugee as victim' view. Thus far, Palestinian refugee camps in Lebanon are the source of the majority of incipient information on refugee-led spatial initiatives. In those camps, the politicised use of space has gained a highly complex and rooted dimension.[24] An interesting study on the production of 'place' in the camps in Beirut is anthropologist Julie Peteet's *Landscape of Hope and Despair*. In it, she states how 'refugees were the driving force in generating places as meaningful constructs within the constraints imposed by structural features and forms of external power. At one brief point in time, . . . power shifted to the interior and gave leeway for Palestinians to transform the camps in their image'.[25] Also, in her *Squatting in Camps: Building and Insurgency in Spaces of Refuge*, Romola Sanyal links refugee-led spatial modifications of the Middle Eastern camps with urban squatting employing Bayat's 'quiet encroachment of the ordinary'[26] to bridge urban theory and humanitarian space.

Yet, studies on refugee-led spatial production in East African camps are still almost non-existent. While studies that centre the view and voice of refugees and their direct local hosts started to appear in the region in the last decade, they focus mainly on economic and political aspects of the refugee-led spatial change.[27] Only a couple of works and authors focus on the space itself: Bram Jansen[28] and Anooradha

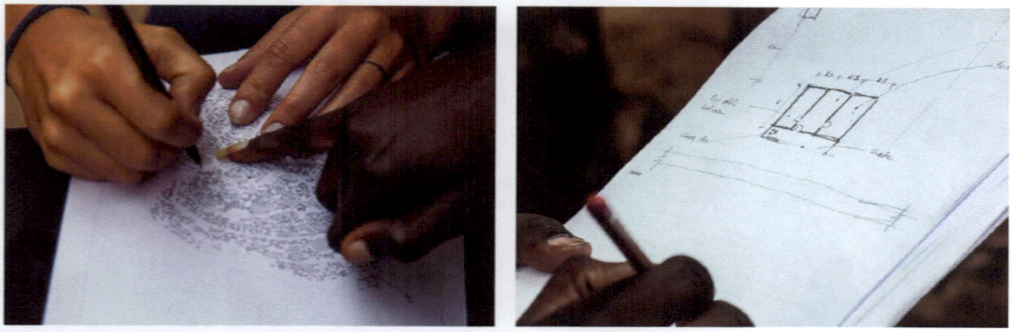

3.3

3.3 Sample of methods of spatial data collection. Map orientation (left) and sketching (right). Rwandan camps, September 2015. © Amorós Elorduy.

Iyer Siddiqi.[29] Both look at the visible and better-sourced operations in Northern Kenya. This book wants to continue turning the tide, providing enough base information and inciting local and regional researchers and built environment professionals to expand this research task in other camps in the region.

Observed quiet encroachment and everyday life practices—Through both permanent and transitory spatial appropriations, refugees repair, modify and adapt all the available spaces to suit their needs. For example, children transform streets, interstitial spaces between houses and front yards into playgrounds; mothers appropriate these same spaces into temporary home-based ECD (HBECD) initiatives.[30]

In my work in the camps in Rwanda since 2011 and during fieldwork trips with my team of research assistants for this book (all students of architecture from the schools in the region), we photographed, measured and sketched the spatial elements that research respondents identified as potential influencers for young children's learning in the camps – both positive and harmful. We specifically asked which features – such as additions to homes, schools and public areas – had refugees and direct local hosts developed, enquiring about the spatial evolution of the whole camp over time (fig. 3.3).

We concluded that refugees – and in some cases direct local hosts – are the main actors modifying the long-term camps over time. Refugees take the lead after the humanitarian community and the host government establish the camp and do the main infrastructural works. They particularly take over when humanitarian resources dwindle, which they do in protracted complex crises and long-term refugee assistance operations. Because the majority of these inhabitant-led changes are small scale, incremental and informal, they largely go unnoticed, especially if viewed from a top-down perspective – such as that of the media, the government and the humanitarian system.

Moreover, we learned that the humanitarian system mainly reacts to refugee-initiated interventions – by ignoring, allowing or encouraging those. In the coming sections, I illustrate those reactions

3.4

3.4 Man repairing the tarp roof to his home in Kiziba. Kiziba refugee camp, September 2017. © Amorós Elorduy.

with examples that are relevant for young children's learning. In this book, I do not document any refugee-led intervention blocked, banned, destroyed or met with blind opposition by the humanitarian system. That does not mean these do not occur. It can be hard to find these examples because, by their nature, most refugee-led initiatives are informal and unobtrusive, not leaving much in the way of evidence. Refugee's successes are largely ignored, and their failures mostly invisible.

Unnoticed: the homes and WASH facilities—Days after a camp is established, the first refugee-led spatial appropriations start taking place (fig. 3.4). These happen at the individual and family level with the construction, expansion and modification of homes, toilets and – if the land allows it – vegetable patches.[31] Notably, the houses are relevant in this book because they constitute the bulk of what I consider as informal learning environments, and they enhance the refugee's 'right to the city'. The humanitarian-government-media assemblage is not just unaware of home changes in the camps in East Africa. These supposedly powerful and in-control actors assume from the start that refugees will be in charge of making and modifying their homes (fig. 3.5).

All research respondents,[32] as well as the literature on young children's learning environments,[33] identify the homes as paramount to young children's learning, especially learning through experience.

Works examining the influence of the home's physical environment on child development began in earnest in 1979.[34] For example, Harold Proshansky and Abbe stated that:

'The home is a critical socio-physical setting in the life of the child because it is the arena in which most early learning occurs. Self-knowledge, knowledge of others, and knowledge of the environment all begin there. Many of these early self-perceptions and place-identity cognitions will persist and determine the kind of experiences the child is likely to have in later settings'.[35]

From an early learning perspective, the humanitarian system's failure to account for the homes as learning spaces leaves the most critical hours and years of child development in the hands of the assemblage of parents and neighbours and of the built environment built by them. Refugees are indeed the makers of one of the most critical learning resources for young children in the camps. Being virtually in charge is empowering for refugees, but at the same time, it also means that policies, funding, humanitarian and government actors obviate this remarkable resource and role. The humanitarian system/host government binomial places elsewhere the materials, advocacy and other resources that would significantly help ECD at home.

In the establishment of the long-term camps in East Africa, the diverse assemblages of UNHCR/host governments provide initial 'shelter infrastructure', which varies from case to case. For example, in the oldest cases – the initial Kakuma phases, Kiziba and Kigeme A[36] – the UNHCR provided tented structures that teams of technicians assembled (or helped refugees assemble) within the boundaries of the camps.[37] A few months later, the UNHCR provided poles and tarpaulins to facilitate the construction of self-built mud houses with tarp roofs. Years later,[38] they provided iron sheets that corresponded with the initial three-by-four-metre footprint of the original shelters.[39]

The recognition of permanence allowed and pressed refugees to make self-improvements to the shelters, transforming them into 'semi-permanent' homes with attached kitchens, extra rooms and fences.[40] In the Southwest Ugandan camps – the largest and least densely populated of the camps here presented – the UNHCR and the Ugandan government provided each arriving family with a plot of land[41] and with poles and tarpaulins to build an initial shelter on their own. In the Ugandan context, the humanitarian system/host government assemblage seems keener at distributing power.[42] It allows refugees relative freedom to work and to move, and it provides them with some land in lusher areas than those offered by Rwanda or Kenya. This is in turn reflected in a broader range of construction materials and shapes in home structures.[43]

Refugees' spatial appropriations of their homes can be observed in real time a few weeks after a camp establishment. For example, in Mugombwa (Rwanda), the newest camp included in this book, the refugees promptly converted the initially tented structures into mud and iron sheeting shelters with a footprint of 12 square metres. Now, seven years on, housings incorporate

3.5

3.5 Adapted homes. Top: two-storey home in Rubondo zone, Nakivale refugee camp, August 2016. Bottom (from left to right): Base Camp, Nakivale refugee camp, August 2016; Mugombwa refugee camp, September 2015; and Juru zone, Nakivale refugee camp, August 2016. © Amorós Elorduy.

interior partitions, attached extra rooms and kitchens, plastered walls and in some cases kitchen gardens and fences. The material evolution of Mugombwa includes businesses, churches and other more 'public' spatial appropriations done in conjunction with NGOs.[44] In older Rwandan camps such as Kiziba and Kigeme, the lack of planning, the scarcity of land and years of home expansion have homes placed within close proximity of each other – from 20 centimetres to a couple of metres apart. To the unaccustomed eye, it is difficult to differentiate between the outdoor area of one house and that of its neighbour (fig. 3.5).

The contextual assemblage of human and non-human actors affects the homes' transformations. For example, in Kakuma in Northwest Kenya, homes and compounds create a spatial quality variation between phases. As they grow older, they become denser and diverse.[45] At establishment, all plots measure 10 square metres and house one family, which is still the case in the recent III and IV phases. However, in Kakuma phase I, uses and time have divided some original plots to house up to three families and have merged others to become big and amorphous in order to host churches and major commercial operations. The modified streets are narrow and curvy. In an expression of their soft power and their 'right to the city', Kakuma's refugees have over time transformed even the grain of the camp's master plan to serve their needs.

The specific physical characteristics of the self-built homes – the number of rooms, style of openings, furniture, flooring, ceiling and the exterior spaces – depend on many overlapping variables, including time, host government policies, resource availability, family size, cultural backgrounds, traditions, climate and geography.

The different refugee origins provide a clear illustration of these intersections. For example, Democratic Republic of Congo (DRC) refugees, who reside in all seven camps that I present here,[46] tend to build similarly fenceless and small rectilinear houses. These mud homes, which comprise two to four rooms, usually have one space as a living and eating area, kitchen and bedroom, and the other space as a bedroom and storage, sometimes shared with animals. The Congolese usually build the extra rooms, attached to the home's main structure, out of wattle and daub or adobe bricks,[47] and typically use them as a sleeping areas (fig. 3.6).[48] Being fenceless reduces the adults' ability to control young children and allows passers-by to interact with the activities that take place in the front and back yards, which, in addition to the small homes' interiors, prompts children to roam the streets.[49] The only fenced Congolese homes I have found are those in Kakuma – the least safe of all the camps that I studied – where all inhabitants build tall fences around their homes. Relatively safe streets can become incredible playgrounds and learning environments for young children.[50] However, when violent and armed conflict and insecurity are rife, parents prevent children from leaving their compounds, which has consequences for their understanding of the world and themselves.[51]

One difference between Congolese refugees can be appreciated in their kitchens. This variation is especially notable in the Rwandan camps. These variances are related to origins within DRC and to the availability of materials and space. Refugees who come from areas close to Lake Kivu[52] seem to build kitchens as thatched-roof *tukuls* half a metre to a metre away from the house if space is available.[53] Those from further afield in North Kivu build the added kitchen usually attached to the main structure and generally with the same type of roofing as the main house.

Another illustration of this are the South Sudanese homes, represented in significant numbers in Kyangwali and Kakuma (fig. 3.7). In the Ugandan camp, they are made of several small and circular *tukuls* spaciously spread throughout the usually extremely well-kept home compound. Refugees expressed that the custom in their region was to build a separate *tukul* for each child older than 12 years old, thus providing distinct sleeping arrangements for adults and children. Some of these homes had skirting boards of moulded designs painted with mud, and separate *tukuls* for

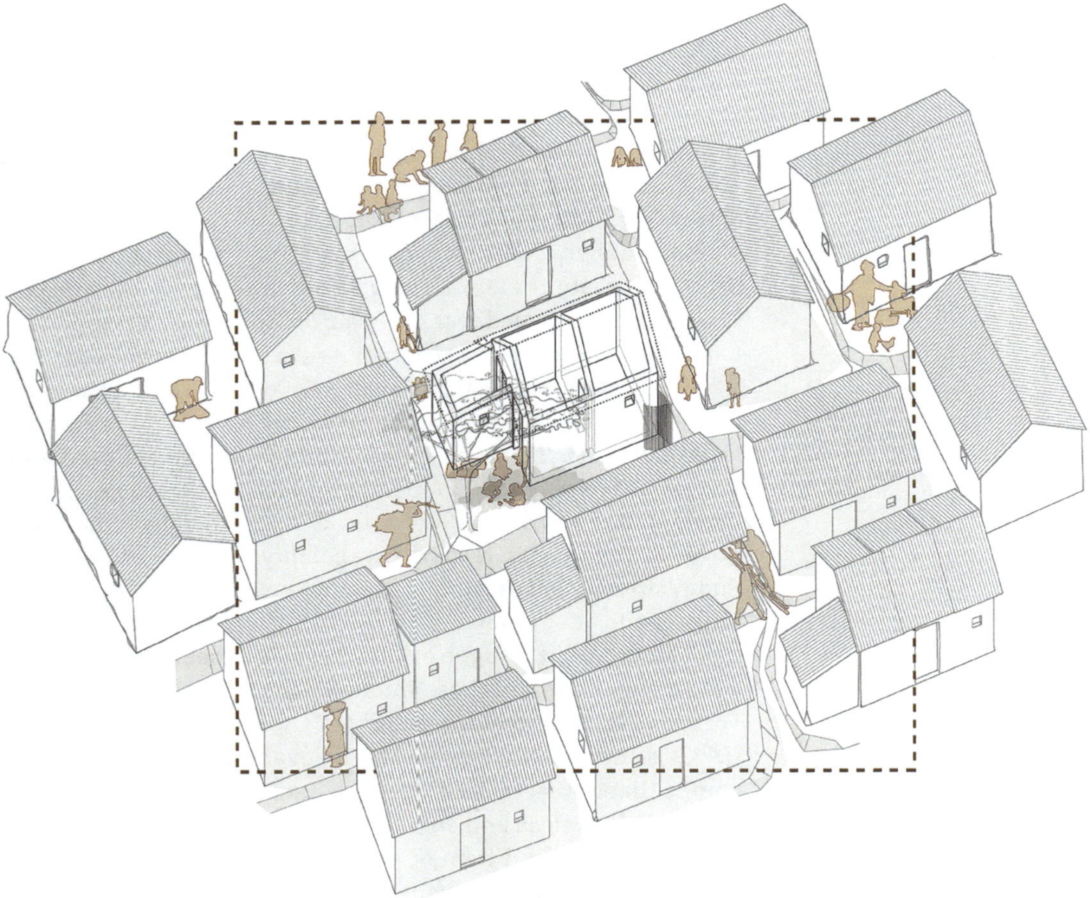

3.6

3.6 Diagrams showing the Congolese refugee homes in the Rwandan refugee camps and the main activities happening during the day and the night within and around them. Left: axonometric overview of homes in Kiziba quarter 2 with day activities. Right: top-down axonometric view of one house in Kiziba quarter 2 showing the sleeping arrangements. © Amorós Elorduy.

hens and grain storage. This separation and the abundance of space tends to benefit children, as the alternative is overcrowded homes with shared sleeping arrangements with some reports of child abuse.[54]

The South Sudanese families in Kakuma do not build in this manner. Reasons such as lack of freedom, smaller plots, insecurity, UNHCR's provision of initial metal roof sheeting, desertification and sandy soil – which consequently meant a lack of construction materials and grass for thatched roofs – force them to construct rectangular homes.

Assemblage thinking helps me to highlight the diverse effects of non-human actors in home construction. Security, availability of materials and climate create diversity, while cultural background, traditions, memory and family structure give more

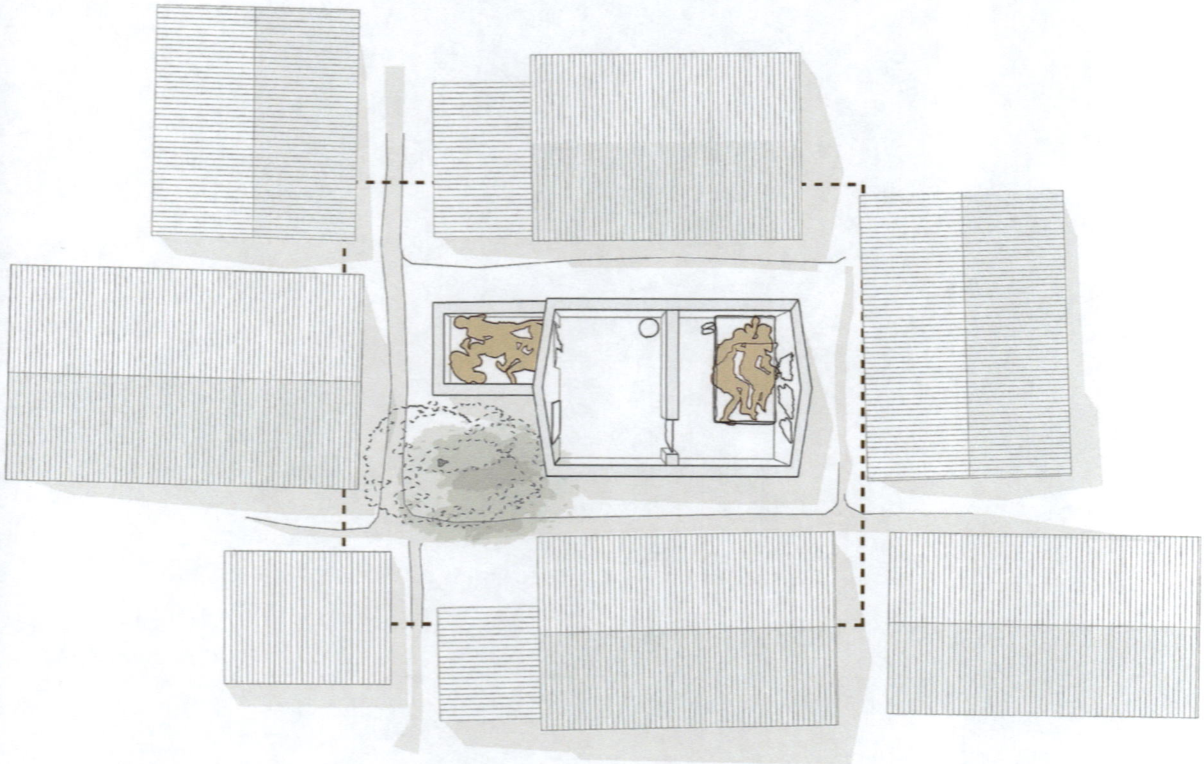

homogeneity. Some factors are territorialising, while others are destabilising. Origins and camps' contexts overlap, creating different assemblages and hence different home structures. Homes are a complex expression of refugees' 'right to the city' and their right to adapt their surrounding built environments to their needs.

WASH facilities are another relevant spatial modification that explicitly affect young children's learning and that the humanitarian assemblage largely obviates.[55] Access to decent, child-friendly, secure and safe water and sanitation facilities affects children's everyday activities. They complain about the dire conditions of WASH in all the camps in which I have worked. They criticise the terrible smell and lack of enough toilets. They are scared of them and hence refrain from using them and

3.7

3.7 Diagrams showing the South Sudanese refugee homes in the Southwest Ugandan refugee camps and the main activities happening during the day and the night within and around them. Left: axonometric overview of homes in Ngurue village in Kyangwali showing daily activities. Right: top-down axonometric view of one house in Ngurue village in Kyangwali showing the sleeping arrangements. © Amorós Elorduy.

excuse themselves elsewhere – with risks involved. Adults also complain about WASH facilities, and even NGO staff agree with the lack of sufficient and child-friendly WASH facilities.[56]

The overall adverse conditions of toilets, showers and points of water access are due to their technical and cultural sophistication, their cost and high maintenance, the host country's policies and the physical characteristics of each camp. For example, in the camps of Southwest Uganda, each family must build its latrine within its allocated plot of land. The camp administration does not provide public latrines or help to construct individual ones. In Kakuma, the NGOs National Council of Churches of Kenya (NCCK) and Norwegian Relief

Committee provide one prefabricated latrine slab per family, but only if the family had previously dug its latrine hole. Families unable to do so – usually the vulnerable, widows or child-led households – remain without a family toilet.[57] In Rwanda, due to the extreme lack of space, latrines and showers are always public and scarce, with one hole for every 45 people in the severe case of Kiziba, and refugee-built ones are exceedingly rare due to the lack of land. It is only in the areas that encroach outside the boundaries of the camps in Kigeme and Kiziba where some families have built private showers and latrines.

The construction of WASH facilities requires more skills and tools, as well as complex negotiations with direct local hosts, neighbours, camp managers and NGOs than is required for the expansion of the homes. They are not as widespread. Yet, their study brings to the fore sophisticated relationships and contextual and cultural characteristics of the various camps.

Allowed: religious temples, educational facilities and commercial structures—A few months after a camp is established, the assemblage of refugees and direct local hosts begin spatial appropriations of a more 'public' nature. Making use of their 'right to the city', refugees, sometimes in conjunction with their direct local hosts and rarely but increasingly in coordination with NGOs, create and maintain those built environment aspects that fall outside of the humanitarian clusters' mandates – elements that the refugee assistance assemblage does not consider essential or life-saving, such as religious facilities, commercial endeavours[58] and culturally relevant educational facilities (fig. 3.8).

In the camps that I have studied, the UNHCR/host government assemblage provides roads, water access, clinics and formal schools during camp establishment. Later, humanitarian-led refurbishments, expansions and new constructions are only punctual and depend on donor agendas and specific funding appeals. As there is not a coordinating body to manage construction works in the camps as a whole once the initial establishment phases are over, architectural interventions are usually one-off, not typically well coordinated and usually designed by NGOs' staff or short-term consultants.[59]

A clear illustration of the intersectionality of assemblages and the diversity of the power structures that exist can be found in Kiziba. Owing to lack of space within the camp boundaries, refugees negotiate with their direct local hosts to acquire or share the land adjacent to the camp to use for farming and to construct shared religious facilities. Over the years, the assemblage of refugees/direct local hosts have built at least nine churches and one madrassa-mosque outside the original camp boundaries, which serve all quarters.[60] Encamped children identify churches and madrassas as some of their favourite spaces in the camps. Workers at both the UNHCR and the Rwandan Ministry of Disaster Management and Refugee Affairs (MIDIMAR, now called MINEMA) have confirmed that these land transactions happen initially without their institutional knowledge or consent, quietly providing spaces for non-formal learning for their children.[61] Once the camp management notices these 'informal' transactions – usually when refugees have already erected a building – they renegotiate the ownership of the land with local and national authorities, and the camps' boundaries expand.[62] Even the more restricted camps have porous borders, and the most destitute refugees have some degree or type of power over their 'managers'.

The Southwest Ugandan camps present good examples of the inhabitant-run educational facilities. The collection of camp planning strategies and government policies in the country allow for close relationships between refugees and their

3.8

3.8 Religious facilities. Top: mosque on Kiziba's outskirts, Kiziba refugee camp, September 2015. Bottom from left to right: church in Kiziba's quarter 8, Kiziba refugee camp, September 2015; Isanja Baptist church, Isanja village, Juru zone, Nakivale refugee camp, August 2016; mosque in Kakuma phase III, Kakuma refugee camp, September 2016. © Amorós Elorduy.

direct local hosts. Within the threshold created by the ambiguous and porous camp boundaries, refugee groups and surrounding Ugandan nationals have initiated non-formal content-based primary and nursery schools. For example, in Kyaka II, direct local hosts had built three of the seven ECD centres that my team and I visited during fieldwork in 2016 and which both refugees and NGOs identified as camp ECD facilities.[63] In Nakivale, in the villages furthest from the camp centre and those shared between refugees and nationals, I found – similarly to Kiziba – churches built by refugees and direct local hosts that doubled as ECD facilities during weekday mornings.[64] In Kakuma, where people of Muslim religion are a majority, I found several madrassas and churches built within the camp fabric in clusters of joint compounds. In Kakuma, unlike in the other case studies, none of these was a shared initiative with the surrounding semi-nomad Turkanas and NGOs. Besides,

3.9

the humanitarian system does not count them as ECD provision.

I classify the religious and self-built schools as non-formal learning environments. They provide a mix of learning by experience and content-based learning, which tends to be culturally adapted and in smaller groups. These fall mainly out of the scope of the assemblage humanitarian system/host government mandate. Hence, they lack material resources and management support. Yet, religious facilities become a node of connection with direct local hosts and a tie to previous lives before refugeehood and encampment (fig. 3.9). They can even become an element of empowerment for refugees. For example, in the case of Rwanda, the mere construction of religious temples has led to the inconspicuous and slow expansion of the camps' boundaries.

One of the most ubiquitous spatial appropriations is the reconversion of homes into businesses and the construction of new commercial buildings (fig. 3.10). These are particularly apparent in the larger, older and more cosmopolitan camp assemblages such as Kakuma phase I and Nakivale. These appropriations take place particularly along the main roads and close to the initially UNHCR-built markets[65] and illustrate the variability among camps. In Kakuma, where refugees have more access to cash than those in other camps[66] and where transport arteries and outside market hubs are further away,[67] commercial facilities abound. Kakuma phase I is indeed an intricate network of commercial avenues. In the camps closer to pre-existing local markets and urban centres – such as Kyangwali, Kyaka II, Kiziba, Kigeme and

3.9 Kiziba's non-formal ECD initiatives taking place in refugee and direct local host-built churches on the camp's outskirts. Kiziba refugee camp, September 2015. © Amorós Elorduy.

3.10

3.10 Commercial activities in Kakuma. Top: small business in Kakuma phase II. Bottom: two commercial roads in Kakuma phase I. Kakuma refugee camp, September 2016. © Amorós Elorduy.

Mugombwa – and where refugees do not receive cash hand-outs or remittances from abroad, commercial spatial appropriations take longer to occur.

These allowed interventions act as informal learning environments.[68] Many children in the larger and older camps in Southwest Uganda and Northern Kenya like the town-like trading centres as places to hang out and play – children in the Southwest Ugandan camps said they liked the 'township life'. They find more stimuli there, in their electricity-run radios and TVs, the varied people and the goods in the shops. However, with the rise in the commercial offer, the land value increases, and

3.11

3.11 One of Kigeme's home-based initiatives in quarter 5. Kigeme refugee camp, September 2017. © Amorós Elorduy.

refugees divide, sublet and expand homes. The front of shelters become shops, and open spaces become scarcer. Public toilets become more crowded and dirtier. Hence, adults tend to keep children away from these spaces.

Encouraged: the case of the home-based ECD centres in Kigeme and Mugombwa, Rwanda—Since 2012 in Kigeme and since 2014 in Mugombwa, for a few hours each day, groups of 10 mothers – with some material support from NGOs – occupy the open spaces that exist between their homes in order to develop HBECD activities.[69] These initiatives each serve around 15 children aged three to five years and take place from 8:00am to 11:00am (fig 3.11).

The nascence of the HBECD initiatives and their success is down to many factors. In 2013, as Kigeme was expanded, the two existing formal ECD centres[70] appeared too far away for many families with young children and were also overcrowded. Besides, some parents wanted to educate children according to their cultural conventions, and CARE International[71] – which was in charge of ECD at the time – had previous successful HBECD experience in rural areas outside the camps.[72] This triggered the first test of HBECD activities in the Rwandan camps. At the end of that year, as Mugombwa was being established, Kigeme's successful HBECD experience enabled better physical planning to allow more space between homes for HBECD activities. In September 2015, around

3.12

3.12 Photographs of Kigeme home-based ECD initiatives in quarters 4 and 5. Kigeme refugee camp, September 2017. © Amorós Elorduy.

940 mothers in Kigeme rotated amongst a constellation of 94 HBECD initiatives – in 2017, there were 74 – occupying an average of 400 square metres in total and hosting 1,146 children between three and five years of age.[73] In Mugombwa, around 600 mothers organised 61 initiatives – in 2017, there were 64 – serving 599 children in an occupied space of about 250 square metres.

At each HBECD initiative, a locally made mat is placed on the floor to define the space and to provide a clean, horizontal platform for the four hours that the activities last (fig. 3.12). The UNHCR and NGOs support these HBECD initiatives with sorghum for the daily porridge, some toys and floor mats. The rotating volunteer mothers cook the porridge for the young HBECD attendants in the mother leader's kitchen. In some cases, the space selected is fenced with found recycled materials such as jerry cans, tarps and wooden poles. In Mugombwa, the mothers provide toilet paper turbans to distinguish the young children while they are taking part in HBECD activities (fig. 3.13). These turbans work as an added component of the place-making; by wearing them, children and neighbours recognise they are now at the HBECD.

The tremendous lack of space in both camps constrains these HBECD spaces to an average of four square metres. The damp mud floors are not adequate to spend several hours sitting on, and the initiatives lack enough toys, furniture and educational materials. There is no protection from the sun, the rain and passers-by unless the area has a fence. Despite these drawbacks, children and mothers successfully occupy the spaces for a few hours every day, and

3.13

3.13 Photographs of home-based ECD initiatives in Mugombwa quarters 5, 6 and 7. Mugombwa refugee camp, September 2015. © Amorós Elorduy.

they prefer these to the centralised formal ECD. HBECD activities help decongest the overcrowded formal ECD centres, empower mothers, entertain and stimulate young children and their older siblings, increase ties amongst neighbours and improve the ECD offer in these two camps.

Even in the HBECD cohesive operation, it is possible to observe the Congolese refugees' heterogeneity. While most appreciate the mother leaders' work, not all the neighbours are happy with the noise and the initiative's daily occupation of space. Likewise, not all the mothers are happy to volunteer one day a week to rotate and take care of the children, despite the benefits this brings them. These differences are a clear illustration of Harrell-Bond's criticism of the over-socialised view of man applied to refugees.

Quietly reproducing informal learning environments—Encamped refugees and their direct local hosts are continuously adapting to the built environments of the camps and are, in turn, adapting these to their needs, embodying their 'right to the city'. While none of the observed spatial appropriations has a political agenda at their core, in the cases that I present, a new degree of consciousness emerges when the assemblage of humanitarian system/host government notices the spatial appropriations and either allows or encourages them for their own goals, as sociologist Asef Bayat explains:

'[As] long as the actors carry on without being confronted seriously by any authority, they are likely to treat their advance as an ordinary, everyday exercise. However, once their gains are threatened, they tend to become conscious of the value of their doings and gains, defending them often in collective and audible fashion'.[74]

The humanitarian system has, for a long time, been mostly unaware of these appropriations. That is due in part to their consideration of the camps solely as humanitarian spaces, with the term 'urban' shunned from humanitarian narratives and the built environment considered of little importance, and also to the only recently contested assumption that refugees are primarily vulnerable victims, dependent and apathetic.[75] As sociologist Zygmunt Bauman expressed:

'... questions could be addressed to refugee life that are ordinary in urban studies but have not been addressed thus far to the assemblies of the refugees, partly because of their tight entanglement in the victimisation and humanitarianism discourses, but also because of the counterfactually assumed transitional nature of the settlements'.[76]

An interesting remark is that refugee-led spatial appropriations seem to thrive in the most impoverished camps as humanitarian resources dwindle. While the unnoticed – homes and WASH facilities – are prevalent at all camps, the allowed – religious and commercial – flourish where humanitarian management is weaker and where resources shrink, especially for refugee assistance of complex long-term conflicts in so-called fragile states – such as DRC, South Sudan and Somalia – where a large section of the inhabitants of long-term camps in East Africa stem from. Wealthier and highly visible aid operations tend to be more hierarchically controlled and provide better centralised facilities. In those, educational spatial appropriations – such as non-formal ECD centres – are fewer. Another noteworthy remark is that operations established after 2010, when the urban approach started to gain traction and the new alternatives to camps began to be promoted, tend to encourage spatial interventions.

Another interesting take from the observed spatial appropriations is that wealthier and more internationally visible humanitarian operations tend – or did so in the past – to provide advantages to refugees over their hosts who are also poor and isolated, causing divides between both groups. In these cases, relationships worsen, and combined spatial appropriations reduce, as is the case of Kakuma. On the contrary, refugees in the long-term camps in Southwest Uganda, and in Rwanda to a lesser degree, have developed more, and more sophisticated, relationships with their direct local hosts. Improved relationships seem to be beneficial for all involved: national and local governments, refugees and direct local hosts, as well as humanitarians. In the last 10 years, refugee assistance operations have started to include direct local hosts in their strategies, improving this trend.

Refugee-led spatial appropriations appear to provide what the resource-scarce humanitarian system is unable or unwilling to deliver through formal alternatives. Up until 2014, camp managements just barely allowed the majority of the refugee-led spatial appropriations they noticed, while in the last six years, many of these have been encouraged. Camp management in the region is opening up to more refugee-led spatial appropriations.

The humanitarian system's shift from detecting to allowing to promoting these interventions is happening everywhere, even if it differs between contexts. Declining humanitarian resources, the failure of encampment policies that force refugees' dependency on aid and the recent austerity measures and neo-liberal policies of many of the donor countries are triggering this shift. For example, both Rwanda and Southwest Uganda have changed from in-kind to cash hand-outs and encourage work for self-reliance as they adhere to the CRRF put forward by the international community in 2016.[77] Even if the value in cash is the same as – or even lower than – the former in-kind aid, access to money and the authorisation to work produces changes in the urban fabric of the camp as homes are refurbished and shelters are turned into shops. The growing urban development is clear in the highly isolated and impoverished Kiziba where new businesses sprouted up overnight with the arrival of cash hand-outs.[78]

Embracing neo-liberal policies, the humanitarian system/host governments assemblage is increasingly focusing on refugees' self-help. It encourages spatial appropriations and employs refugees' agency to achieve its assistance goals more efficiently. However, it is unclear whether these strategies will contribute to loosening the grip that agencies and governments have on refugees' freedoms. It remains to be seen if the CRRF will enhance refugees' human rights and will promote holistic solutions devised together with refugees, taking into account the assemblage of human and non-human actors that partake in refugee assistance.

So far, the same powerful actors cherry-pick only the elements of the *Alternatives to Camps* or the CRRF that interest them in order to keep control over the refugees. New interventions sometimes twist the idea of refugees' capability to force them into self-help while keeping them under similar tight sets of devised rules – camps, special economic zones and other methods of containment.[79] These neo-liberal strategies seem to ignore that while refugees are capable, motivated and skilled individuals, they do not play on even ground. Approaches that rely on physical containment are an attempt on refugees' human rights and freedoms, marginalising them and leaving them with minimal access to resources.

Refugees are a heterogeneous constellation of often skilled individuals who are a key component of their own well-being. Hopefully, the encouragement of refugee-led interventions that we see in the long-term camps is a sign of the humanitarian system and the host governments truly embracing that refugees are a necessary and active actor in their assistance. However, the implementation of new containment strategies suggests that those powerful actors are still reluctant to recognise refugees' agency. To some degree, it just does not compute in the normative development/aid world view that poor, vulnerable and displaced populations can be capable of contributing to and leading their development while simultaneously needing help defending their human rights and accessing food, money, shelter and education. The neo-liberal thought ties monetary and material capability with human capability.

Moreover, in the East African case, the post-colonial hangover of the Security Council–dominated international community still ties Africans with need and dependency. The UNHCR's imposition of refugee containment for years – now embraced by host governments – was based on this view of the continent. Forcing the establishment of camps in exchange of aid was an approach rooted in a lack of trust in new African states and the continent's assumed helplessness. Moreover, the paternalistic and patriarchal international community ties women and children – who form the majority of encamped refugees in the continent – with victimhood and dependence. The fact that currently most of the literature, scholars and organisations working in humanitarian aid still hail from Europe and America and are funded by them only helps to continue this cycle. There is a need for more voices, particularly feminist and decolonising perspectives. There is a need for more situated knowledges.

Refugee-imagined radical incrementalism—Throughout fieldwork in 2015, 2016 and 2017, my team and I asked research respondents which spatial interventions they would propose to make their camp a more stimulating mosaic of child-friendly learning environments.[80] Their proposals focused on three main intervention areas: the camp/neighbourhood, the ECD initiatives and the home. I translated these proposals into drawings and photomontages and showed the proposals back to the refugee respondents and camp managers to discuss further whether the interventions were addressing young children's learning (fig. 3.14).

The camp/neighbourhood—The most prominent proposal – and the only one consistent throughout camps and respondents – was 'to have more young-children-friendly spaces with play equipment at the neighbourhood/village level'. All adult respondents[81] and a quarter of all child respondents mentioned this proposal as one of their priority interventions.[82]

In general, children focused on experiential interventions that bring joy, entertainment, variety of options and education. In Kakuma phases II and III, they clearly and consistently proposed to have a similar life to the 'commercial centre' of Kakuma phase I with the 'development of "township life"; access to electricity, TV, groceries, bars and police'. In addition, children in Kakuma phase III suggested 'setting up a motorised transport system to get to school'.[83] Children in the Southwest Ugandan camps proposed 'having more, closer, bigger and better quality ECD centres and health centres'. In contrast, those at Nakivale suggested 'having more cows and birds'.

Adults instead focused on reducing accidents and improving the educational and WASH infrastructure. The adult respondents in the Rwandan camps (the most active in terms of camp proposals) wanted to 'secure slopes and other risk areas – ravines, dumpsters and open septic tanks – with handrails and paving'; to 'curate

3.14

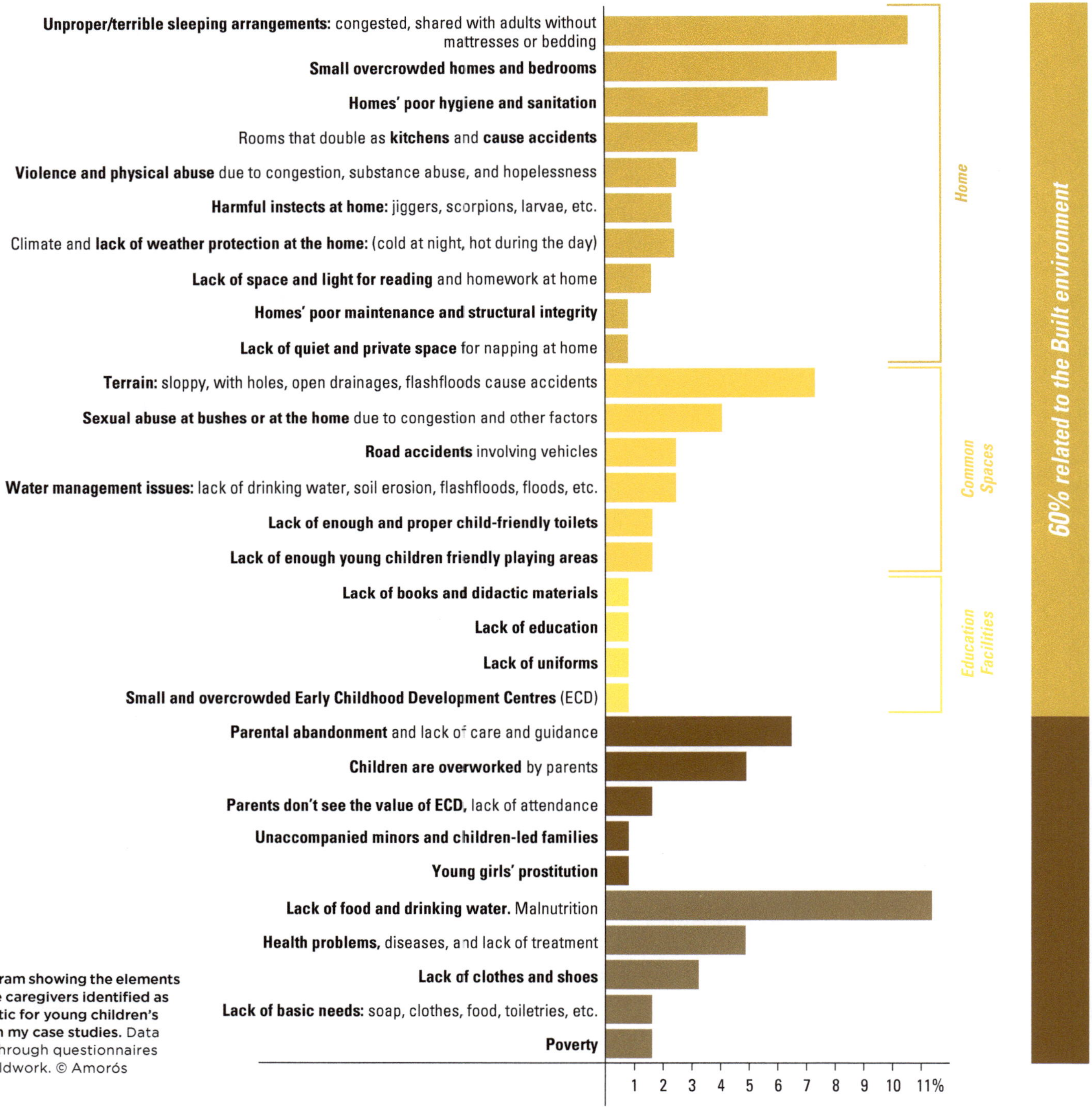

3.14 Diagram showing the elements that home caregivers identified as problematic for young children's learning in my case studies. Data sourced through questionnaires during fieldwork. © Amorós Elorduy.

3.15

3.15 (A+B) **Before-and-after photomontage of pavement and drainage solutions in Kiziba refugee camp.** © Amorós Elorduy.

and make safer the paths that children use to access schools'; to 'cover and improve the stormwater drainages'; and to 'maintain and make latrines safer'. In particular, Kiziba's adult respondents suggested 'more ECD centres that are good quality and more easily accessible' (fig. 3.15).[84]

Very few children in the Rwandan camps, few adult respondents in the Southwest Ugandan ones and almost none of the adult respondents in Kakuma proposed changes at camp level.[85] This indifference might show a certain disempowerment or disengagement with common life, reinforcing Harrell-Bond's opposition to the idea of the over-socialised view of man.[86] As useful as it would be to understand the triggers for this seeming disinterest and how it compares to the diversity of the camps, I do not have enough information to make firm conclusions on this point.

The formal and non-formal ECD initiatives—The respondents who were actively involved in the formal and non-formal ECD initiatives – caregivers, mother leaders and young community mobilisers – gave answers geared towards improving their quality. They proposed 'stimulating and didactic', 'child-friendly designed', 'structurally sound and durable', 'sheltered from the sun and the rain', 'easy to maintain and clean' centres. These facilities could 'have openings for ventilation and light', be 'fenced for security' and 'have enough well-designed child-friendly playgrounds appropriately equipped with play objects' (figs. 3.16 and 3.17).[87]

The parents and guardians – less involved in the ECD initiatives – focused on quantity: the size, position and security of the ECD spaces. All the parents and guardians except those in Kakuma phase III suggested 'building more child-friendly, high-quality ECD centres closer to the people'. They also proposed 'improving the existing ECD centres to serve all neighbourhoods' and 'expanding the existing ECD centres to include more classrooms, a fence with a gate, green areas and access to water'.

Child respondents focused their ECD-related proposals on the play and educational materials available and on the provision of food and water. In Kakuma phase III, Nakivale and Kyaka II, children suggested 'classrooms with sturdy wall materials with openings and good iron sheet roofs'.[88] All the children in Kakuma, Kyaka II and Kiziba proposed an 'ECD kitchen with provisions of sweetened porridge'. The children at Kyaka II, Kyangwali, Kigeme and Kakuma phase III suggested 'access to water and clean toilets with hand-washing basins'.[89]

The home—The home was central in the refugees' proposals for improvement. All respondents in Kakuma and Southwest Uganda agreed on the need for 'better well-furnished bedrooms'. The children wanted to 'have bed structures, mattresses, bedding and mosquito nets'. It is striking that the Rwandan camps' inhabitants barely mentioned bedroom improvements when in more than half of the households, adults and children share overcrowded bedrooms that lack mattresses,[90] and the bedroom can be a source of sexual and physical abuse of children (fig. 3.18).[91]

The adults in Nakivale and the children in Kakuma phases I and II, Kiziba, Nakivale and Kyangwali suggested having 'cement floors inside the homes'. Children in Kyaka II, Kyangwali, Kigeme and Kakuma phases II and III also proposed the placement of 'furniture and furnishings like towels, carpets and shelves'. Children living in the Southwest Ugandan camps suggested setting up 'solar power to provide electricity for lighting and TV' and agreed with the suggestion by the children at Rwandan camps of 'building more easily accessible water points to clean things and drink from'. Only the children in Mugombwa and Kyaka II asked for 'nicer and cleaner latrines'. This point is interesting, since the quantitative analysis indicated that Kiziba's WASH facilities were the worst of all camps studied.

All adult respondents across all camps suggested building 'bigger and better houses, inside and out'. This proposal indicates pronounced differences in perception between camps, since the size and quality of the homes vary greatly from camp to camp.[92] Kakuma's home interiors are on average 20 square metres and the private or semi-private compounds are on

3.16

3.16 (A+B) Before-and-after photomontage of the formal ECD centre in Kiziba quarter 8, with new windows manufactured in the camp. © Amorós Elorduy.

3.17 (A+B) Before-and-after photo-montage of classroom interior in the *maternelle* in Kiziba quarter 4, with new windows and ceiling.
© Amorós Elorduy.

3.17

average 80 square metres. The homes at the Southwest Ugandan camps have interiors that are 20–30 square metres. Their average plot size is 600 square metres for those who arrived before the 2000s, and around 250 square metres for more recent arrivals. The homes on the Rwandan camps on average have two rooms, with interiors that are 12 square metres and shared exterior spaces that are three square metres. In fact, the adult respondents in the Rwandan camps suggest the 'need for a fence'.[93]

The collection of suggestions and proposals for the homes by both adults and children shows an appetite for better bedrooms and WASH facilities. While some recommendations, such as having bigger houses and plots, are more complex to achieve, others, such as having beds, mattresses, pavements and power, are all doable and achievable through diverse affordable strategies.

The homes are generally in poor condition and yet have both positive and negative effects on young children. On the one hand, children and their support networks agree that homes provide children with a safe space to be with family members. Children explicitly state that they feel united and that it feels good to be close to their mothers and siblings. On the other hand, these structures tend to imprint on children negative experiences and prevent their long-term learning mainly due to poor sleeping conditions, lack of hygiene, lack of privacy and accidents related to open kitchens, which are the root of physical and socio-emotional trauma. Refugee respondents stated that sleeping on dusty, damp floors in unventilated and overcrowded rooms was the cause much illness.[94] Chronic anaemia, diarrhoea and parasites such as hookworms and jiggers are also related to the insalubrious indoor home environments. All these negative influences have an impact on the brain and physical development of young children, affecting amongst other things their attention span and neural connections.

Homes should be central in efforts to improve children's lifelong learning and their physical and socio-emotional well-being. Health, education and protection initiatives that strive to be successful will gain insight by looking at the home as a paramount influence for young children and their caregivers.[95] Failure to do so has the potential to frustrate efforts and waste millions. Deworming campaigns and nutritional programmes are doomed if homes are unpaved and children sleep on the dusty floors of humid unventilated and overcrowded homes. Sexual abuse and gender-based violence sensitisation programmes will hardly succeed if non-family adults and children continue to share bedrooms and bed structures and access to safe toilets is not ensured. In contrast, small interventions such as paving homes, providing or fabricating bed structures on site as well as sturdy windows and doors, providing power and access to well-lit, secure, safe, clean and accessible WASH facilities can have critical positive effects in supporting those initiatives.

A mosaic of imagined utopias—Adults and children have a wealth of knowledge and ideas on how to improve their lives and their children's well-being through small, medium and large spatial interventions.

3.18

3.18 Home interiors in the Rwandan refugee camps, September 2015 and 2017. © Amorós Elorduy.

Recording and documenting these proposals can provide policymakers, camp managers, NGO workers, academics and refugees with a catalogue of options to begin improving young children's learning in these long-term camps. It is necessary and worthwhile to research potential ways of carrying out these interventions, supporting refugees and direct local hosts to develop them and implement some of these changes from a camp management position.

Moreover, the refugee proposals recorded[96] open the door to a new understanding about the role of the refugees and of built environment technicians in the planning and maintenance of camps. They reveal refugees as capable of imagining and planning a better settlement that improves young children's learning, and of meaningfully participating in discussions and plans about the camps' built environment. The collection of the imagined utopias described raises several questions related to empowerment, biases, assumptions and cultural influences. Each proposal would require more time, information and in-depth research to understand the underlying causes of the different perceptions between groups of respondents and to investigate means for their implementation.

Speculated transversal spatial appropriations—Participatory Action Research (PAR) methodologies rely on an iterative four-step cycle: gathering data, analysing it, planning an action and carrying it out. I developed this cycle in the past while working as an architect with my teams in the camps. We collected data, designed and built ECD centres based on its analysis, learned from the process and repeated the cycle for the next ECD centre design and construction. I continued with this strategy for the development of maps and visual information about the camps that I present here, the development of fieldwork trips, the analysis of the data and finally the PAR exercises.

In 2017, I developed participatory research with children and their support network of adults in Kiziba and Kigeme refugee camps. I chose these two sites due to budget, time, accessibility, the wealth of information and connections I had in both (I had worked in Kiziba since 2011 and in Kigeme since 2013) and their length of operation (Kiziba for 20 years and Kigeme for 12 years in 2017). PAR seemed relevant because the limited research about children in refugee camps recommends its use[97] and because the educator Paulo Freire[98] and UNESCO's Growing Up in Cities[99] and MOST Programmes recommend the use of PAR with children.[100]

Some of the strengths of using PAR in these two camps was their compactness, their relatively small size and their location among hills, which enable a comprehensive view of the camps from adjacent hills and roads. In both settlements, all residents and most PAR participants spoke Kinyarwanda and French, had a similar culture and upbringing (Congolese from Eastern DRC from three central provinces) and had similar ancestry and customary practices.

During the PAR exercises, I tried to engage all the human actors who could potentially be involved in young children's learning processes: children, their parents, caregivers and teachers, young refugees and local graduate architects, artists and NGO workers. I used arts and crafts, traditional and new technologies, and the diversity of the participants' skills and knowledge to disseminate information, develop targeted actions, discuss and create new knowledge. Due to the obstacles involved in participatory research with young children living in refugee camps, to address ethical matters and for organisational reasons, I developed art-based PAR exercises.[101]

I chose to organise the PAR into three interconnected and sequential exercises: (1) the discussion about research findings amongst research participants, (2) the development of a spatial appropriation in Kiziba using participatory murals[102] and (3) the development of a research-based public interest design (PID) studio with architecture master's students from Kigali's African Design Centre (ADC) and Kigeme's inhabitants. The exercises built upon each other and

3.19

3.19 (composition workshop 1st day) Inception workshop in Kiziba refugee camp. Left page: adult participants engaged in a discussion about the common and open spaces young children currently use as playground. Right page, clockwise: discussing the photomontages; listing the diverse needs and qualities for each of the locations identified; the diverse locations for potential child-friendly spaces (CFS) identified marked on the 3D-printed model; children and adult participants identifying current and potential playgrounds for young children in the camp. Kiziba refugee camp, 5 September 2017. © Amorós Elorduy.

overlapped in time. The ADC fellows were involved in all PAR exercises, and hence the learnings from one exercise fed the following.

PAR 1: discussing maps, proposals and needs—In the long-term Congolese refugee camps in Rwanda, there is a lack of practice – amongst refugees and refugee camp workers – in talking and thinking about the built environment. For that reason, I devised three tools that could facilitate discussions amongst participants: a 3D-printed model, printed photomontages representing the utopic proposals imagined by the refugee respondents and a website.[103]

I began by showing participants the 2D map. Only the MIDIMAR camp manager and one of the UNHCR participants were able to read it. I then showed the 3D-printed physical model. This time, even the young participants – aged between three and five years old – were able to locate their homes and their go-to play areas on it (fig. 3.19). The model allowed an intergenerational and interdisciplinary discussion where all the actors had their say. Finally, I showed

a few of the selected refugee proposals as photomontages, which displayed bigger openings in the wattle-and-daub classrooms, playgrounds made from local materials and paths paved with river pebbles and gravel found close to the camp. These images initiated a dialogue amongst participants about their diverse priorities and the potential of the built environment and their skills to improve daily life.[104]

PAR 2: mural making—Next, the PAR participants developed a series of murals using the 300-year-old Rwandan mural art tradition *imigongo* that stems from what is now Rwanda's Eastern province.[105] In the Congolese refugee camps in Rwanda, many families already use mud and natural pigments (both materials used in the *imigongo*) to decorate the interiors – and sometimes the exteriors – of their homes (fig. 3.20). Many even imitate the traditional Rwandan *imigongo* designs, in part because these refugees are mostly Banyarwanda who immigrated into the North and South Kivu regions in DRC at the end of the nineteenth

3.20

3.20 Diverse uses of mud colours and other natural pigments in the decoration of home interiors and exteriors in Kiziba refugee camp, September 2015 and 2017.
© Amorós Elorduy.

century and naturalised. They speak Kinyarwanda and share several common traditions and culture.[106] As well as those reasons, we chose to do *imigongo* murals because arts and crafts have been tested in a variety of different settings as useful elements of PAR to overcome language and cultural barriers in order to engage a variety of actors and to trigger change within public spaces in urban settings.[107] Moreover, painted murals are used widely as educational displays in schools in the region and the camp, and most child respondents stated they liked them during our previous data collection fieldwork trips.

Two months were required to prepare all the paperwork and logistics to be able to develop the murals,[108] which involved around 20 refugee participants[109] and nine *imigongo* artisans.

The initial PAR exercise was also the first day of the two-week-long mural-making activity. The site selection process was a joint effort between all participants. After holding talks with the NGOs in charge of ECD, child protection and education,[110] the group decided that the murals should contain didactic information about learning environments, raise awareness and trigger the development of child-friendly spaces (CFS) around the camp.[111]

The team used the 3D-printed model to locate all the main spaces where young children play. From the 30 initially selected sites, they pinpointed 10 for the potential CFSs according to distances between locations, the need for at least one site per quarter and the qualities and risks of each site. Following this, the whole party visited, photographed and measured all 10 selected areas and chose two sites with three to four murals in each to create synergies.[112] They chose the *maternelle* in quarter 4 – the formal ECD centre – and a space close to the market in quarter 2 where many children already played.

Next, all refugee participants learnt from the *imigongo* artisans how to develop different traditional geometrical designs, make the dung and ash mixture, and apply it to walls and small wooden pieces (figs. 3.21 and 3.22). Over the next five days, the team developed the first set of murals in the *maternelle*'s courtyard. Children, caregivers, parents and artisans chose the themes, the different designs and how they might be organised on the walls; the artisans and the rest of the adults developed them. The privacy provided by the enclosed courtyard facilitated the learning of all participants and encouraged the children's involvement (fig. 3.23).

We replicated a similar system at the neighbourhood location during the second week. Being in a public space incentivised curiosity and dialogue amongst neighbours and other camp inhabitants. This time, the neighbours selected the designs that would go on the walls of their homes from a set of traditional *imigongo* designs. Some of the neighbours were sceptical at first, hesitant about attracting even more children to the relatively quiet area, while others participated actively in the painting (figs. 3.24 and 3.25).

The murals' design and production sessions were active and creative. They incited informal conversations about the built environment, child development and the importance of CFSs. They also strengthened ties between the *imigongo* artisans, the refugees, the architecture fellows and me.

The murals triggered positive spatial change around them. At the end of the 12 days, the caregivers at the *maternelle* began to plant flowers around the paintings. In addition, most neighbours surrounding the other site used the remaining materials to paint the interiors of their homes with help from the *imigongo* artisans.

A couple of weeks after the completion of the murals, during informal conversations, the children highlighted that the *maternelle* was now 'much nicer', and they touched the murals every time they went in and out of the classrooms. The designs that they had chosen and that their parents and caregivers had built triggered conversations amongst the young refugees on different animals, colours, objects and shapes. The set of murals close to the market attracted neighbours from other quarters. They expressed a desire to implement wall decorations in their neighbourhoods and discussed with the *imigongo* artisans how to get the necessary materials from the camp surroundings. The creative and participatory activities seemed to be generating tangible and positive change for the children and their close community. They increased the awareness amongst the wider community about the relevance of space for young children's learning (fig. 3.26).

A few years after the intervention, most murals are still standing and have survived several rainy seasons,[113] although I do not have information on the impact of the murals long term. Have they improved the children's learning situation in those particular spaces? Have the surrounding neighbours recognised those spaces as first and foremost child-friendly areas? Have they triggered the creation

3.21

3.21 First day of learning the *imigongo* technique. Left page: applying the dung-and-ash mixture to a preprepared wooden frame. Right page, from top to bottom and left to right: studying the different traditional *imigongo* designs and their meanings; preparing a wooden frame with a geometric framework to develop an *imigongo* design; refugees filming the dung-and-ash application with their mobile phones; and an *imigongo* artisan teaching a group from the youth arts club. Kiziba refugee camp, 6 September 2017. © Amorós Elorduy.

of other child-friendly areas in other neighbourhoods?

PAR 3: PID—PID is a human-centred and participatory design teaching practice that originated in the USA in the 1990s. PID studios emphasise topics and processes that enhance sustainable designs and include ecological, economic and social issues.[114] The PID studio I developed from September through to November 2017 in the camps of Kiziba and Kigeme in Rwanda involved three recent graduates of architecture – from Rwanda, Uganda and South Sudan[115] – and teams of 10–15 refugees from both camps (fig. 3.27).

The PID aimed to explore potential collaborations between schools of architecture and refugee assistance in the region. It engaged the refugee and student participants into trying varied methods of data collection and analysis, it fostered their creativity and innovation in dealing with a complex issue and it helped them understand the ethics of a research project by

applied architectural design with human subjects. It was intended to help students and refugees master the use of architecture and design as tools to create and transmit new knowledge, emotions and stories.

This PAR exercise required much prior planning.[116] The PID studio was comprised of initial desk-based research and the writing of a research proposal; a two-week workshop in Kiziba with field visits to Kigeme and Mugombwa to learn the common traits and differences between camps; a two-month iterative design research process where both refugees and students worked together in a hypothetical project to improve young children's learning in the case studies; and the presentation of the findings to the broader refugee and humanitarian communities.

During the two-week-long intensive initial workshop, the team decided to focus on devising a set of design guidelines for the construction, upgrade and maintenance of CFS in the refugee camps in Rwanda.[117]

3.22

3.22 *Imigongo* learning process. Left page: sanding the sun-dried dung-and-ash wooden boards. Right page, from top to bottom and left to right: sun-drying the wooden boards with the top layer of dung-and-ash mixture already applied; sanding the dried dung-and-ash mixture; applying a first coat of grey mud before painting; and the finished board. Kiziba refugee camp, 7–15 September 2017. © Amorós Elorduy.

The refugee-architect team undertook desk-based research, walked around the camp and sketched, measured and photographed the selected sites. They held informal conversations during the mural-making activities and developed three iterative workshops where they proposed ideas. They identified six different criteria – aligned with national and international CFS standards – to analyse the existing and the potential CFSs in the camps.[118] They used these six criteria to devise a set of incremental design guidelines[119] and tested them in utopic CFS projects in two selected sites in Kiziba.[120] We then presented the findings to the refugees, the NGOs and camp management in the UNHCR field offices, gave the camp managers the 3D-printed model and gathered feedback on the CFS guidelines proposal.

The architect fellows then began an intense two-week-long period of desk-based

research, interviewed experts from PLAN International, the UNHCR and CARE International and talked to refugees. They decided to use the remaining two months to develop a set of standards and design guidelines for the HBECD initiatives in conjunction with a group of refugees in Kigeme, the camp with the oldest HBECD initiatives. The fellows and their Kigeme counterparts – 10 mother leaders, four youth community mobilisers, two members of the refugee leadership and one worker from the NGO ADRA[121] – met at the camp on three occasions. During those meetings, they held informal conversations while visiting a variety of HBECD sites, discussed design options during the workshops and took design decisions together.

We visited, sketched and photographed 14 of the 74 HBECD in Kigeme. We listened to the pros and cons from the users of each site and collected spatial data. The team of

3.23

3.23 Mural-making process on the first and second walls of the *maternelle* site. Left page: a geometric piece during the sun-drying process. Right page, from top to bottom and left to right: usual number of children surrounding the mural-making process during their break time; detail of corner between first and second walls; the application of the mixture should be done by adding water to the mixture; an overview of the first and second walls at *maternelle* in the afternoon. Kiziba refugee camp, 8 and 9 September 2017. © Amorós Elorduy.

refugees and fellows then analysed the spatial qualities, challenges and potential ways to improve each of the HBECD visited. Using that information, they devised seven overarching design guidelines with 26 specific elements that an HBECD site in a Rwandan camp must, should and may have. They tested the guidelines and standards with two hypothetical HBECD projects: one in quarter 1 and one in quarter 5.

PAR triggers new knowledge and transformation—Humanitarian actors do not usually engage refugee adults – even less children – in initiatives that are connected to the built environment and to young children's learning. Despite the endemic lack of participation in the Rwandan refugee camps, refugees participating in the PAR exercises were curious and eager to enter conversations about how to improve their camp through design

and creative interventions. The iterative character of the PID studio feedback sessions contributed to engaging refugee participants in spatial and design-based dialogues. Throughout the process, the participants' knowledge grew on topics of spatial language and refugee camp issues with conversations of varied content and breadth. Refugees initiated discussions on circulation flows, rain and wind direction, and the quality and sourcing of local construction materials, amongst other topics.

It was remarkably valuable but also challenging to develop participatory processes in the Congolese refugee camps. This was due to bureaucracies, security protocols and the humanitarian assemblage's primary commitment to donors and host countries' agendas rather than to their refugee beneficiaries, as well as to what Andrew Pearse and Barbara Harrell-Bond

3.24

3.24 First steps of the mural-making process on neighbourhood site. Left page: two of the walls at the neighbourhood mural site during the process of sun-drying the dung-and-ash mixture. Right page, bottom left: the neighbourhood site prior to the mural-making activity. Bottom right: *imigongo* artisan, community mobiliser and owner of one of the homes to get an *imigongo* mural on its walls discussing the potential outcomes portrayed in the photomontages. Kiziba refugee camp, 11 and 12 September 2017. © Amorós Elorduy.

call the 'anti-participatory ideologies' of the humanitarian system.[122] This attitude adds to the extreme lack of information available on the built environment and on young children's learning on the long-term camps. It took me four years of work in the Rwandan camps as an architect in addition to the two-and-a-half years of fieldwork research to collect enough base information and personal knowledge to be prepared to develop a rather small PAR exercise focused only in Kiziba and Kigeme. This demonstrates how demanding it is to do participatory research with young children and their support networks and to do it in these settings.

Two other obstacles to real participation in the camps were the encamped refugees' heterogeneity and research fatigue.[123] Refugees' opinions and priorities are varied. For example, those involved in young children's learning stated a desire

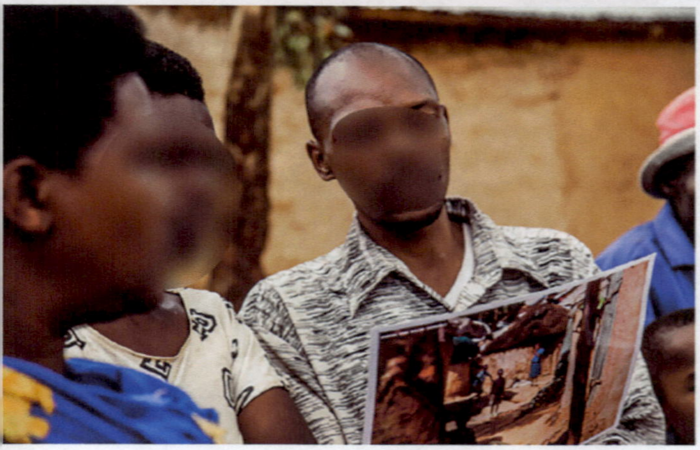

to have CFSs closer to their homes, while adjacent neighbours sometimes disliked the possibility of an increase in young children playing around their homes. Furthermore, repeated consultations that extract knowledge from refugees but that rarely end up contributing back cause fatigue and a refusal to participate in projects, especially amongst youth.[124] This practice is sadly quite widespread in academic and humanitarian research.[125]

The values of the PAR exercises are multiple. The involvement of young architects and artists through an iterative process improved the level of information available to refugee parents, children, caregivers and leadership on the role of space in young children's learning. The participatory exercises opened up new opportunities for the PID studio participants to collaborate in future multi-authored spatial appropriations.[126] PAR

3.25

3.25 Painting process on first and second walls at neighbourhood site. Left page: working atmosphere. Right page: painting process (through layers) applied after sanding the sun-dried dung-and-ash mixture. Application of base coat in dark grey mud, application of other colours, application of detailing in black, and final detail. Kiziba refugee camp, 12 and 13 September 2017. © Amorós Elorduy.

participants stated that they were pleased to partake and had enjoyed and learned from the experience. They had had fun and felt that their ideas were recognised and encouraged. These participants also gained new skills such as developing murals in the *imigongo* technique and design and technical approaches to improve the HBECD spaces.

The use of traditional and new technologies, arts and crafts, and the design and discussion processes afforded the inclusion of more voices into the conversation. These universal languages facilitated communication with a broader audience in a universal language enabling their active engagement. The PAR exercises might have helped create some cracks in the barriers built by assumptions that refugees are vulnerable, apathetic and a homogeneous group. The PID's proposed improvements show that the refugees are able to create

spaces, evaluate their environments and recommend thoughtful ways of improving them.

Despite the positive outcomes of the PAR exercises, I am unable to tell if and how the strategies used would work in other refugee camps. For example, would the 3D-printed model technique work in the flat, sparsely populated and vast camps in Southwest Uganda and Northwest Kenya? How will PAR exercises affect the participants' long-term commitment to the initiated spatial appropriations?

Even though I did not measure it, the confidence to apply their social and ethical convictions and to act on their dreams and needs grew in most of the PAR participants, which were already some of the most active members of their communities. They transformed the murals, the CFS and the HBECD designs that had initially seemed rather ordinary and quotidian into

3.26

3.26 Finished murals. Left page: neighbourhood site with its three murals. Right page, bottom left: two walls at *maternelle*'s entrance; bottom right: mural facing *maternelle*'s playground. Kiziba refugee camp, 15 September 2017. © Amorós Elorduy.

discussion points. Even if not quickly qualitatively evaluated and almost impossible to quantify, these discussions and informal conversations during the PAR exercises suggest their positive influence on the participants' further empowerment.

Most refugees are not usually called upon to participate in the camps' improvement and development, and they are generally trapped in an extremely unjust system. Consequently, they typically have very little leverage over the human and non-human actors who govern them. Yet, they are the main characters modifying the camps – a role that is mostly unrecognised, unpraised and hidden under humanitarian discourses of victimisation and dependency. Artistic and architectural interventions elsewhere suggest that the involvement of local young artists and architects in participatory projects with marginalised populations have the

potential to increase pre-existing ethical, social and political awareness amongst those participating.[127]

Each individual and group involved in the spatial appropriations highlighted in this chapter approached the same questions differently and asked different questions.[128] The students of architecture were mesmerised at the discovery of the camps in their own countries and enjoyed the interactions with people from such diverse backgrounds and origins. The artists and artisans were glad to see the similarities between the refugees' culture and their own, to try something so different from what they are used to and to contribute to the improvement of other people's lives through their art. Children and the rest of the refugee participants enjoyed the artistic activities. They liked being involved in the thought and design processes during the PID and the mural making, having a say

3.27

3.27 Public interest design studio workshops. Left page: discussion around findings and potential design guidelines for home-based ECD spaces in the Rwandan refugee camps. Kigeme refugee camp, 6 November 2017. Right page: session to discuss the findings and the design guidelines for future CFS in the Congolese refugee camps in Rwanda. Kiziba refugee camp, 9 September 2017. © Amorós Elorduy.

and contributing to a creative process. The immediate influence of the PAR exercises on participants – including the research team – is the unveiling of a more positive sense of self, a better understanding of the needs of others, new social networks, new skills and enjoyment.

Conscious radical incrementalism—The rich research by an architectural design approach offers many possible angles. For example, it enables participation using architectural tools and the use of an assemblage thinking lens to create new spatial knowledge. In our case, it has helped to unveil some of the complex realities of the camps while including more voices in the process and potentially triggering change.

I have found limited refugee camp studies where researchers had tried to develop such substantive ways of making their research immediately beneficial to

the people with whom they work.[129] Too often, researchers and academics get hung up on changing the world with their ideas and findings, forgetting the opportunity that lies in the research process itself. In my practice and research work, through research by architectural design, I take specific decisions, make great efforts and try hard to create a cycle from experience to theory to research to tangible outcomes, even if minor.

This chapter contests widespread assumptions that refugees are a smooth fabric with no agency and not enough skill. Refugees continuously use their 'right to the city'. They build and modify all of their homes, many of the schools and ECD initiatives, and all the religious facilities, which often double as ECD spaces. They also create all the small shops that exist in the camps. They negotiate rent and acquire land inside and outside the predesignated camp borders, expanding the footprint of the camps.

It seems evident that Colin Ward's idea of the urban setting as a school without walls could be attainable.[130] Some ways of transforming the camps' architectures into stimulating learning resources are the ones that I speculated about here, harnessing the refugees' knowledge of the camps and of the diverse communities that inhabit them, bringing in refugees' varied cultures, imagination and wishes – especially those of children and their support networks – and employing local creative minds such as young architects, artisans and makers.

Some organisations and individuals are already tapping into existing opportunities to transform the camps into stimulating learning environments. They do so to improve formal schooling such as is the work of Active Social Architecture (ASA) developing formal ECD centres in the Congolese camps in Rwanda,[131] to provide CFSs such as the work of East African Playgrounds in the Southwest Ugandan camps and to improve home environments such as Opportunigee in Nakivale or Creative Assemblages in Mugombwa.[132]

Stimulating environments might look slightly different in each camp setting. Specifically, in the Rwandan camps, safer streets will be those with proper storm water drainage, with handrails and proper paving in the steep areas. In the Kenyan camps, stimulating and secure streets would assimilate Kakuma phase I, smaller with more vegetation and shade, and where clusters of neighbours can take care of their younger members. Better homes could improve across the board with natural light and ventilation, dust-free and dry pavements and enough furniture such as bedframes and mattresses, creating home environments that foster children's safety, privacy and enjoyment of family life.

I have relished working with refugees and local artisans and students of architecture in different ways through the years. The speculations and interventions that I describe in this chapter suggest ways of using the built environment as a valuable resource for learning. Through speculative actions based on observation of each specific settlement, architecture can transform the long-term camps and design the new alternatives to camps in order to cultivate an environment conducive to young children's learning more effectively. A new chapter for the long-term camps is possible. That is particularly true in East Africa as Uganda[133] and Rwanda[134] both embrace the new CRRF and the GRC approach to include refugees into national programming. If those in charge of ECD – both humanitarians and refugees – are able to learn the camps' architectural qualities and harness those, if they can value architecture and see it as an opportunity, it might be possible to transform the camps into 'schools without walls'.[135]

Notes

1. Since the early 1980s, critics of the camp have argued that they should be a last resort – advice that is also highlighted throughout the UNHCRs different versions for the*Handbook for Emergencies*. However, physical containment and isolation are still the go-to strategy for humanitarian operations.
2. UNHCR, 'The implementation of UNHCR's policy on refugee protection and solutions in urban areas'; UNHCR, UNHCR policy on refugee protection and solutions in urban areas.

3. UNHCR, 'Comprehensive refugee response framework'.
4. See, for example, the new strategies in Rwanda and Uganda. Government of Uganda, UN Uganda, and World Bank, 'REHOPE – Refugee and host population empowerment'; UNHCR, 'MIDIMAR-UNHCR joint strategy partners'. UNHCR, 'Protracted refugee situations: The search for practical solutions'.
5. Hyndman, 'Geographies of displacement'; Hyndman, *Managing Displacement.*
6. Deleuze, and Guattari, *A Thousand Plateaus.*
7. Herz, 'Refugee camps in Chad'; Scott-Smith, 'The humanitarian-architect divide', 2017.
8. Pieterse, *City Futures*, 6.
9. 'To think about alternative possibilities, we need utopias. . . . Transduction is an intellectual operation which can be methodically carried out and which differs from classical induction, deduction, the construction of "models", simulation as well as the simple statement of hypothesis. Transduction elaborates and constructs a theoretical object, a possible object from information related to reality and a problematic posed by this reality. Transduction assumes an incessant feedback between the conceptual framework used and empirical observations. Its theory (methodology) gives shape to certain spontaneous mental operations of the planner, the architect, the sociologist, the politician and the philosopher. It introduces rigour in invention and knowledge in utopia'. Lefebvre, *Writings on Cities*, 21.
10. 'The conviction of the oppressed that they must fight for their liberation is not a gift bestowed by the revolutionary leadership, but the result of their own *conscientizaçao.* Humankind "emerge" from their "submersion" and acquire the ability to "intervene" in reality as it is unveiled. "Intervention" in reality – historical awareness it-self – thus represents a step forward from "emergence", and results from the *conscientizaçao* of the situation. *Conscientizaçao* is the deepening of the attitude of awareness characteristic of all "emergence"'. Freire, *Pedagogy of the Oppressed*, 67 and 109.
11. Colin Ward and Anthony Fyson elaborate on the idea of urban areas as 'schools without walls' in their book 'Streetwork: The Exploding School', 1973.
12. Pieterse, *City Futures*, 7.
13. Amorós Elorduy, 'Mapping refugee spaces'; Amorós Elorduy, 'Learning in and through the long-term refugee camps'.
14. Architects Constantin Petcou and Doina Petrescu used Lefebvre's term 'transduction' in their work 'R-Urban or how to co-produce a resilient city', 2015.
15. McFarlane, 'Learning assemblages'.
16. Simone, 'On cityness', 38–9.
17. UNHCR, 'Comprehensive refugee response framework'.
18. Scott, 'Everyday forms of resistance', 1986, 42.
19. Scott, 42.
20. Scott, 'Weapons of the Weak', xvi–xvii.
21. Bayat, 'From "dangerous classes" to "quiet rebels"', 2000; Bayat, 'The quiet encroachment of the ordinary', 2007.
22. Bayat, 'From "dangerous classes" to "quiet rebels"', 2000, 545, 546 and 548.
23. Harrell-Bond, 'Weapons of the weak', 2004, 1–2. In this quotation, Harrell-Bond actually refers to Roger Baker's 1984 unpublished paper 'Is loss and crisis theory relevant to understanding refugees in Africa?' That resonates as well with James Scott's work that Harrell-Bond chooses as the title for her response to Kibreab.
24. Abourahme and Hilal, 'The production of space'; Martin, 'From spaces of exception to "campscapes"', 2015; Peteet, 'Producing place, spatializing identity, 1948–68'.
25. Peteet, *Landscape of Hope and Despair*, 130.
26. Bayat, 'From "dangerous classes" to "quiet rebels"', 2000.
27. Kagwanja and Pérouse de Montclos, 'Refugee camps or cities?', 2000; Jansen, 'The accidental city', 2009; Oka, 'Unlikely cities in the desert', 2011.
28. Jansen, 'The accidental city', 2009; Jansen, 'The protracted refugee camp', 2015.
29. Siddiqi, 'L'historire architecturale d'un territoire non identifie'.
30. Fieldwork in Rwanda September 2015, September to November 2017, from Southwest Uganda August 2016, and Kakuma in Kenya September 2016.
31. Fieldwork in Rwanda September 2015, September to November 2017, from Southwest Uganda August 2016, and Kakuma in Kenya September 2016.
32. Amorós Elorduy, 'Mapping refugee spaces'; Amorós Elorduy, 'The impact of humanitarian shelter', 2017.
33. Rodriguez and Tamis-Lemonda, 'Trajectories of the home learning environment', 2011; Halldén, 'Children's views of family'; Gottfried and Gottfried, 'Home environment and cognitive development'; Johnson, 'The developmental implications of home environments'.

34. Heft, 'Background and focal environmental conditions', 1979; Gottfried and Gottfried, 'Home environment and cognitive development'.
35. Proshansky and Fabian, 'The development of place identity in the child', 27.
36. Dates of establishment: Kakuma phase I in 1992, Kakuma phase II in 1997, Kakuma phase III in 2009, Kakuma phase IV in 2014, Kiziba in 1996 and Kigeme A in 2005.
37. Many of these camps were not planned using humanitarian grided standards.
38. In Rwanda, the UNHCR was allowed to distribute iron sheeting amongst refugees in 2013. UNHCR, 'UNHCR's global shelter and settlement strategy, 2014–2018'.
39. Anecdotal evidence collected in Rwanda from February 2011 to November 2014 and cross-checked with data collected through fieldwork in September 2015, September to November 2017 and August and September 2016.
40. In 2013, Kiziba and Gihembe had been running for more than 15 years and Kigeme A and Nyabiheke for more than eight years.
41. In the 1960s and 1980s, these were around 50×50 metres; currently, they tend to be to 20×30 metres.
42. Rwanda began a shift in its strategy, aligning with the CRRF and also owing to the drying up of international funding due to the European refugee crisis. UNHCR, 'Rwanda country refugee response plan 2019–2020'.
43. Fieldwork in Rwanda September 2015, September–November 2017, from Southwest Uganda August 2016, and Kakuma in Kenya September 2016.
44. In 2019, the NGO Give Directly began a programme of large direct cash disbursements to refugees in Mugombwa refugee camp. Most of the refugees used this cash to make home improvements, some of those being pavements. In line with that and using the findings from my PhD research (some of which is contained in this book), I began a project with a local organisation that develops improved earthen floors to pave more than 200 shelters in the camp and to train more than 20 masons on this cheap, local and durable technique.
45. As gathered from the spatial analysis of the map I had created for Kakuma using AutoCAD and GIS and based on satellite imagery and existing population data sets gathered from the UNHCR data manager at Kakuma, Kakuma phase I is the densest phase, and Kakuma phase IV is the least dense.
46. Congolese make up 99% of the inhabitants in the Rwandan camps.
47. Wattle and daub is a construction technique that uses wooden poles and cane to create a structure and to support the mud from which the walls are composed.
48. The reasons and means for home expansion, and the uses and functions of the home's spaces, were collected through home caregiver questionnaires and focus group discussions (FGD) carried out during fieldwork in all my Rwandan case studies in September 2015 and from September to November 2017.
49. In Rwanda, most of the Congolese refugees are Banyamulenge. In Kyangwali, most are from different ethnicities from Ituri and North Kivu provinces, who actually built fences around their homes and took their children to the ECD activities. The refugee president in Kyangwali provided this information during a semi-structured interview on 20 August 2016.
50. Ward, 'Children of the streets', 1986; Ward and Fyson, *Streetwork: The Exploding School*; Karsten and Van Vliet, 'Children in the city', 2006.
51. Ward, *Caught in the Crossfire*; Matthews, 'The street as liminal space'; Valentine and McKendrck, 'Children's outdoor play', 1997.
52. Goma and Bukavu are the two major cities in North and South Kivu, respectively. Lake Kivu is a natural border between DRC and Rwanda.
53. Thatched roofs have been forbidden in Rwanda since the Bye-bye Nyakatsi campaign took place in the early 2010s.
54. AVSI and InfoAid, 'Child protection KAP survey in Rwandan refugee camps'.
55. Amorós Elorduy, 'Mapping refugee spaces'; Consultative Group on Early Childhood Care and Development and INEE, 'The path of most resilience'.
56. Amorós Elorduy, 'Mapping refugee spaces'.
57. This has changed in Kalobeyei where the latrines are now shared between several plots, which provide all refugees with access to a toilet. However, as experience shows in other camps, shared toilet facilities suffer from poor maintenance and increase the chances of abuse.
58. Usually, the UNHCR provides with an initial market structure (a platform with a roof) or an open space for commercial use at the camp's establishment, providing the host country allows it.
59. For example, in Kakuma, the NCCK and the Lutheran World Federation both had an

engineer in their teams in charge of infrastructure. In Rwanda, UNICEF had either an architect or an engineer on its staff or a consultant who provided support to infrastructural needs in education, child protection and health.

60. The NGO Global Help to Heal (GHH) has used them to develop community-based ECD activities since 2014, and the refugees and direct local hosts teach Sunday school in them every weekend. Data collected through fieldwork in Kiziba from 11 to 14 September 2015 and from 5 to 15 September 2017.
61. For more information, see: Amoros Elorduy, 'East African refugee camps as learning assemblages'.
62. Data gathered through semi-structured face-to-face interviews with the camp coordinator of Kiziba refugee camp on 4 October 2017.
63. These schools were close to the main roads in the Sweswe and Alfajiri zones. It is possible that in other zones in the camp, there might have been more of this type of ECD centre. These schools served refugees and direct local hosts who were able to pay a small fee. Data collected through a multi-method qualitative approach during fieldwork in Kyaka II from 9 to 12 August 2016.
64. Amongst the 11 centres we visited, 'Baptist Isanja' in Isanja village in the Juru zone and 'Ruhoko Nursery' in Ruhoko village in the Rubondo zone were non-formal. Both refugees and NGOs recognised these as ECD. Nakivale has three zones: Juru, Base Camp and Rubondo.
65. This type of spatial appropriation is particularly prominent in Nakivale's Base Camp neighbourhoods of Sudan, Kigali and Little Congo.
66. Examples of situations where refugees have access to cash include aid hand-outs in cash, access to NGO jobs and access to loans and remittances. Aid hand-outs are the aid that the UNHCR provides regularly to each refugee family. Hand-outs used to be in-kind, such as food, construction materials and hygienic items, but now they are increasingly monetary due to the decreasing funds of the humanitarian operations in the region. Guyatt, Rosa, and Spencer, 'Refugees vulnerability study Kakuma, Kenya', 23.
67. Fieldwork in Kakuma from 2 to 10 August 2016.
68. For more information, see: Amoros Elorduy, 'East African refugee camps as learning assemblages'.
69. With the help of the UNHCR, ADRA (which took over ECD management from CARE International in 2016) provides the HBECD mother groups with sorghum for porridge and with some toys and mats. ADRA stands for Adventist Development and Relief Agency.
70. In 2012, there was only one formal ECD centre, and it was located in Kigeme A.
71. CARE: Cooperative for Assistance and Relief Everywhere, formerly Cooperative for American Remittances to Europe.
72. Between 2012 and 2016, the HBECD programmes in both camps were influenced by CARE's prior experience in rural Rwanda, particularly by the 'Nkundabana model'. The HBECD programme was incorporated into national policy in 2007. CARE, 'A model geginning', 4.
73. HBECD initiatives have existed in Kigeme since its expansion in September 2012 and in the establishment of Mugombwa in October 2013.
74. Bayat, 'The quiet encroachment of the ordinary', 2007, 6.
75. Turner, 'Lukole (Tanzanie)'; Fresia, 'Performing repatriation?', 2014; Grbac, 'Civitas, polis, and urbs'.
76. Bauman, 'In the lowly nowherevilles of liquid modernity', 2002, 344.
77. UNHCR, 'Comprehensive refugee response framework'.
78. For example, in Rwanda, until 2017, direct local hosts were not allowed to shop in the refugee camps, and refugees were not allowed to work outside the camps. Since 2017, the policy and aid strategy has shifted with MIDIMAR and UNHCR's joint strategy on livelihoods. Hand-outs are now in cash, and refugees are encouraged to work. ONE UN, 'MIDIMAR and UNHCR affirm plan'.
79. Barbelet et al., 'How to ensure Ethiopia's "Jobs Compact" works for refugees'; Crawley, 'Why jobs in special economic zones'; Castle-Miller, 'The law and policy of refugee cities', 2018.
80. We asked respondents for their opinions on three different areas to improve young children's learning: (1) the whole settlement – the streets, common spaces and WASH facilities, (2) the homes and (3) the educational facilities – ECD, pre-primary and *maternelle*.
81. Adult respondents include home caregivers, community leaders, community mobilisers and ECD caregivers.
82. Only the children from Kakuma phases I and II and Nakivale did not mention it as a priority. Data gathered from game-based questionnaires in all case studies: in Rwanda in September 2015, in Uganda in August 2016 and in Kenya in September 2016.

83. The newly established Kalobeyei uses a similar master plan design as that of Kakuma phases III and IV. Both those phases are the ones where children propose more changes, most of which are aimed at making Kakuma phases III and IV become similar to Kakuma phase I (the initial phase that is denser and more organic). The grid-like planning of Kakuma phases II, III and IV means they are less dense and have less commercial activities than Kakuma phase I. Data collected through fieldwork in Kakuma from 2 to 10 September 2016.
84. Kiziba is the only one of the three Rwandan camps that I studied that does not have home-based ECD initiatives run by refugee groups.
85. Half of these respondents did not know what to suggest, and the others said they would not change anything.
86. Harrell-Bond, 'Weapons of the weak', 2004, 1–2.
87. With the exception of Mugombwa that has a new, well-equipped and child-friendly ECD centre, built in December 2014. For more information see Amorós Elorduy, 'Mapping refugee spaces'; ASA Studio, 'Early childhood facilities in refugee camps'.
88. Some of Kakuma phase III's ECD centres are built from metal sheeting – the walls and roofs – or are tented structures. In Nakivale and Kyaka, most of the ECD centres, especially the community-run ones that use community-built churches, are made out of wattle and daub. They lack proper roofs, pavements, openings and playground spaces or facilities. Data collected through fieldwork in Kakuma from 2 to 10 September 2016.
89. Amorós Elorduy, 'Mapping refugee spaces'; Amorós Elorduy, 'Learning in and through the long-term refugee camps'.
90. The rooms are normally four square metres in size and are shared between five people, with no mattresses or proper bed structures. Fieldwork in Rwanda September 2015, September–November 2017, from Southwest Uganda August 2016, and Kakuma in Kenya September 2016.
91. AVSI and InfoAid, 'Child protection KAP survey in Rwandan refugee camps'.
92. At the end of our FGD, we showed images of the other case studies to the respondents. The residents of Kakuma and the Southwest Ugandan camps were shocked at the overcrowding in the Rwandan camps. Meanwhile, the residents of Kakuma and the Rwandan camps were impressed at the conditions in Uganda due to the generous amount of space. Fieldwork in Rwanda September 2015, September–November 2017, from Southwest Uganda August 2016, and Kakuma in Kenya September 2016.
93. Most of the inhabitants in the Southwest Ugandan camps and all Kakuma's inhabitants have a fence and a secure door surrounding their home compound. This is particularly prominent in the congested areas. Fieldwork in Rwanda September 2015, September–November 2017, from Southwest Uganda August 2016, and Kakuma in Kenya September 2016.
94. Respondents cited the presence of worms and other parasitic insects that get under the children's skin, as well as other skin illnesses and respiratory illnesses such as asthma and bronchitis. Data collected from FGD from the Rwandan cases in September 2017 and from September to November 2017, from the Ugandan cases in August 2016 and from Kakuma in September 2016.
95. Amorós Elorduy, 'Mapping refugee spaces'; Amorós Elorduy, 'The impact of humanitarian shelter', 2017; Amorós Elorduy, 'Learning in and through the long-term refugee camps'.
96. Aside from spatial proposals, many of the suggestions from parents and children revolved around factors such as school fees, paying caregivers, having more toys, more scholastic materials and better food. However, I am centring this study on the spatial and material interventions only. Fieldwork in Rwanda September 2015, September–November 2017, from Southwest Uganda August 2016, and Kakuma in Kenya September 2016.
97. Chawla and Driskell, 'The Growing Up in Cities project', 2006; Riggio and Kilbane, 'The International Secretariat for Child-Friendly Cities', 2000, 201–5.
98. Freire, *Pedagogy of the Oppressed*.
99. Lynch and Banerjee, *Growing Up in Cities*.
100. UNESCO, 'Management of Social Transformations (MOST) Programme'.
101. The PAR participants in Kiziba were: (1) three recent graduates of architecture, developing a fellowship at the African Design Centre (ADC) based in Kigali; (2) eight humanitarian workers and camp managers involved in Kiziba's education and child protection programmes, (3) one member from MIDIMAR, two from UNHCR, two from ADRA, one from PLAN International, one from GHH and one from Handicap

International; (4) 11 *imigongo* artisans, three caregivers from GHH's *maternelle* and five community mobilisers; (5) refugee parents and young adults organised by PLAN International; (6) four young children from GHH's ECD initiatives; and (7) myself. In Kigeme, the PAR participants were: (1) the three architect fellows, three humanitarian workers and camp managers involved in Kigeme's HBECD delivery; (2) one member from MIDIMAR, one from UNHCR and one from ADRA; (3) five mother leaders who ran HBECDs and five community mobilisers; (4) refugee parents and young adults organised by PLAN International; and (5) myself.

102. This activity entailed the creation of murals made from cow dung, ash and mud with the participation of Rwandan artisans and refugee parents, caregivers, youth, and children.

103. The website was meant to make accessible some of the research findings to audiences far from the camps: students and researchers, humanitarian workers and institutions and also host governments and local authorities that had at that moment very little information about young children's learning and the built environments of these long-term camps.

104. Data collected through a multi-method qualitative approach on 5 September 2017.

105. In the early nineteenth century, King Karira decorated his own hut palace with this technique that uses the dung of young calves mixed with ash to create relief on the wall's surface. This is later painted with mud, lime and burnt aloe vera. *Imigongo* also means ridge, or elongated protrusion in Kinyarwanda. This art was later incorporated into the Banyarwanda kingdom and culture. After the Rwandan genocide, the technique practically disappeared. Kodumuki, 'History of imigongo'.

106. Prunier, *From Genocide to Continental War*.

107. Hamdi, *The Spacemaker's Guide to Big Change*, 79–82; Derr, Chawla and Mintzer, *Placemaking with Children and Youth*, 73–7.

108. This included: (1) presenting the idea to UNHCR, the *imigongo* artisans, the NGO workers and the refugee leadership; (2) asking MIDIMAR permission to access the camps and develop the murals in Kiziba; (3) organising funding through UCL Culture and the Beacon Bursary; and (4) putting together a team of nine *imigongo* artisans from Rwanda's Eastern province, three young architect graduates on a fellowship in Kigali, an English artist and a Spanish photographer.

109. Specifically, six mother leaders, six community mobilisers, two caregivers and six young people from the youth arts club. The participants from the youth arts club dropped out of the activities after the first two days of *imigongo* training. The youth arts club coordinator and the community mobilisers were unable to contact them to ask them why they left.

110. PLAN International was the NGO in charge of child protection – and by extension the CFS spaces – in the Congolese camps in Rwanda in 2017. Fieldwork in Kiziba from September to November 2017.

111. This topic became the entry point for the PID studio and guided the first two-week intensive workshop of the ADC fellows.

112. That was a total of approximately six walls, since most walls in the Kiziba are 12 square metres.

113. In mid-2018, due to heavy rainfall, one of the school buildings at the *maternelle* in quarter 4 was destroyed. However, the murals on the other locations are still standing, and the NGO in charge of the *maternelle* is looking for funds to replace the destroyed construction.

114. Feldman et al., 'Wisdom from the field'; Elliott and Kemp, 'Building social building'.

115. The young architects were Victor Ikaremye (a Rwandan graduate from the CST University of Rwanda), Lydia Kanakulya (a Ugandan graduate from Ardhi University in Dar es Salaam) and Moses Mawa (a South Sudanese graduate from the Juba University School of Architecture). I trained them on ethics, information procedures and consent forms, photography, film and recording techniques and authorisations, sample selection processes, FGD, questionnaire building and interview techniques. They were developing a fellowship at the ADC based in Kigali. The ADC fellow Moses Mawa had been a refugee, living in three different refugee camps in Northern Uganda for 10 years. Victor Iyakaremye and Lydia Kanakulya, despite living close to refugee camps, had never set foot in one and had very limited knowledge of life in the camps. Mawa noted how different life in the Rwandan camps was from the one he had lived in Northern Uganda.

116. I had to develop a syllabus, present my work to all the ADC fellows who could select my

topic amongst other potential research paths, prepare all the required authorisations and other paperwork to enter and develop research in the camps, and organise the logistics needed to make the whole process happen.

117. See, for example: Ager and Metzler, 'Child friendly spaces'; Metzler et al., 'Evaluation of child friendly spaces'; Wessells and Kostelny, 'Child friendly spaces', 2013.
118. The six criteria were: (1) safety and security, (2) accessibility, (3) sanitation, (4) stimulation, (5) cost effectiveness and (6) management and maintenance.
119. This incremental approach was based on: Hirano, 'Child friendly schools'.
120. The ADC fellows' and refugees' proposals could cost as little as US$500 and used materials available in the camp or in the nearby town of Kibuye.
121. ADRA stands for Adventist Development and Relief Agency.
122. Harrell-Bond, *Imposing Aid*, 3.
123. Social anthropologist Elizabeth Cooper describes young refugees' research fatigue: 'too many researchers had come in the past, asked their questions and left without ever reporting back to the research participants and without the refugees ever seeing the benefits of participating. Researchers are not the only guilty party in abusing refugees' cooperation: youths describe how humanitarian agencies sporadically invite their input to planning processes, but do not report back to participants on decisions or progress'. Cooper, 'What do we know about out-of-school youths?', 2005, 468.
124. Cooper, 466.
125. Pyles, 'Participation and other ethical considerations', 2015.
126. Data collected from the iterative workshops developed for the PID studio, from the initial inception session and the last meeting with camp management, and from informal conversations during the *imigongo* mural making during fieldwork trips to Kiziba, Kigeme and Mugombwa from 30 August to 15 September, 1–7 October and 5–11 November 2017.
127. Hamdi, *The Spacemaker's Guide to Big Change*; Derr, Chawla, and Mintzer, *Placemaking with Children and Youth*.
128. This refers to the refugees and their direct local hosts, the 18 research assistants, the three ADC fellows, the photographer, the English artist, the Spanish pedagogue, the 11 *imigongo* artisans, the camp management teams and the hundreds of NGO workers, other actors and me who have been involved in this PhD project to varying degrees.
129. Petti and Hilal, 'Architecture of exile'; Petti and Hilal, 'Decolonizing architecture art residency'; Maqusi, 'Space of refuge', 2017.
130. Ward, 'The child in the city', 1978; Ward and Fyson, *Streetwork: The Exploding School*.
131. ASA Studio, 'Early childhood facilities in refugee camps'.
132. Amorós Elorduy and Madete, 'Building refuge', 2020.
133. UNHCR, 'Uganda, comprehensive refugee response plan 2017'.
134. UNHCR, 'Rwanda country refugee response plan 2019–2020'.
135. Ward, 'The child in the city', 1978; Ward and Fyson, *Streetwork: The Exploding School*.

Conclusions | through the eyes of an architect

With this book, I try to bring nuance, contextualisation and empathy to the study and management of the long-term refugee camps in East Africa. I believe that it is empathy that will help to change mind-sets, decolonise humanitarian refugee assistance and its study, and ultimately improve the learning of millions of young children. As someone between the worlds of architecture, humanitarian aid and early childhood development (ECD), I hope that this book provides many practical learnings.

For starters, considering long-term camps as proto-urban may be more useful – for analytical and practical reasons – than merely seeing them as humanitarian spaces, limbo and spaces of exception. The effort presented in this book is a testament that the incorporation of

C.1

C.1 Children playing with bottle tops on the street. Kiziba refugee camp, September 2015. © Amorós Elorduy.

urban logics and assemblage thinking lens as a means to study and improve existing long-term refugee camps yields remarkable and useful results. In fact, gradually, academics, humanitarian practitioners and policymakers have been incorporating urban logics into refugee camp study and refugee assistance. For example, the new *Rwanda Country Refugee Response Plan 2019–2020* gears towards converting camps into villages,[1] which is in stark contrast to the country's early approaches that separated refugees from Rwandan nationals and deprived them of some of their freedoms. Acknowledging the power of the urban will hopefully continue to change human containment strategies at their core.

Moreover, considering long-term camps in their own right as different from recently established ones, valuing their urban-like characteristics and learning from their spatial qualities can shed light into their complex realities. Learning from the long-term camps can contribute to their transformation towards healthy human settlements and inform new humanitarian strategies. Ideally, this new perspective can improve the livelihoods of refugees and the surrounding communities.

Through an urban lens, the built environment gains centrality and agency. Treating the built environment as an active agent of camp life affords its inquiry and manipulation and gives planners, refugees and academics a relevant avenue to study and improve refugee assistance. Understanding the camps' growth patterns and having detailed, open-source and readily available spatial information might trigger more studies, improve their planning and management, and lead to more effective alternatives to them. One example of this is how the construction – and the appearance on maps – of formal ECD centres promotes awareness about ECD's relevance amongst refugees, direct local hosts, non-governmental organisations (NGOs), donors and local authorities. I expect that the maps, website and publications that I have developed might further enhance the discussion about the significance of the built and learning environments and about young children's education in refugee assistance triggering more locally led research.

Harnessing camps' spatial qualities can transform these settlements into positive and stimulating learning environments for young children. Understanding the built environment as an added educator for young children opens the door to applying the teachings of authors such as Ward,[2] Lynch[3] or Chawla[4] to the camps. Such a move can allow researchers and humanitarians to study the influence of the camps' physical environments on the lifelong learning of millions of children. It might give practitioners more tools to transform the camps from deprived and damaging into stimulating added educators.

Focusing on the built environment, it becomes evident that refugees are the leading builders of these settlements. Together with their direct local hosts, they appropriate and reproduce the camps,[5] particularly their shelters, commercial and religious facilities and many educational structures. Therefore, while the humanitarian system might be the de facto government of these settlements,[6] control over their spaces is shared with the refugees, their direct local hosts and numerous geopolitical, climatic and socio-economic actors. As refugees change their surroundings, they simultaneously adapt to those in a continuous co-modification. This co-modification is especially prevalent in the older and most resource-limited camps, where aid hand-outs and humanitarian control are rapidly dwindling.[7]

The built environment of the home predominantly but also of the streets and other common areas – what I classify as informal learning environments – are paramount to young children's learning. In these settings, children acquire skills, behaviours, values and knowledge through experience. This learning and these environments surpass the influence of formal and non-formal content-based learning environments. Unfortunately, these contexts have mostly adverse effects, which go unaccounted for, as the education cluster focuses principally on the formal ECD facilities.

Informal learning environments could improve with support to the refugee-led spatial upgrading. A child-friendly and stimulating home environment could be one where the pavements are dirt free, where there is enough light and ventilation, and where the sleeping areas are safe, secure and comfortable. WASH facilities could positively influence young children when well-lit at night, clean, secure and used only by small groups. Moreover, children will significantly benefit from child-friendly neighbourhoods where streets are safer and designed for those shorter than 95 centimetres tall, where smaller playgrounds and child-friendly spaces (CFSs) dot the landscape and where initiatives such as the home-based ECD (HBECD) in Kigeme and Mugombwa have dedicated spaces for child stimulation.

Non-formal and formal educational facilities will serve better those who attend them if children and their support networks take centre stage, thus becoming contextualised. A step to achieving that would be to consider, fund and support the already existing initiatives led by refugees and direct local hosts. These enterprises tend to give more weight to cultural upbringings, are smaller and are closer to the diverse communities.[8] Moreover, humanitarian NGOs could learn from these grass-roots initiatives and support existing Parent–Teacher Associations in the choice of location, the design and management of formal ECD facilities in case those are needed. Another avenue would be – as I have tested through the public interest design (PID) studio in Rwanda – to have local and regional designers, engineers, artists and other experts involved, and even leading, the design and construction of learning environments, always with the children's well-being and stimulation as the central goal.

Architecture can help to transform the long-term camps and create new alternatives to camps in order to cultivate more effectively an environment conducive to young children's learning, for example developing speculative actions based on the qualities of each specific camp, and developing interventions bearing in mind the six spatial attributes of the long-term camps – growing heterogeneity and complexity, co-functioning/interconnectedness, ever-becoming, porosity, land scarcity and weak soils, and isolation and proximity to the border. If people in charge of ECD – both humanitarians and refugees – can value architecture and see it as an opportunity and harness the camps' architectural qualities, if they practice meaningful participatory processes, it might be possible to convert the camps into 'schools without walls'.[9]

In my quest to unravel the long-term camp paradox, assemblage thinking has helped me substantially. It has revealed long-term camps as multi-authored, polyrhythmic, heterogeneous and ever-evolving proto-urban learning assemblages. It has exposed the heterogeneity of the encamped groups of individuals: some are dependent and passive, many are active and self-motivated, others are resourceful entrepreneurs, some are vulnerable and oppressed victims, others are perpetrators and looters, and many are energetic and hard-working.[10] Thinking through assemblage, the power and agency that refugees have becomes evident, which does not take away from the oppressive dominance that the humanitarian system/host governments assemblage imposes on them. In the long-term camps as in other urban settings, diverse levels and kinds of power and agency work simultaneously.

Using assemblage thinking, I have seen connections that might otherwise be missed, such as the camps' static and interactive spatial characteristics and the continuous spatial modifications that refugees lead. Acknowledging the constellation and overlapping of assemblages allows action on these, such as the murals we developed in Kiziba. It paves the way to create new and better assemblages such as those imagined by the students of architecture and the refugees during the PID studio in Kigeme and Mugombwa.

Contributing to research by architectural design—The series of which this volume is a part is instrumental to those involved in architecture with a social purpose. Practising architecture, I have discovered the value of using design as an avenue to investigate social matters. Developing research through design has helped the teams that I work with and me to evaluate our work better, connect with our clients and the users of our buildings better and understand their cultural, natural, social and political ecosystems better. The three-year-long research that feeds this book continued with that approach and aligned with refugee camp research ethics. It investigates what Barbara Harrell-Bond called the anti-participatory ideologies and practices of the humanitarian system.[11] It builds on the idea that research on the subject of refugees and migrant populations should, in addition to the principle of causing no harm, benefit academia, policy development and refugee livelihoods.[12,13]

Architectural tools have facilitated the translation and reassemblage of information into cartographic and pictorial representations of long-term refugee camps that did not exist before, and the collection of refugee accounts about the problems that young children face in the camps. For example, mapping and spatial analysis allowed the discovery of trends, patterns and particularities of the interactive and static spatial characteristics of the long-term camps in the region and their influence on young children's learning. The translation and interpretation qualities of tools such as models and photomontages have enabled and enhanced participatory processes. These instruments highlighted the relevance of space on young children's learning and brought this relevance to the current refugee-led spatial appropriations. The participatory action research (PAR) exercises that I present in this book demonstrate that architecture, low- and high-tech tools, art and crafts might allow the inclusion of various relevant actors in knowledge production cycles. Specifically, they afforded a collective process of spatial speculation testing the Lefebvrian notion of transduction[14] through the creation of *imigongo* murals, the representation of imagined and desired proposals in photomontages and the development of a PID studio in Kiziba, Kigeme and Mugombwa refugee camps to design CFSs and HBECD facilities.

The situated knowledges that I created with the research by architectural design approach are vital tools to question underlying assumptions and generate new information. Through participatory research, facilitated with design tools, I included voices that are usually marginalised, both non-human (the built environment) and human (refugees and students of architecture), in knowledge production cycles. Including these actors usually bereaved of agency highlights their role in the development of contextualised theory, policy and practice of refugee assistance and refugee education.

This type of approach to research and architecture focuses on the process rather than solely on the results. A relevant take on research by architectural design is, in my experience, that research per se can be impactful and meaningful in many and varied ways. Focusing attention on the process and considering its relevance and effects can prevent issues such as widespread research fatigue amongst refugees. Moreover, this focus enables the researcher to gauge the research team's influence on the results. The research team becomes part of the assemblages that it studies. The choices that a principal investigator makes and the relationships she or he has with research assistants, regulations, translations and translators, data dissemination, ethics and logistics all affect the results.

The approach that I have taken is not new. It has been widely applied in urban settlements across the globe.[15] It has even been used in refugee settlements in the Middle East.[16] It could be replicated in new and long-term camps elsewhere to decolonise refugee studies and refugee assistance further.

Situating refugee studies—In my quest to contribute – even to a slight degree, given my European background – to the decolonisation of the fields of architecture, ECD and refugee assistance, I made a special effort to help the careers and enhance the skills of young architects in the region. They were my research assistants throughout my architectural practice and my fieldwork. They have been invaluable collaborators. They might be involved in the future designing and building infrastructures or participating in drafting policy related to making better and safer places for refugees, their direct local hosts, as well as young children.

I also strove to include the voices of young refugee children living in encampment and their support networks meaningfully, highlighting their role in making the refugee camps and ECD, and harnessing their agency to trigger positive change on both fronts.

This book demonstrates that more locally and regionally led research is needed – research that could better navigate the socio-political dynamics of the East African camps. Such studies could contribute to further decolonising the research and practise of refugee assistance and should be encouraged. Contextualised studies by African universities and lead researchers could improve the understanding of the camps. Also, at the policy and theory level, there should be an effort to decolonise the field further. It is necessary to bring more voices into play, develop more situated knowledges and disseminate those. Some steps to achieve that could be to promote open-source publications, create accessible discussions and seminars, and move the centres of knowledge creation, collection and distribution closer to the refugee-hosting areas.

Research grounded on iterative, multi-stakeholder and participatory knowledge creation processes is necessary. Studies are needed that include local creative minds, and where – as this book has demonstrated – arts and crafts can work as a universal language and as tools to involve more actors and create change in the long-term refugee camps. Investigations need to take into account parents', caregivers' and children's perceptions, and acknowledge the whole built environment as a learning source. This is a research body that is mostly yet to be developed.

Looking for real alternatives to camps—Suppose refugee children are to have a fair take on their futures. In that case, the humanitarian system/host government assemblage should consider banning the physical confinement of refugees in contained and isolated areas – planned camps, settlements and special economic zones.

As politics and advocacy efforts work on that front, new approaches should be taken for those camps and containment spaces that already exist: the long-term camps. Moreover, practitioners should provide real alternatives to camps which do not rely on isolating and physically containing refugees.

From an architectural and urban standpoint, long-term camps could work as other urban hubs, placing relevance on the built environment with a body in charge of its urban and architectural development, with a holistic view of the whole. Power and responsibilities should be distributed and should include refugees, their direct local hosts and the local authorities. That does not mean that assistance to the vulnerable or international support should stop. Instead, power dynamics should change, as it happens in urban settlements across the globe.

With my work, I do not intend to provide linear solutions to clearly defined problems. I want to offer situated bits of knowledge that might be useful to policy and practice on refugee ECD, to the transformation of long-term camps in East Africa and also to research on refugee studies and the built environment. For example, could the harnessing of the long-term camps' spatial characteristics highlighted in this book help envision a humanitarian strategy without the forceful containment of people? An approach that promotes a participatory, decentralised and contextualised assistance? That promotes real alternatives to camps? Could the collaboration between local creative minds – higher education institutions for example – humanitarian organisations and refugees improve and contextualise assistance as we did with our PAR exercises? Furthermore, could the support to already existing refugee-led strategies and interventions contribute to better housing, child-friendly education and opportunities for both refugees and hosts?

More situated knowledges – and less overarching and generalising standard solutions – are what, in my opinion, will get us to an increasingly child-friendly and situated approach to housing and educational infrastructures in long-term camps and the rethinking of spatial strategies for refugee assistance.

This book presents an empathic approach to knowledge creation and a nuanced image of seven long-term refugee camps in the East African Rift. It opens up the possibility for more contextualised responses to the spatial, socio-political and educational challenges they present. It has shown that ECD initiatives, camp planning and maintenance have the potential to affect young children's lifelong learning positively. However, this potential is now underused. I hope that the avenues that I have presented here to harness the built environment's potential as a positive added educator for young children are useful and used.

Notes

1. UNHCR, 'Rwanda country refugee response plan 2019–2020'.
2. Ward and Fyson, *Streetwork: The Exploding School*; Ward, 'The child in the city', 1978.
3. Lynch and Banerjee, *Growing Up in Cities*.
4. Chawla, *Growing up in an Urbanising World*; Chawla and Malone, 'Neighbourhood quality in children's eyes'; Derr, Chawla and Mintzer, *Placemaking with Children and Youth*.
5. Spatial appropriations take place through what Asef Bayat calls 'quiet encroachment of the ordinary', AbdouMaliq Simone and James Scott call 'everyday resistance', Teresa Caldeira calls 'peripheral urbanism' and Edgar Pieterse calls 'radical incrementalism'. Bayat, 'From "dangerous classes" to "quiet rebels"', 2000; Scott, 'Beyond the war of words'; Simone, 'On cityness'; Pieterse, *City Futures*.
6. Slaughter and Crisp, 'New issues in refugee research'.
7. IRIN, 'Food Aid 2018'.
8. Amorós Elorduy, 'Learning in and through the long-term refugee camps'.
9. Ward, 'The child in the city', 1978; Ward and Fyson, *Streetwork: The Exploding School*.
10. Slaughter and Crisp, 'New issues in refugee research'; UNHCR, 'Emergency handbook. Camp planning standards. (Planned settlements)'.
11. Harrell-Bond, *Imposing Aid*, 3.
12. Turton, 'Refugees, forced resettlers and other forced migrants'.
13. Jacobsen and Landau, 'The dual imperative in refugee research', 2003.
14. Lefebvre, *Le Droit a La Ville Suivi de Espace et Politique*.
15. Derr, Chawla and Mintzer, *Placemaking with Children and Youth*; Unt and Bell, 'The impact of small-scale design interventions', 2014; Hamdi, *The Spacemaker's Guide to Big Change*.
16. Ziliacus, 'With the Jarahieh Refugee School'; Petti and Hilal, 'Architecture of exile'; Maqusi, 'Space of refuge', 2017.

Glossary

Assemblage thinking—Gilles Deleuze and Félix Guattari presented the assemblage theory in 1987 with the publication of *Mille Plateaux: Capitalisme et Schizophrénie*. Assemblage thinking rejects the interpretation of the social and natural worlds as made up of finite and definable entities organised in fixed, linear, hierarchical and stable structures. It considers conceptualisation a reductionist generalisation and a synthesis to facilitate analysis.[1] Assemblage theory proposes instead that natural and social formations are assemblages of complex configurations that are interrelated, composed of other complex configurations and in turn create more extended configurations. [2]

Relativism is assemblage thinking's main criticism. However, it has allowed me detail and contextualisation, opening the door for the creation of situated bits of knowledge. I use assemblage thinking as a post-structural framework for analysing social complexity, emphasising non-linear approaches to social systems based on mutability, exchangeability and interconnectedness to contend both totalising and relativist discourses.[3] The assemblage lens becomes emancipatory, rendering visible diverse levels and kinds of power and agency, where refugees' power and agency does not take away from the oppressive dominance that the humanitarian system/host governments assemblage imposes on them.

Built environment—In this book, I define the term 'built environment' as the human-made physical structures created to influence human activities.

Co-constitutive—'Co-constitutive' is when two or more events, actors or elements are necessary for each other's creation and structure. One is necessary for the others to exist and be organised in a specific way. In our case, camp inhabitants and camp spaces are co-constitutive; as they modify each other, they adapt to each other.

Early childhood development—I use the acronym 'ECD' to refer to early childhood development from conception through to six years of age in four main domains: socio-emotional, cognitive, physical and language development. The sustainable development goals (SDGs) of the United Nations (UN) endorsed these four domains in 2015.[4] As refugee assistance tightens its connection with development efforts,[5] this interpretation of ECD is likely to define refugee ECD for at least the next 10 years.[6] ECD initiatives in refugee camps ideally include the supply of nutritious food, health care, shelter, psychosocial care and early learning education, as well as the provision of services to pregnant and lactating women, parents and other caregivers. For this research, I am focusing only on the 'early learning' piece of the ECD framework.[7] Despite this conscious specificity, I nonetheless still use the acronym 'ECD' because of its prevalence amongst the education cluster[8] leads on ECD (United Nations Children's Fund (UNICEF) and Save the Children), and education implementing partners (IPs)[9] working in refugee camps.[10]

Ecosystemic—This term emphasises the interaction between the human and non-human actors of a setting: the individual and the family, and the social, urban and natural contexts. Originally, the term was used by Urie Bronfenbrenner and focused on the environment as a context for child development. It represented a broader conception of human development where the individual is as important as the context (spatial, temporal and natural) where it develops. The term emphasises interrelatedness and interdependency.

Long-term refugee camp—I define 'long-term refugee camps' as those that have lasted for more than three years and that host more than 5,000 refugees from 'protracted refugee situations' as defined by the United Nations High Commissioner for Refugees (UNHCR) in 2004.[11] They are not temporal emergency settings. According to a study made in 1990, 117 camps had been established since UNHCR first started intervening in the continent, and of those, 59 were still standing.[12] From the 1990s to date, in East Africa, camps have only been dismantled if requested by the host country. This is partly due to the protracted nature of some conflicts, as well as the camps being reoccupied over time by different waves of refugees stemming from diverse countries and conflicts.

Multi-scalar—Social and natural phenomenon take place and are constituted on different scales. They might act differently on each of those scales; continuity on one scale can be interruption at another. Scales can be spatial, temporal or socio-economic. Doing a multi-scalar analysis of refugee camps and their inhabitants allows a deeper and richer understanding of a phenomenon – refugee camps – that has historically been quite flat and one-sided. It might help in the decolonisation of the refugee camp studies to bring in transdisciplinarity and a higher variety of voices.

Polyrhythmic—The term 'polyrhythmic' in this book illustrates the simultaneous (two or more rhythms present) in the life of a camp – the daily rhythms of life, the rhythms found in the spatial patterns and plans of the camps and the diverse rhythms of lifelong learning that children experience.

Proto-urban—I use the term 'urban' to mean 'within or of distinctly demarcated human settlements'. I specifically use the term 'proto-urban', borrowing from Manuel Herz,[13] since the political community in these settings is not fully formed, and there is no real refugee representation in the camps' management. At present, both transnational humanitarian organisations and national sovereign states share the governance and the management of these spaces and people. The current structure prevents refugees' political participation within the nation states that host them and the accountability of the humanitarian organisations that de facto govern them. These camps are not a polis, not yet.[14] Besides, despite the move to recognise these as not just 'humanitarian' spaces or 'limbo', the humanitarian system/host government assemblage is reluctant to admit them as urban. That recognition could legitimise these spaces as permanent – as 'cities' – and their inhabitants as citizens.

Radical incrementalism—Professor Edgar Pieterse of the African Center for Cities coined the term 'radical incrementalism', meaning:

'Surreptitious, sometimes overt, and multiple small revolutions that at unanticipated and unexpected moments galvanise into more profound ruptures that accelerate tectonic shifts of the underlying logics of domination.... A disposition and sensibility that believes in deliberate actions of social transformation but through a multiplicity of processes and imaginations, none of which assumes or asserts a primary significance over other struggles'.[15]

Refugee—In this book, the term 'refugee' aligns with the definitions found in the 1951 Convention Relating to the Status of Refugees and the subsequent 1967 Protocol. Article I, points 1 and 2, define a 'refugee' as:

'... every person who, owing to a well-founded fear of being persecuted for reasons of race, religion, nationality, membership of a particular social group or political opinion, is outside the country of his nationality and is unable or, owing to such fear, is unwilling to avail himself of the protection of that country, or who, not having a nationality and being outside the country of his former habitual residence as a result of such events, is unable or, owing to such fear, is unwilling to return to it.... Every person who, owing to external aggression, occupation, foreign domination or events seriously disturbing public order in either part or the whole of his country of origin or nationality, is compelled to leave his place of habitual residence in order to seek refuge in another place outside his country of origin or nationality'.

African states had been using the term 'refugee' even before the signature of the 1969 Convention Governing the Specific Aspects of Refugee Problems in Africa.

Right to the city—This notion coined by philosopher and sociologist Henri Lefebvre discussed how city space and inhabitants are co-constitutive and use their agency to modify each other.[16] Furthermore, Lefebvre explained space as a complex social construction based on socially produced values and meanings that affected spatial practices of the everyday and the inhabitants' perceptions.[17]

Transduction—Henry Lefebvre developed 'transduction' as a methodology aimed 'to encourage the creation of "experimental utopias". Framed by existing reality, introduce "rigour in invention and knowledge in utopia" as a way of avoiding "irresponsible idealism"'.[18]

Urban turn—The 'urban turn' is a relatively new study avenue in refugee camp studies. It conceives camps as what I call proto-urban spaces. Post-structuralist transdisciplinary authors are the leading proponents of this branch of works, which includes – in addition to humanities and social sciences academics – geographers, architects and urban planners since the early 2000s. It includes a relevant representation of academics who aim at decolonising the field.[19] Urban turn works are especially prevalent in highly visible cases, such as the Palestinian camps in Lebanon, and bring to the forefront the complexity, variability and overlapping authorships of the long-term camp spaces. The urban turn approach renders visible human and non-human actors largely bereft of agency and overlooked under discourses of humanitarian spaces and spaces of exception.

Young children's learning—I define 'young children's learning' as the concepts, skills, values, knowledge and behaviour patterns that children acquire. Content-based direct learning, incidental or indirect learning, and learning through experiencing the human–human, human–built environment and human–natural environment interactions are different means to assimilate knowledge.

Notes

1. Anderson and McFarlane, 'Assemblage and geography', 2011, 124–7.
2. Deleuze and Parnet, Dialogues II, in de Landa, *Assemblage Theory*, 2016, 1.
3. 'Both assemblage thinking and ANT have much to say about the spatial dimensions of power and politics. That is because both approaches are concerned with why orders emerge in particular ways, how they hold together, somewhat precariously, how they reach across or mold space and how they fall apart'. Müller, 'Assemblages and actor-network', 2015, 27.
4. In 2016, the international community committed to the SDGs, in which ECD was explicitly mentioned in target 4.2. This target states that by 2030, countries should 'ensure that all girls and boys have access to quality early childhood development, care and pre-primary education so that they are ready for primary education'. Global Education Cluster, 'Global education cluster 2015 report'; Global Education Cluster, 'Education cluster strategic plan 2015 to 2018'; Woodhead, 'Early childhood development in the SDGs', 6.
5. Dryden-Peterson, 'Refugee education: A global review', 478.
6. Global Education Cluster, 'Education cluster strategic plan 2015 to 2018'.
7. For more information about the ECD framework as understood by the United Nations Children's Fund (UNICEF) and the United Nations Educational, Scientific and Cultural Organization (UNESCO) and of the different definitions of ECD in emergencies, see: Woodhead, 'Early childhood development in the SDGs'; Cappa, 'The formative years', 4; UNICEF, 'Building better brains', 2014.
8. United Nations Office for the Coordination of Humanitarian Affairs clusters are 'groups of humanitarian organizations, including but not limited to the UN, in each of the main sectors of humanitarian action'. OCHA, 'United Nations Office for the Coordination of Humanitarian Affairs'.
9. IPs are public and non-public entities to which the United Nations entrust resources (funds and materials) to implement programme activities. UN Joint Inspection Unit, 'Review of the management of implementing partners in United Nations system organizations'.
10. UNESCO's conception of ECD has its foundations in four pillars established in 1996: (1) socio-emotional, (2) cognitive, (3) physical and (4) language development. UNICEF's conception of ECD is guided by six developmental domains that were established in 2008: (1) language, (2) cognitive, (3) physical, (4) social, (5) emotional and (6) approaches to learning.

Both UNESCO's pillars and UNICEF's domains encompass Gardner's theory of the Seven Intelligences developed throughout a person's life: (1) interpersonal, (2) intrapersonal, (3) logical-mathematical, (4) bodily-kinaesthetic, (5) musical, (6) linguistic and (7) spatial.

11. The UNHCR defines 'protracted refugee situations' as 'refugee populations of 25,000 persons or more who have been in exile for five or more years in developing countries without immediate prospects for implementation of durable solutions'; 'in protracted situations, refugee populations have moved beyond the emergency phase – where the focus is on life-saving protection and assistance – but cannot expect durable solutions in the foreseeable future'. UNHCR, 'Protracted refugee situations: Revisiting the problem', 2008; UNHCR, 'Protracted refugee situations: The search for practical solutions', 105–97; UNHCR, 'Protracted refugee situations', 2004.
12. Stein and Clark, 'Refugee integration and older refugee settlements in Africa'.
13. Herz uses this term to refer to the long-term refugee camps in the Western Sahara. Herz, 'Refugee camps of the Western Sahara', 2013, 383.
14. Jansen, 'The accidental city', 2009, 11–2; Agier and Lecadet, *Un Monde de Camps*; Feldman, 'What is a camp?', 2014, 244–52; Jansen, 'The protracted refugee camp', 2016.
15. Pieterse, *City Futures*, 6.
16. Lefebvre, *Le Droit à La Ville*.
17. Lefebvre, *La Production de l'Espace*.
18. Lefebvre, *Writings on Cities*, in Petcou and Petrescu, 'R-URBAN or how to co-produce a resilient city', 2015, 256.
19. Paraphrasing cultural anthropologist Bram Jansen, I call the 'urban turn' the epistemic and ontological shift that occurred in refugee camp studies that associated long-term refugee camps with urbanisation. The inclusion of geographers, architects, urban planners and urban theorists into the study of refugee camps brought with it this new perspective. Jansen, 'The protracted refugee camp,' 2015.

Acronyms

AAH	Action Africa Help
ADRA	Adventist Development and Relief Agency
ANT	actor-network theory
ASA	Active Social Architecture
CARE	Cooperative for Assistance and Relief Everywhere
CFS	child-friendly spaces
DRC	Democratic Republic of Congo
ECD	early childhood development
EFA	Education for All
HBECD	home-based early childhood development
IP	implementing partners
MIDIMAR	Ministry of Disaster Management and Refugee Affairs (Rwanda)
MOST	Management of Social Transformations and the Environment
NCCK	National Council of Churches Kenya
NGO	non-governmental organisation
OCHA	United Nations Office for the Coordination of Humanitarian Affairs
OPM	Office of the Prime Minister (Uganda)
PAR	participatory action research
PID	public interest design
SDGs	sustainable development goals
UN	United Nations
UNESCO	United Nations Educational, Scientific and Cultural Organization
UNHCR	United Nations High Commissioner for Refugees
UNICEF	United Nations Children's Fund
WASH	water and sanitation

Bibliography

Abourahme, Nasser. 'Assembling and spilling-over: Towards an "ethnography of cement" in a Palestinian refugee camp'. *International Journal of Urban and Regional Research* 39 (2015): 200–17.

Abourahme, Nasser, and Sandi Hilal. 'The production of space, political subjectification and the folding of polarity: The case of Deheishe Camp, Palestine'. Campus in Camps, 2008. Accessed 17 November 2020, http://www.campusincamps.ps/wp-content/uploads/2012/12/Nasser-Abourahme-and-Sandi-Hilal_Deheishe-Paper.pdf.

Agamben, Giorgio. *Homo Sacer. Sovereign Power and Bare Life*. Stanford, CA: Stanford University Press, 1998.

Ager, Alastair, and Janna Metzler. 'Child friendly spaces: A structured review of the current evidence-base.' Uxbridge: World Vision International, 2012. Accessed 17 November 2020. https://www.wvi.org/sites/default/files/CFS%20Literature%20Review%20final%20Aug%202012.pdf.

Agier, Michel. 'Afterword: What contemporary camps tell us about the world to come'. *Humanity: An International Journal of Human Rights, Humanitarianism, and Development* 7 (2016): 459–68.

Agier, Michel. 'Between war and city: Towards an urban anthropology of refugee camps'. *Ethnography* 3 (2002): 317–41.

Agier, Michel, and Clara Lecadet. *Un Monde de Camps*. Paris: La Découverte, 2014.

Amorós Elorduy, Nerea. 'East African refugee camps as learning assemblages: The built environment as an educational resource for encamped young children in the East African Rift'. University College London, 2018. Accessed 17 November 2020. https://discovery.ucl.ac.uk/id/eprint/10057316/.

Amorós Elorduy, Nerea. 'The impact of humanitarian shelter and settlements on child protection'. *Forced Migration Review* 55 (2017): 41–3.

Amorós Elorduy, Nerea. 'Learning in and through the long-term refugee camps in the East African Rift'. In *Refugee in a Moving World: Refugee and migrant journeys across disciplines*, edited by Elena Fiddian-Qasmiyeh, 362–81. London: UCL Press, 2020.

Amorós Elorduy, Nerea. 'Mapping refugee spaces'. Mapping Refugee Spaces, 2017. Accessed

17 November 2020. https://www.mappingrefugeespaces.com.
Amorós Elorduy, Nerea, and Etta Madete. 'Building refuge'. *The Architectural Review* no.1477 (2020): 36–41.
Anderson, Allison and Marian Hodgkin. 'The creation and development of the global IASC education cluster.' Paper commissioned for the EFA Global Monitoring Report 2011, *The hidden crisis: Armed conflict and education*. Paris: UNESCO, 2010.
Anderson, Ben, and Colin McFarlane. 'Assemblage and geography'. *Area* 43 (2011): 124–7.
Appadurai, Arjun. 'Grassroots globalization and research imagination'. *Public Culture* 12 (2000): 1–19.
ASA Studio. 'Early childhood facilities in refugee camps'. 2013. Accessed 17 November 2020. http://www.activesocialarchitecture.com/refugee-camps-educ.
AVSI, and InfoAid. 'Child protection KAP survey in Rwandan refugee camps.' Milan: AVSI, 2013. Accessed 17 November 2020. https://www.avsi.org/upload/publication/0/24.pdf?_636348590910931508.
Ayiemba, Elias H. O. 'Refugees in post-conflict reconstruction: A study of Kakuma and Dadaab refugees in Kenya'. In *Conference on African Transnational and Return Migration in the Context of North–South Relations*, 29–30. Coventry, UK: University of Warwick, 2009.
Bagenda, Emmanuel, Angela Naggaga and Elliott Smith. 'Land problems in Nakivale settlement and the implications for refugee protection in Uganda'. Refugee Law Project Working Paper 8, 2003. Accessed 17 November 2020. https://www.refugeelawproject.org/files/working_papers/RLP.WP08.pdf.
Bakewell, Oliver. 'Repatriation and self-settled refugees in Zambia: Bringing solutions to the wrong problems'. *Journal of Refugee Studies* 13 (2000): 356–73.
Ban, Shigeru. 'Paper emergency shelters for UNHCR – Byumba refugee camp, Rwanda, 1999'. Shigeru Ban Architects. Disaster Relief Projects, 1999. Accessed 17 November 2020. http://www.shigerubanarchitects.com/works/1999_paper-emergency-shelter/index.html.
Barbelet, Veronique, Jessica Hagen-Zanker, Eva Ludi, Freddie Carver and Dirk Willem te Velde. 'How to ensure Ethiopia's "Jobs Compact" works for refugees'. Overseas Development Institute, 2018. Accessed 17 November 2020. https://www.odi.org/blogs/10716-how-ensure-ethiopia-s-jobs-compact-works-refugees.
Basiime, Felix. '6 injured as refugees clash with locals in Kyegegwa'. *Daily Monitor Uganda*, 23 November 2017. Accessed 17 November 2020. http://www.monitor.co.ug/News/National/6-injured-as-refugees-clash-with-locals-in-Kyegegwa/688334-4200532-3ef8lt/index.html.
Bauman, Zygmunt. 'In the lowly nowherevilles of liquid modernity: Comments on and around Agier'. *Ethnography* 3 (2002): 343–9.

Bayat, Asef. 'From "dangerous classes" to "quiet rebels": Politics of the urban subaltern in the Global South'. *International Sociology* 15 (2000): 533–57.

Bayat, Asef. 'The quiet encroachment of the ordinary'. *The Chimumrenga Chronic* 3 (2007): 1–8.

Berlanda, Toma. 'Umujyi: Cities and human settlements in Rwanda'. Proceedings of *Sustainable Futures: Architecture and Urbanism in the Global South*. Kampala, Uganda, 27 – 30 June 2012, 136–41. Accessed 17 November 2020. http://www.sfc2012.org/berlanda.pdf.

Betts, Alexander, Gil Loescher and James Milner, eds. *The United Nations High Commissioner for Refugees (UNHCR): The politics and practice of refugee protection*. 2nd ed. London: Routledge, 2012.

Betts, Alexander, Louise Bloom, Josiah Kaplan and Josiah Naohiko. *Refugee Economies: Forced displacement and development*. Oxford: Oxford University Press, 2016.

Betts, Alexander, and Naohiko Omata. *Refugee Economies: Rethinking popular assumptions*. Oxford: Refugee Studies Centre, University of Oxford, 2015.

Bonta, Mark, and John Protevi. *Deleuze and Geophilosophy: A guide and glossary*. Edinburgh, UK: Edinburgh University Press, 2004.

Bronfenbrenner, Urie. 'Contexts of child rearing: Problems and prospects'. *American Psychologist* 34 (1979): 844–50.

Bronfenbrenner, Urie. *The Ecology of Human Development: Experiments by nature and design*. Cambridge, MA: Harvard University Press, 1979.

Bühmann, Dörthe, and Barbara Trudell. 'Mother tongue matters: Local language as a key to effective learning'. Paris: UNESCO Division for the Promotion of Basic Education, Education Sector, 2008.

Bush, Kenneth David, and Diana Saltarelli, eds. *The Two Faces of Education in Ethnic Conflict: Towards a peacebuilding education for children*. Florence, Italy: UNICEF Innocenti Research Centre, 2000.

Caldeira, Teresa P. R. 'Peripheral urbanization: Transversal logics, and politics in cities of the Global South'. *Society and Space* 35 (2016): 3–20.

Cappa, Claudia. 'The formative years: UNICEF's work on measuring early childhood development'. New York: UNICEF Data & Analytics Section Division of Policy and Strategy, 2014.

CARE International. 'A model beginning: CARE's early childhood development for Rwanda's most vulnerable children'. Geneva: CARE International, 2015.

Castle-Miller, Michael. 'The law and policy of refugee cities: Special economic zones for migrants'. *Chapman Law Review* 21 (2018): 303.

Chambers, Robert. 'Hidden losers? The impact of rural refugees and refugee programs on poorer hosts'. *International Migration Review* 20 (1986): 245–63.

Chambers, Robert. 'Rural refugees in Africa: What the eye does not see'. *Disasters* 3 (1979): 381–92.

Chawla, Louise. *Growing Up in an Urbanising World*. London: Routledge, 2001.

Chawla, Louise. 'Growing Up in Cities: A report on research under way'. *Environment and Urbanization* 9 (1997): 247–52.

Chawla, Louise, and David Driskell. 'The Growing Up in Cities project'. *Journal of Community Practice* 14 (2006): 107–23.

Chawla, Louise, and Karen Malone. 'Neighbourhood quality in children's eyes'. In *Children in the City: Home neighbourhood and community*, edited by Pia Christensen and Margaret O'Brien, 118–42. London: RoutledgeFalmer, 2003.

Chiles, Prue. 'The classroom as an evolving landscape." In *Children's Spaces*, edited by Mark Dudek, 101–13. London: Architectural Press, 2005.

Chkam, Hakim. 'Aid and the perpetuation of refugee camps: The case of Dadaab in Kenya 1991–2011'. *Refugee Survey Quarterly* 35 (2016): 79–97.

Christensen, Pia, and Margaret O'Brien, eds. *Children in the City: Home neighbourhood and community*. London: RoutledgeFalmer, 2003.

Consultative Group on Early Childhood Care and Development, and INEE. 'The path of most resilience: ECCD in emergencies principles and practice'. Paris: UNESCO, 2010.

Coombs, Philip H. *World Educational Crisis: A systems approach*. New York: Oxford University Press, 1968.

Coombs, Philip H., and Manzoor Ahmed. 'Attacking rural poverty: How nonformal education can help'. Washington, D.C.: International Council for Educational Development and World Bank, 1975. Accessed 6 April 20201. http://documents1.worldbank.org/curated/en/656871468326130937/pdf/multi-page.pdf.

Cooper, Elizabeth. 'What do we know about out-of-school youths? How participatory action research can work for young refugees in camps'. *Compare: A Journal of Comparative and International Education* 35 (2005): 463–77.

Crawford, Nicholas, John Cosgrave and Irina Mosel. '10 things to know about refugees and displacement'. Overseas Development Institute and the Humanitarian Policy Group, Policy Brief. London, 2015.

Crawford, Nicholas, John Cosgrave, Simone Haysom and Nadine Walicki. 'Protracted displacement: Uncertain paths to self-reliance in exile'. Overseas Development Institute and the Humanitarian Policy Group, Commissioned Report. London, 2015.

Crawley, Heaven. 'Why jobs in special economic zones won't solve the problems facing the world's refugees'. The Conversation, 2017. Accessed 17 November 2020. https://theconversation.com/why-jobs-in-special-economic-zones-wont-solve-the-problems-facing-the-worlds-refugees-75249.

Crisp, Jeff. 'Forced displacement in Africa: Dimensions, difficulties, and policy directions'. *Refugee Survey Quarterly* 29 (2010): 1–27.

Crisp, Jeff. 'A state of insecurity: The political economy of violence in refugee-populated areas of Kenya'. *African Affairs* 99 (2000): 601–632.

Daley, Patricia. 'Refugees and underdevelopment in Africa: The case of Barundi refugees in Tanzania'. PhD Thesis submitted in The Faculty of Anthropology and Geography, University of Oxford Trinity Term, St Anthony's College, 1989.

David, Thomas G., and Carol Simon Weinstein. 'The built environment and children's development'. In *Spaces for Children: The built environment and child development*, edited by Thomas G. David and Carol Simon Weinstein, 3–18. New York: Plenum Press, 1987.

David, Thomas G., and Carol Simon Weinstein, eds. *Spaces for Children: The built environment and child development*. New York: Plenum Press, 1987.

Deleuze, Gilles, and Felix Guattari. *A Thousand Plateaus*, translated by Brian Massumi. Minneapolis: University of Minnesota Press, 1987.

De Landa, Manuel. *Assemblage Theory*. Edinburg: Edinburg University Press, 2016.

Derr, Victoria, Louise Chawla and Mara Mintzer. *Placemaking with Children and Youth*. New York: New York University Press, 2018.

Dewey, John. 'Experience and education'. *The Educational Forum* 50 (1986): 241–52.

Diken, Bülent. 'From refugee camps to gated communities: Biopolitics and the end of the city'. *Citizenship Studies* 8 (2004): 83–106.

Diken, Bülent, and Carsten B. Laustsen. 'The camp'. *Geografiska Annaler, Series B: Human Geography* 88 (2006): 443–52.

Diken, Bülent, and Carsten B. Laustsen. *The Culture of Exception: Sociology facing the camp*. Abingdon, UK: Routledge, 2005.

Dovey, Kim, and Ross King. 'Forms of informality: Morphology and visibility of informal settlements'. *Built Environment* 37 (2011): 11–29.

Dryden-Peterson, Sarah. 'Refugee education: A global review'. Geneva: UNHCR Policy Development and Evaluation Service (PDES), 2011.

Dryden-Peterson, Sarah. 'Refugee education: The crossroads of globalization'. *Educational Researcher* 45 (2016): 473–82.

Dudek, Mark. *Kindergarten Architecture: Space for the imagination*. 2nd ed. London: Spon Press, 2000.

Elliott, Emily Roush, and Leah Faulk Kemp. 'Building social building: Public interest design as a catalyst for change'. In *Globalizing Architecture: Flows and disruptions*, edited by John Stuart and Mabel Wilson, 411–8. Washington, DC: ACSA, 2014.

Emuria, Lotethiro Peter. 'Clashes between refugees and host communities: The case study of Kakuma Refugee Camp, 1992–2013'. Masters thesis, University of Nairobi, 2015. Accessed 17 November 2020. http://erepository.uonbi.ac.ke/handle/11295/93215.

Ennead, Ennead Lab, UNHCR, and Stanford University. 'Rethinking refugee communities'. Ennead Lab, 2015. Accessed 17 November 2020. http://www.enneadlab.org/projects/rethinking-refugee-communities.

Evans, Gary W. 'The environment of childhood poverty'. *American Psychologist* 59 (2004): 77.

Evans, Gary W., and Susan Saegert. 'Residential crowding in the context of inner city poverty'. In *Theoretical Perspectives in Environment-Behavior Research*, edited by Seymour Wapner, Jack Demick, C. Takiji Yamamoto and Hiroufmi Minami, 247–67. New York: Springer, 2000.

Fafunwa, Aliu B. 'Education in the mother tongue: A Nigerian experiment'. *Journal of African Studies* 1 (1974): 285.

Feldman, Ilana. 'What is a camp? Legitimate refugee lives in spaces of long-term displacement'. *Geoforum* 66 (2014): 244–52.

Feldman, Roberta, Sergio Palleroni, David Perkes and Bryan Bell. 'Wisdom from the field: Public interest design architecture in practice. A guide to public interest practices in architecture'. Washington: American Institute of Architects, College of Fellows, 2014.

Feldman, Sara, Meredith Hunter, Karen Jacobsen, Nicholas Crawford, John Cosgrave, Simone Haysom, Nadine Walicki, Humanitarian Policy Group and Way Forward. 'The failure of self-reliance in refugee settlements'. *POLIS Journal* 33 (2013): 4.

Freire, Paulo. *Education for Critical Consciousness*. London: Continuum, 1973.

Freire, Paulo. *Pedagogy of the Oppressed*. 30th anniversary ed. New York: Continuum, 2006.

Fresia, Marion. 'Performing repatriation? The role of refugee aid in shaping new beginnings in Mauritania'. *Transition and Justice: Negotiating the Terms of New Beginnings in Africa* 45 (2014): 41–63.

Fresia, Marion, and Andreas Von Kanel. 'Beyond space of exception? Reflections on the camp through the prism of refugee schools'. *Journal of Refugee Studies* 29 (2015): 250–72.

Gale, Lacey Andrews. 'The invisible refugee camp: Durable solutions for Boreah "residuals" in Guinea'. *Journal of Refugee Studies* 21 (2008): 537–52.

Gardner, Tom. 'Beneath the surface of Uganda's "exemplary" refugee settlement, tensions simmer'. Reuters, 2016. Accessed 17 November 2020. https://www.reuters.com/article/us-uganda-refugees-landrights/be ... andas-exemplary-refugee-settlement-tensions-simmer-idUSKBN13A1UW.

Global Education Cluster. 'Education cluster strategic plan 2015 to 2018'. Geneva: Global Education Cluster, 2015.

Global Education Cluster. 'Global education cluster 2015 report'. Geneva: Global Education Cluster, 2015.

Gottfried, Allen W., and Adele Eskeles Gottfried. 'Home environment and cognitive development in young children of middle-socioeconomic-status families'. In *Home Environment and Early Cognitive Development: Longitudinal research*, edited by Allen

W. Gottfried, 57–115. Orlando, Florida: Academic Press, 1984.

Gottwald, Martin. 'Burden sharing and refugee protection'. In *The Oxford Handbook of Refugee and Forced Migration Studies*, edited by Elena Fiddian-Qasmiyeh, Gil Loescher, Katy Long and Nando Sigona, 1–16. Oxford: Oxford University Press, 2014.

Government of Rwanda, and UNDP. '2014 National human development report. Decentralisation and human development: Accelerating socio-economic transformation and sustaining accountable governance'. Kigali: Government of Rwanda, 2015.

Government of Uganda. 'Uganda: Control of Alien Refugees Act, Cap. 64 of 1960'. *Laws of Uganda* Vol. 2, 1960. Accessed 8 April 2021. https://www.refworld.org/cgi-bin/texis/vtx/rwmain/opendocpdf.pdf?reldoc=y&docid=544e48d84.

Government of Uganda, UN Uganda and World Bank. 'REHOPE – Refugee and host population empowerment: Strategic framework – Uganda'. Kampala: Government of Uganda, 2017. Accessed 6 April 2021. https://data2.unhcr.org/en/documents/details/64166.

Grbac, Peter. 'Civitas, polis, and urbs: Reimagining the refugee camp as the city'. Working Papers Series No. 96 (2013): 1–36. The Refugee Studies Centre, University of Oxford. Accessed 5 April 2021. https://www.refworld.org/pdfid/55c9f3504.pdf.

Guattari, Félix, and Gilles Deleuze. 'Introduction: Rhizome'. In *A Thousand Plateaus: Capitalism and schizophrenia*, trans. Brian Massumi, 3–25. Minneapolis: University of Minnesota Press, 1987.

Guyatt, Helen, Flavia Della Rosa and Jenny Spencer. 'Refugees vulnerability study Kakuma, Kenya'. World Food Program, United Nations High Commissioner for Refugees and Kimetrica, 2016.

Halldén, Gunilla. 'Children's views of family, home and house'. In *Children in the City: Home neighbourhood and community*, edited by Pia Christensen and Margaret O'Brien, 29–46. London: RoutledgeFalmer, 2003.

Hamdi, Nabeel. *The Spacemaker's Guide to Big Change: Design and improvisation in development practice.* Earthscan. New York: Routledge, 2014.

Haraway, Donna J. 'Situated knowledges: The science question in feminism of partial and the privilege'. *Feminist Studies* 14 (2009): 575–99.

Harrell-Bond, Barbara. 'Camps: Literature review'. *Forced Migration Review* 2 (1998): 22–3.

Harrell-Bond, Barbara. *Imposing Aid: Emergency assistance to refugees.* Oxford: Oxford University Press, 1986.

Harrell-Bond, Barbara. 'UNHCR – Are refugee camps good for children?' *New Issues in Refugee Research*, Working Paper No. 29. Geneva: UNHCR, 2000.

Harrell-Bond, Barbara. 'Weapons of the weak. Response to Kibreab'. *Journal of Refugee Studies* 17 (2004): 1–2.

Hart, Roger, David Satterthwaite, Ximena De La Barra, Sheridan Bartlett and Alfredo Missair, eds. *Cities for Children: Children's rights, poverty and urban management*. London: Earthscan, 1999.

Heft, Harry 'Background and focal environmental conditions of the home and attention in young children'. *Journal of Applied Social Psychology* 9 (1979): 47–69.

Herz, Manuel. *From Camp to City: Refugee camps of the Western Sahara*. Zurich: Lars Müller, 2013.

Herz, Manuel. 'Refugee camps in Chad: Planning strategies and the architect's involvement in the humanitarian dilemma'. *New Issues in Refugee Research*. Policy Development and Evaluation Service, Research Paper No. 147. Geneva: UNHCR, 2007.

Herz, Manuel. 'Refugee camps of the Western Sahara'. *Humanity: An International Journal of Human Rights, Humanitarianism, and Development* 43 (2013): 365–91.

Herz, Manuel. 'Refugee camps or ideal-cities in dust and dirt'. In *Urban Transformation*, edited by Ilka Ruby and Andreas Ruby, 315–22. Berlin: Ruby Press, 2005.

Hilhorst, Dorothea, and Bram J. Jansen. 'Humanitarian space as arena: A perspective on the everyday politics of aid'. *Development and Change* 41 (2010): 1117–39.

Hilhorst, Dorothea, and Mathijs van Leeuwen. 'Emergency and development: The case of imidugudu, villagization in Rwanda'. *Journal of Refugee Studies* 13 (2000): 264–80.

Hirano, Seki. 'Child friendly schools infrastructure standards and guidelines primary and tronc commun schools'. Rwanda Ministry of Education, Working Draft, 2009.

Holzer, Elizabeth. *The Concerned Women of Buduburam: Refugee activists and humanitarian dilemmas*. Ithaca, NY: Cornell University Press, 2015.

Holzer, Elizabeth. 'What happens to law in a refugee camp?' *Law and Society Review* 47 (2013): 837–72.

Human Rights Watch. 'Rwanda: A year on, no justice for refugee killings'. Human Rights Watch, 23 February 2019. Accessed 17 November 2020. https://www.hrw.org/print/327730.

Hyndman, Jennifer. 'Geographies of displacement: Gender, culture and power in UNHCR refugee camps. Kenya'. Thesis, University of British Columbia, 1996.

Hyndman, Jennifer. *Managing Displacement: Refugees and the politics of humanitarianism*. Minneapolis: University of Minnesota Press, 2000.

IRIN. 'Food Aid 2018: The never-ending crisis'. IRIN News, 2018. Accessed 17 November 2020. http://archive.irinnews.org/multimedia/food-aid-2018/index.html.

Isin, Engin F., and Kim Rygiel. 'Of other global cities: Frontiers, zones, camps'. In *Cities of the South: Citizenship and exclusion in the 21st century*, edited by Barbara Drieskens, Franck Mermier and Heiko Wimmen, 170–209. London: Saqi Books, 2007.

Iveson, Kurt, and Ruth Fincher. '"Just diversity" in the city of difference'. In *The New Blackwell Companion to the*

City, edited by Gary Bridge and Sophie Watson, 407–18. Wiley Online Library, 2012.

Jacobsen, Karen, and Loren Landau. 'The dual imperative in refugee research: Some methodological and ethical considerations in social science research on forced migration'. *Disasters* 27 (2003): 185–206.

Jansen, Bram J. 'The accidental city: Urbanisation in an East-African Refugee Camp'. *Urban Agriculture* 21 (2009): 11–12.

Jansen, Bram J. 'The protracted refugee camp and the consolidation of a "humanitarian urbanism"'. *International Journal of Urban and Regional Research* (2015). Accessed 6 April 2021. https://www.ijurr.org/spotlight-on/the-urban-refugee-crisis-reflections-on-cities-citizenship-and-the-displaced/the-protracted-refugee-camp-and-the-consolidation-of-a-humanitarian-urbanism/.

Jansen, Bram J. 'The refugee camp as warscape: Violent cosmologies, "rebelization", and humanitarian governance in Kakuma, Kenya'. *An International Journal of Human Rights, Humanitarianism, and Development* 7 (2016): 429–41.

Johnson, Laura C. 'The developmental implications of home environments'. In *Spaces for Children: The built environment and child development*, edited by Thomas G. David and Carol Smith Weinstein, 139–57. New York: Plenum Press, 1987.

Kagwanja, Peter Mwangi, and Marc-Antoine Pérouse de Montclos. 'Refugee camps or cities? The socio-economic dynamics of the Dadaab and Kakuma camps in Northern Kenya'. *Journal of Refugee Studies* 13 (2000): 205–22.

Kaiser, Paul J. 'Structural adjustment and the fragile nation: The demise of social unity in Tanzania'. *The Journal of Modern African Studies* 34 (1996): 227–37.

Karsten, Lia, and Willem Van Vliet. 'Children in the city: Reclaiming the street'. *Children, Youth and Environments* 16 (2006): 151–67.

Katz, Irit. 'Between bare life and everyday life: Spatializing Europe's migrant camps'. *Architecture Media Politics Society* 12 (2017): 1–20.

Kayizzi-Mugerwa, Steve, and Jorgen Levin. 'Adjustment and poverty: A review of the African experience'. *African Development Review* 6 (1994): 1–39.

Kibreab, Gaim. *African Refugees: Reflections on the African refugee problem*. Trenton, NJ: Africa World Press, 1985.

Kibreab, Gaim. 'Forced migration in the Great Lakes and Horn of Africa'. In *The Oxford Handbook of Refugee and Forced Migration Studies*, edited by Elena Fiddian-Qasmiyeh, Gil Loescher, Katy Long and Nando Sigona. Oxford Handbooks Online. Oxford: Oxford University Press, 2014. https://doi.org/10.1093/oxfordhb/9780199652433.013.0046.

Kodumuki. 'History of imigongo'. Kodumuki Wordpress, 2015. Accessed 17 November 2020. https://kodumuki.wordpress.com/history-of-imigongo/.

Koralek, Ben, and Maurice Mitchell. 'The schools we'd like: Young people's participation in architecture'. In *Children's Spaces*, edited by Mark Dudek, 114–54. London: Architectural Press, 2005.

Kreibaum, Merle. 'Their suffering, our burden? How Congolese refugees affect the Ugandan population'. *World Development* 78 (2016): 2–29.

Kupfer, Meital. 'Accessibility and quality of education for refugees: A case study of Kyangwali refugee settlement'. The School for International Training, 2016, Independent Study Project (ISP) Collection, Paper 2346.

Landau, Loren. 'The humanitarian hangover: Transnationalization of governmental practice in Tanzania's refugee-populated areas'. *Refugee Survey Quarterly* 21 (2002): 260–99.

Latour, Bruno. 'From the world of science to the world of research?' *Science* 280 (1998): 208–9.

Lefebvre, Henri. *La Production de l'Espace*. Paris: Éditions Anthropos, 1974.

Lefebvre, Henri. *Le Droit à La Ville*. Vol. 3. Paris: Éditions Anthropos, 1968.

Lefebvre, Henri. *Le Droit à La Ville Suivi de Espace et Politique*. Éditions Anthropos. Paris: Seuil, 1972.

Lefebvre, Henri. *Writings on Cities*. Edited by Eleonore Kofman and Elizabeth Lebas. Oxford: Blackwell, 1996.

Loescher, Gil. 'The emerging independence of the UNHCR under Auguste Lindt'. In *The UNHCR and World Politics: A perilous path*. Oxford Scholarship Online. Oxford: Oxford University Press, 2001. https://doi.org/10.1093/0199246912.003.0004.

Loescher, Gil. 'International recognition of refugees'. In *The UNHCR and World Politics: A perilous path*. Oxford Scholarship Online. Oxford: Oxford University Press, 2001. https://doi.org/10.1093/0199246912.003.0002.

Loescher, Gil. 'The new cold war and the UNHCR under Poul Hartling'. In *The UNHCR and World Politics: A perilous path*. Oxford Scholarship Online. Oxford: Oxford University Press, 2001. https://doi.org/10.1093/0199246912.003.0007.

Loescher, Gil. 'The UNHCR at 50: Pressures and institutional autonomy'. In *The UNHCR and World Politics: A perilous path*. Oxford Scholarship Online. Oxford: Oxford University Press, 2001. https://doi.org/10.1093/0199246912.003.0001.

Lomo, Zachary, Angella Naggaga and Lucy Hovil. 'The phenomenon of forced migration in Uganda: An overview of policy and practice in an historical context'. Refugee Law Project Working Paper no. 1, 2001. Accessed 4 April 2021. https://refugeelawproject.org/files/working_papers/RLP.WP01.pdf.

Lubega, Henry. 'The coming of Rwandan refugees and why Ugandans turned against them'. *Daily Monitor Uganda*, 23 April 2017. Accessed 17 November 2020. http://www.monitor.co.ug/Magazines/PeoplePower/Rwandan-refugees-Mpororo-Batutsi-Hima/689844-3899258-1d5rpnz/index.html.

Lynch, Kevin. 'The form of cities'. *Scientific American* 190 (1954): 54.

Lynch, Kevin. *The Image of the City.* Cambridge, MA: MIT Press, 1960.

Lynch, Kevin, and Tridib Banerjee. *Growing Up in Cities: Studies of the spatial environment of adolescence in Cracow, Melbourne, Mexico City, Salta, Toluca, and Warszawa.* Cambridge, MA: MIT Press, 1977.

Macgregor, Duncan. 'History of the development of the East African Rift System: A series of interpreted maps through time'. *Journal of African Earth Sciences* 101 (2015): 232–52.

Malkki, Liisa H. *Purity and Exile: Violence, memory, and national cosmology among Hutu refugees in Tanzania.* Chicago: University of Chicago Press, 2012.

Malkki, Liisa H. 'The rooting of peoples and the territorialization of national identity among scholars and refugees'. *Cultural Anthropology* 7 (1992): 24–44.

Mamdani, Mahmood. *When Victims Become Killers: Colonialism, nativism, and the genocide in Rwanda.* Princeton, NJ: Princeton University Press, 2020.

Maqusi, Samar. 'Space of refuge: Negotiating space with refugees inside the Palestinian camp'. *Humanities* 6 (2017): 60.

Marie, Delphine, and Kelvin Shimo. 'Zambia initiative: Making refugees agents of development'. *Conflict Trends*, no. 2 (2002).

Martell, Pete. *First Raise a Flag: How South Sudan won the longest war but lost the peace.* Oxford: Oxford University Press, 2018.

Martin, Diana. 'From spaces of exception to "campscapes": Palestinian refugee camps and informal settlements in Beirut'. *Political Geography* 44 (2015): 9–18.

Matsiko, Haggai. 'Museveni shocked at Kyangwali eviction'. *The Independent, Uganda*, 20 September 2013. Accessed 17 November 2020 https://www.independent.co.ug/museveni-shocked-kyangwali-eviction/.

Matthews, Hugh. 'The street as liminal space: The barbed spaces of childhood'. In *Children in the City: Home neighbourhood and community*, edited by Pia Christensen and Margaret O'Brien, 101–18. London: RoutledgeFalmer, 2003.

Mazrui, Ali. *Africa Since 1935: General history of Africa.* Vol. VIII. Edited by Ali Mazrui and C. Wondji. Oxford: Heinemann and UNESCO, 1993.

McFarlane, Colin. 'Learning assemblages'. In *Learning the City: Knowledge and translocal assemblage*, 15–31. Chichester, UK: Wiley-Blackwell, 2011.

Merkx, Jozef. 'Refugee identities and relief in an African borderland: A study of Northern Uganda and Southern Sudan'. *Refugee Survey Quarterly*, vol. 21. Geneva, Switzerland: United Nations High Commissioner for Refugees, 2000.

Metzler, Janna, Kevin Savage, Marisa Vojta, Makiba Yamano, Alison Schafer and Alastair Ager. 'Evaluation of child friendly spaces Ethiopia field study summary report February 2013'. Mailman School of Public Health, Columbia University and World Vision, 2013.

MIDIMAR. 'Rwanda Ministry of Disaster Management and Refugees'. 2017.

Accessed 17 November 2020. http://midimar.gov.rw/index.php?id=69.

Minca, Claudio. 'Geographies of the camp'. *Political Geography* 49 (2015): 74–83.

Ministry of Education Government of Rwanda. 'Integrated early childhood development strategic plan 2011–2016'. Kigali: MINIEDUC, 2011.

Ministry of Infrastructure Government of Rwanda. 'Updated version of the national human settlement policy in Rwanda'. Kigali: MININFRA, 2009.

Ministry of Internal Security Government of Rwanda. 'Main orientations of the Policy of Regrouped Settlement Sites in the rural areas of Rwanda'. Kigali: MININTER, 1997.

Ministry of Planning and National Development Government of Kenya. 'Turkana district development plan (2002–2008): Effective management for sustainable economic growth and poverty reduction'. Nairobi: MPND, 2001.

Montessori, Maria. *The Absorbent Mind*. New York: Dell, 1984.

Muggah, Robert. *No Refuge: The crisis of refugee militarization in Africa*. London: Zed, in association with the Bonn International Center for Conversion and the Small Arms Survey, 2006.

Müller, Martin. 'Assemblages and actor-network: Rethinking socio-material power, politics and space'. *Geography Compass* 9 (2015): 27–41.

Müller, Martin, and Carolin Schurr. 'Assemblage thinking and actor-network theory: Conjunctions, disjunctions, cross-fertilisations'. *Transactions of the Institute of British Geographers* 41 (2016): 217–29.

Mutegeki, Geoffrey, and Felix Basiime. 'Refugee camp chief killed in land dispute'. *Daily Monitor Uganda*, 2012.

Nallari, Anupama. 'The meaning, experience, and value of "common space" for women and children in urban poor settlements in India'. Thesis, CUNY Academic Works, 2014. Accessed 17 November 2020. https://academicworks.cuny.edu/gc_etds/80.

Napier-Moore, Rebecca. 'Entrenched relations and the permanence of long-term refugee camp situations'. Sussex Migration Working Paper No. 28 (2005): 1–21. Brighton: University of Sussex.

Newhouse, Léonie S. 'More than mere survival: Violence, humanitarian governance, and practical material politics in a Kenyan refugee camp'. *Environment and Planning A: Economy and Space* 47 (2015): 2292–307.

Niane, Djibril T. *General History of Africa. Vol. IV. Africa from the twelfth to the sixteenth century*. Paris: Heinemann Educational and UNESCO, 1981.

OCHA. 'United Nations Office for the Coordination of Humanitarian Affairs'. UN OCHA, 2015. Accessed 17 November 2020. https://www.unocha.org/legacy/what-we-do/coordination-tools/cluster-coordination.

Office of the Prime Minister of Uganda. The Refugees Act 2006. Accessed 1 April 2021. https://www.refworld.org/pdfid/4b7baba52.pdf.

Ogot, Bethwell. *General History of Africa. Vol. V. Africa from the sixteenth to the eighteenth century.* Paris: Heinemann Educational and UNESCO, 1992.

Oka, Rahul Chandrashekhar. 'Coping with the refugee wait: The role of consumption, normalcy, and dignity in refugee lives at Kakuma refugee camp, Kenya'. *American Anthropologist* 116 (2014): 23–37.

Oka, Rahul Chandrashekhar. 'Unlikely cities in the desert: The informal economy as causal agent for permanent "urban" sustainability in Kakuma refugee camp, Kenya'. *Urban Anthropology* 40 (2011): 223–62.

Omata, Naohiko, and Josiah Kaplan. 'Refugee livelihoods in Kampala, Nakivale and Kyangwali refugee settlements. Patterns of engagement with the private sector'. Refugee Studies Centre, Oxford, Working paper Series no. 95, 2013.

ONE UN. 'MIDIMAR and UNHCR affirm plan to include refugees in Rwanda's national development'. ONE UN, 2017. Accessed 17 November 2020. http://www.rw.one.un.org/press-center/news/midimar-and-unhcr-affirm-plan-include-refugees-rwanda's-national-development.

OpenStreetMap. 'Humanitarian Openstreetmap team'. Participatory mapping toolkit, n.d. Accessed 17 November 2020. https://www.hotosm.org/updates/participatory-mapping-toolkit-a-guide-for-refugee-contexts/.

Paulson, Julia. *Education, Conflict and Development.* Vol. 20. Oxford Studies in Comparative Education. Oxford: Symposium Books, 2011.

Pence, Alan R., and Hollie Hix-Small. 'Global children in the shadow of the global child'. *International Journal of Educational Policy, Research and Practice* 8 (2007): 83–100.

Pérouse de Montclos, Marc-Antoine. 'Humanitarian aid, war, exodus, and reconstruction of identities: A case study of Somali "minority refugees" in Kenya'. *Nationalism and Ethnic Politics* 14 (2008): 289–321.

Petcou, Constantin, and Doina Petrescu. 'R-URBAN or how to co-produce a resilient city'. *Ephemera: Theory and Politics in Organization* 15 (2015): 249–62.

Peteet, Julie Marie. *Landscape of Hope and Despair: Palestinian refugee camps.* Philadelphia: University of Pennsylvania Press, 2005.

Peteet, Julie Marie. 'Producing place, spatializing identity, 1948–68'. In *Landscape of Hope and Despair,* 93–130. Philadelphia: University of Pennsylvania Press, 2009.

Petti, Alessandro, and Sandi Hilal. 'Architecture of exile'. Campus in Camps, 2016. Accessed 17 November 2020. http://www.campusincamps.ps/architecture-exile/.

Petti, Alessandro, and Sandi Hilal. 'Decolonizing architecture art residency'. DAAR, 2015. Accessed 17 November 2020. http://www.decolonizing.ps/site/.

Picker, Giovanni, and Silvia Pasquetti. 'Durable camps: The state, the urban, the everyday'. *City* 19 (2015): 681–88.

Pieris, Anoma. 'Encampments: Spatial taxonomies of Sri Lanka's civil war'. *Architectural Theory Review* 19 (2014): 393–413.

Pieterse, Edgar. *City Futures: Confronting the crisis of urban development.* Cape Town: University of Cape Town Press, 2008.

Pieterse, Edgar. 'Grasping the unknowable: Coming to grips with African urbanisms'. *Social Dynamics* 37 (2011): 5–23.

Pieterse, Edgar. 'Introduction: Rogue urbanisms'. *Social Dynamics* 37 (2011): 1–4.

Proshansky, Harold M., and Abbe K. Fabian. 'The development of place identity in the child'. In *Spaces for Children: The built environment and child development*, edited by Carol Simon Weinstein and Thomas G. David, 21–40. New York: Plenum Press, 1987.

Proshansky, Harold M., Abbe K. Fabian and Robert Kaminoff. 'Place-identity: Physical world socialization of the self'. *Journal of Environmental Psychology* 3 (1983): 57–83.

Prunier, Gérard. *From Genocide to Continental War: The 'Congolese' conflict and the crisis of contemporary Africa.* London: Hurst, 2009.

Prunier, Gérard. *The Rwanda Crisis, 1959–1994: History of a genocide.* London: Hurst & Co., 1995.

Pyles, Loretta. 'Participation and other ethical considerations in participatory action research in post-earthquake rural Haiti'. *International Social Work* 58 (2015): 628–45.

Ramadan, Adam. 'Spatialising the refugee camp'. *Transactions of the Institute of British Geographers* 38 (2013): 65–77.

Rasmussen, Kim. 'Places for children – Children's places'. *Childhood* 11 (2004): 155–73.

Refugee Law Project. 'Refugees in Kyangwali settlement: Constraints on economic freedom'. Refugee Law Project Working Paper no. 7, 2002.

Riggio, Eliana, and Theresa Kilbane. 'The International Secretariat for Child-Friendly Cities: A global network for urban children'. *Environment and Urbanization* 12 (2000): 201–5.

Rithi, Alex Mati. 'Conflict amongst refugees: The case of Kakuma refugee camp, 1992–2014'. Thesis, University of Nairobi, 2015. Accessed 17 November 2020. http://erepository.uonbi.ac.ke/bitstream/handle/11295/93371/Rithi_Conflict%20Amongst%20Refugees%20The%20Case%20Of%20Kakuma%20Refugee%20Camp,%201992-2014.pdf?sequence=3.

Rodriguez, Eileen T., and Catherine S. Tamis-Lemonda. 'Trajectories of the home learning environment across the first 5 years: Associations with children's vocabulary and literacy skills at prekindergarten'. *Child Development* 82 (2011): 1058–75.

Rogge, John. 'Africa's resettlement strategies'. *The International Migration Review* 15 (1981): 195–212.

Roy, Ananya, and Nezar AlSayyad. *Urban Informality: Transnational perspectives from the Middle East, Latin America, and South Asia.*

Transnational Perspectives on Space and Place. Oxford: Lexington Books, 2004.

Rutinwa, Bonaventure. 'Beyond durable solutions: An appraisal of the new proposals for prevention and solution of the refugee crisis in the Great Lakes Region'. *Journal of Refugee Studies* 9 (1996): 312–25.

Rutinwa, Bonaventure. 'The Tanzanian government's response to the Rwandan emergency'. *Journal of Refugee Studies* 9 (1996): 291–302.

Sanyal, Romola. 'Refugees and the city: An urban discussion'. *Geography Compass* 6 (2012): 633–44.

Sanyal, Romola. 'Squatting in camps: Building and insurgency in spaces of refuge'. *Urban Studies* 48 (2011): 877–90.

Sanyal, Romola. 'Urbanizing refuge: Interrogating spaces of displacement'. *International Journal of Urban and Regional Research* 38 (2014): 558–72.

Scott, James C. 'Beyond the war of words: Cautious resistance and calculated conformity'. In *Weapons of the Weak: Everyday forms of peasant resistance*, 241–303. New Haven, CT: Yale University Press, 1985.

Scott, James C. 'Everyday forms of resistance'. *Copenhagen Journal of Asian Studies* 4 (1986): 33–62.

Scott, James C. 'Preface'. In *Weapons of the Weak: Everyday forms of peasant resistance*, xv–xxii. New Haven, CT: Yale University Press, 1985.

Scott, James C. *Seeing Like a State: How certain schemes to improve the human condition have failed*. New Haven, CT: Yale University Press, 1998.

Scott-Smith, Tom. 'The humanitarian-architect divide'. *Forced Migration Review* 55 (2017): 67–8.

Siddiqi, Anooradha Iyer. 'L'historire architecturale d'un territoire non identifie'. In *Un Monde de Camps*, edited by Michel Agier and Clara Lecadet, 149–63. Paris: La Découverte, 2014.

Simone, AbdouMaliq. 'Cities and change'. In *For the City Yet to Come: Changing African life in our cities*, 213–43. Durham, NC: Duke University Press, 2004.

Simone, AbdouMaliq. 'Movement: The Zawiyyah as the city'. In *For the City Yet to Come: Changing African life in our cities*, 119–35. Durham, NC: Duke University Press, 2004.

Simone, AbdouMaliq. 'On cityness'. In *City Life from Jakarta to Dakar: Movements at the crossroads*, 424. New York: Routledge, 2009.

Skeels, Anna. 'March activities in the Kyaka II refugee settlement (part 2)', 2012 (blog). Accessed 17 November 2020 https://www.elrha.org/project-blog/march-activities-kyaka-ii-refugee-settlement-part-2/.

Slaughter, Amy, and Jeff Crisp. 'New issues in refugee research. A surrogate state? The role of UNHCR in protracted refugee situations'. *New Issues in Refugee Research*, Research Paper No. 281. Geneva: UNHCR, 2009.

Smith, Linda Tuhiwai. *Decolonizing Methodologies*. London: Zed Books, 1999.

Smithson, Alison, and Peter Smithson. *Ordinariness and Light: Urban theories and their application in a building project*. London: Faber, 1970.

Stearns, Jason. *Dancing in the Glory of Monsters: The collapse of the Congo and the Great War of Africa*. New York: Public Affairs, 2010.

Stearns, Jason. *Mai-Mai Yakutumba: Resistance and racketeering in Fizi, South Kivu*. London: Rift Valley Institute, 2013.

Stein, Barry N., and Lance Clark. 'Refugee integration and older refugee settlements in Africa'. In *1990 Meeting of the American Anthropological Association*. New Orleans, 1990.

Turner, Simon. 'The barriers of innocence: Humanitarian intervention and political imagination in a refugee camp for Burundians in Tanzania'. Thesis, Roskilde Universitet, 2001. Accessed 17 November 2020. https://rucforsk.ruc.dk/ws/portalfiles/portal/57417344/The_Barriers_of.pdf.

Turner, Simon. 'Lukole (Tanzanie). Victimes ou fauteurs de troubles: Humanitaire et politique dans les camps'. In *Un Monde de Camps*, edited by Michel Agier and Clara Lecadet, 73–86. Paris: La Découverte, 2014.

Turton, David. 'Refugees, forced resettlers and other forced migrants: Towards a unitary study of forced migration'. UNHCR *New Issues in Refugee Research*, Working Paper no. 94. Geneva: UNHCR, 2003.

UNESCO. 'The Dakar Framework for Action'. Paris: UNESCO, 2000.

UNESCO. 'The hidden crisis: Armed conflict and education'. EFA Global Monitoring Report. Paris: UNESCO, 2011.

UNESCO. 'Management of Social Transformations (MOST) programme'. UNESCO, n.d. Accessed 17 November 2020. http://www.unesco.org/new/en/social-and-human-sciences/themes/most-programme/.

UNESCO. 'Strong foundations: Early childhood care and education'. Vol. 11. Paris: UNESCO, 2007.

UNHCR. 'Camp planning standards (planned settlements)'. *Handbook for Emergencies*. Geneva: UNCHR, 2015. Accessed 17 November 2020. https://emergency.unhcr.org/entry/45582/camp-planning-standards-planned-settlements.

UNHCR. 'Comprehensive refugee response framework: From the New York Declaration to a global compact on refugees', Geneva: UNHCR, 2016.

UNHCR. 'Dadaab refugee camps, Kenya UNHCR Dadaab bi-weekly update'. Nairobi: UNHCR, 2017.

UNHCR. 'Education. Field guidelines'. Geneva: UNHCR, 2003.

UNHCR. 'Global strategy for settlement and shelter: A UNHCR strategy'. Geneva: UNHCR, 2014.

UNHCR. 'The implementation of UNHCR's policy on refugee protection and solutions in urban areas'. Vol. 21. Geneva: UNHCR, 2012.

UNHCR. 'Kalobeyei settlement'. UNHCR, 2016. Accessed 17 November 2020. http://www.unhcr.org/ke/516-kalobeyei-settlement.html.

UNHCR. 'MIDIMAR-UNHCR joint strategy partners for economic inclusion of refugees'. UNHCR, 2017. Accessed 17 November 2020. http://www.unhcr

.org/rw/12173-midimar-unhcr-joint-strategy-partners-economic-inclusion-refugees.html.

UNHCR. 'OAU Convention governing the specific aspects of refuge problems in Africa'. Geneva: UNHCR, 1969.

UNHCR. 'Operational update – Rwanda 2017'. Kigali: UNHCR, 2017.

UNHCR. 'Policy on alternatives to camps'. Geneva: UNHCR, 2014.

UNHCR. 'Policy on emergency preparedness and response.' *Handbook for Emergencies*. Geneva: UNHCR, 2007.

UNHCR. 'Population statistics'. UNHCR, 2020. Accessed 17 November 2020. https://www.unhcr.org/refugee-statistics/download/?url=E1ZxP4.

UNHCR. 'Protracted refugee situations'. Geneva: UNHCR, 2004.

UNHCR. 'Protracted refugee situations: Revisiting the problem'. Geneva: UNHCR, 2008. Accessed 3 April 2021. https://www.refworld.org/docid/486903142.html.

UNHCR. 'Protracted refugee situations: The search for practical solutions'. In *The State of the World's Refugees*, 105–97. Geneva: UNHCR, 2006.

UNHCR. 'Refugee children: Guidelines on protection and care preface'. Geneva: UNHCR, 1994.

UNHCR. 'Rwanda country refugee response plan 2019–2020'. Kigali: UNHCR, 2020.

UNHCR. 'Statistical summary refugees and asylum seekers in Kenya as of January 31st 2018'. Geneva: UNHCR, 2018.

UNHCR. 'Uganda, comprehensive refugee response plan 2017: Humanitarian needs and requirements'. Kampala: UNHCR, 2017.

UNHCR. 'UNHCR calls for calm and restraint after Rwanda refugee camp protests'. Kigali: UNHCR, 2018.

UNHCR. 'UNHCR policy on refugee protection and solutions in urban areas, 21'. Geneva: UNHCR, 2009.

UNHCR. 'UNHCR Rwanda monthly population statistics'. Kigali: UNHCR, 2017.

UNHCR. 'UNHCR's global shelter and settlement strategy, 2014–2018'. Geneva: UNHCR, 2014.

UNHCR. 'UNHCR welcomes Kenya statement, urges flexibility on timeframes for Somali refugees'. UNHCR, 2016. Accessed 17 November 2020. http://www.unhcr.org/uk/news/press/2016/11/582d614a4/unhcr-welco . . . -flexibility-timeframes-somali-refugees.html?query=Dadaab 2016.

UNHCR Kenya. 'Dadaab refugee complex – UNHCR Kenya'. UNHCR, 2018. Accessed 17 November 2020. http://www.unhcr.org/ke/dadaab-refugee-complex.

UNHCR, and MIDIMAR. 'Economic inclusion of refugees in Rwanda'. Kigali: UNHCR, 2016.

UNHCR, and Office of the Prime Minister Uganda. Uganda Refugee Response Portal. Refugees and nationals per district, 2018. Accessed 17 November. 2020. https://ugandarefugees.org/analysis/refugees-and-hosts/.

UNHCR Rwanda. 'Mahama refugee camp, one year on'. UNHCR Rwanda, 22 April 2016. Accessed 17 November 2020. http://www.unhcr.org/rw/93

-watch-video-mahama-refugee-camp-one-year-on.html.

UNHCR Rwanda. 'Participatory assessment 2017'. Kigali: UNHCR, 2017.

UNHCR Uganda. 'Kyaka II fact sheet'. Kampala: UNHCR, 2014.

UNHCR Uganda. 'Nakivale fact sheet'. Kampala: UNHCR, 2014.

UNHCR Uganda. 'Statistical summary refugees and asylum seekers in Uganda'. Kampala: UNHCR, 2017.

UNICEF. 'Building better brains: New frontiers in early childhood development'. Geneva: UNHCR, 2014.

UNICEF. *Transitional Learning Spaces (TLS): Resilient design and construction in emergencies*, New York: UNICEF, 2013.

United Nations. 'Convention on the Rights of the Child'. New York: United Nations, 2001.

United Nations. *New York Declaration for Refugees and Migrants*. Vol. 16163. New York: United Nations, 2016. Accessed 17 November 2020. http://www.un.org/en/development/desa/population/migration/generalassembly/docs/globalcompact/A_RES_71_1.pdf.

United Nations General Assembly. 'Convention relating to the status of refugees'. *Treaty Series* 606. New York: United Nations, 1951.

UN Joint Inspection Unit. 'Review of the management of implementing partners in United Nations system organizations'. Geneva: UN, 2013.

Unt, Anna Liisa, and Simon Bell. 'The impact of small-scale design interventions on the behaviour patterns of the users of an urban wasteland'. *Urban Forestry and Urban Greening* 13 (2014): 121–35.

Valentine, Gill, and John McKendrck. 'Children's outdoor play: Exploring parental concerns about children's safety and the changing nature of childhood'. *Geoforum* 28 (1997): 219–35.

Van Damme, Wim. 'Do refugees belong in camps? Experiences from Goma and Guinea'. *The Lancet* 364 (1995): 360–2.

van Leeuwen, Mathijs. 'Rwanda's imidugudu programme and earlier experiences with villagisation and resettlement in East Africa'. *Journal of Modern African Studies* 39 (2001): 623–44.

Vasquez, Carlos, and Anika Grafwerk. 'Compendium. Transitional learning spaces, design and construction in emergency'. New York: UNICEF, 2011.

Vincent-Geslin, Stephanie, Yves Pedrazzini, Hossam Adly and Yafiza Zorro, eds. *Translating the City: Interdisciplinarity in urban studies*. Oxford: EPFL Press, 2015.

Walter, Freith, and Francis Wrester. 'Early childhood development: The key to a full productive life'. *The Journal of Childhood Development* 23 (2009): 23.

Ward, Colin. *Caught in the Crossfire: Children and the Northern Ireland conflict*. Belfast, UK: Appletree Press, 1987.

Ward, Colin. 'The child in the city'. *Society* 15 (1978): 84–91.

Ward, Colin. 'Children of the streets'. *New Society* 77 (1986): 23.

Ward, Colin, and Anthony Fyson. *Streetwork: The exploding school*.

London: Routledge and Kegan Paul, 1973.

Wessells, Michael, and Kathleen Kostelny. 'Child friendly spaces: Toward a grounded, community-based approach for strengthening child protection practice in humanitarian crises. Natural helpers play a critical role in ensuring children's safety during and in the aftermath of crises'. *Child Abuse and Neglect* 37 (2013): 29.

Winter, Roger. 'Uganda – Creating a refugee crisis'. *Cultural Survival Quarterly* June (1983): 1–13.

Wood, Stephen, and Kim Dovey. 'Creative multiplicities: Urban morphologies of creative clustering'. *Journal of Urban Design* 20 (2015): 52–74.

Woodhead, Martin. 'Early childhood development in the SDGs'. Young Lives Policy Brief 28, January 2016. University of Oxford.

Zeiher, Helga. 'Shaping daily life in urban environments'. In *Children in the City: Home neighbourhood and community*, edited by Pia Christensen and Margaret O'Brien, 66–82. London: RoutledgeFalmer, 2003.

Zetter, Roger. 'Incorporation and exclusion: The life cycle of Malawi's refugee assistance program". *World Development* 23 (1995): 1653–67.

Ziliacus, Ariana. 'With the Jarahieh Refugee School, CatalyticAction demonstrates the true potential of temporary structures'. Arch Daily, 2017. Accessed 17 November 2020. http://www.archdaily.com/806427/with-the-jarahieh-refugee-school-catalyticaction-demonstrates-the-true-potential-of-temporary-structures.

Zumthor, Peter. 'A way of looking at things'. In *Thinking Architecture*, 9–27. Basel, Switzerland: Birkhauser, 1998.

Index

Note: Page numbers in italics denote figures.

www.ingramcontent.com/pod-product-compliance
Lightning Source LLC
LaVergne TN
LVHW070146270926
848888LV00013B/39
9781800080126